Plays by
Susan Glaspell

TRIFLES
THE OUTSIDE
THE VERGE
INHERITORS

Edited with an introduction by
C. W. E. Bigsby

Additional textual notes by Christine Dymkowski

CAMBRIDGE
UNIVERSITY PRESS

PUBLISHED BY THE PRESS SYNDICATE OF THE UNIVERSITY OF CAMBRIDGE
The Pitt Building, Trumpington Street, Cambridge, United Kingdom

CAMBRIDGE UNIVERSITY PRESS
The Edinburgh Building, Cambridge CB2 2RU, UK
40 West 20th Street, New York, NY 10011-4211, USA
477 Williamstown Road, Port Melbourne, VIC 3207, Australia
Ruiz de Alarcón 13, 28014 Madrid, Spain
Dock House, The Waterfront, Cape Town 8001, South Africa

http://www.cambridge.org

This edition first published 1987
Ninth printing 2006

Printed in the United Kingdom at the University Press, Cambridge

British Library cataloguing in publication data

Glaspell, Susan
Plays. – (British and American playwrights 1750-1920)
I. Title   II. Bigsby, C. W. E.   III. Series
812'. 52   PS3513.L35

Library of Congress cataloguing in publication data

Glaspell, Susan, 1876-1948
Plays. – (British and American playwrights, 1750-1920)
Bibiliography.
Contents: Trifles - The Outside - The Verge- [etc.]
I. Dymkowski, Christine, 1950- .   II. Title   III. Series.
PS3513.L35A6   1987   812'.52   86-30986

ISBN 0 521 31204 3

GENERAL EDITORS' PREFACE

It is the primary aim of this series to make available to the British and American theatre plays which were effective in their own time, and which are good enough to be effective still.

Each volume assembles a number of plays, normally by a single author, scrupulously edited but sparingly annotated. Textual variations are recorded where individual editors have found them either essential or interesting. Introductions give an account of the theatrical context, and locate playwrights and plays within it. Biographical and chronological tables, brief bibliographies, and the complete listing of known plays provide information useful in itself, and which also offers guidance and incentive to further exploration.

Many of the plays published in this series have appeared in modern anthologies. Such representation is scarcely distinguishable from anonymity. We have relished the tendency of individual editors to make claims for the dramatists of whom they write. These are not plays best forgotten. They are plays best remembered. If the series is a contribution to theatre history, that is well and good. If it is a contribution to the continuing life of the theatre, that is well and better.

We have been lucky. The Cambridge University Press has supported the venture beyond our legitimate expectations. Acknowledgement is not, in this case, perfunctory. Sarah Stanton's contribution to the series has been substantial, and it has enhanced our work. Later volumes in the series have benefited from the care and attention of Kevin Taylor.

Martin Banham
Peter Thomson

Susan Glaspell (1938, courtesy of the Theatre Arts Library, Harry Ransom Humanities Research Center, The University of Texas at Austin)

BRITISH AND AMERICAN PLAYWRIGHTS
1750–1920
General editors: Martin Banham and Peter Thomson

Susan Glaspell

A co-founder of the Provincetown Players – the group which acted as
midwife to the American theatre – Susan Glaspell (1876–1948) can also lay
claim to be a major figure in her own right. Her early plays were in many
respects as challenging and original as those with which O'Neill made his
debut. Her concern with language as subject, with character as an
expression of social role, with plot as a mechanism which may ensnare
rather than locate the self, made her very much a modern. In *Trifles* (1916)
she developed a feminist critique of social role. In *The Outside* (1917) she
staged a debate between the life force and a perverse celebration of death.
In both plays silence becomes an eloquent expression of meaning. *The
Verge* (1921) is an experimental work of considerable proportions, more
daring in many ways than anything attempted by O'Neill. And though
Inheritors (1921) is far more conventional it touched a contemporary nerve,
questioning the nature and reality of American pieties.

Long known only for a single play, Susan Glaspell now emerges as a
significant figure in the history of American drama, a woman of genuine
creative daring.

CONTENTS

vii

INTRODUCTION

Davenport, Iowa, in the early part of the century, was a surprising city. Though situated in a conservative part of the country and reflecting that fact in a stern and unforgiving moralism, it also retained something of the radicalism of its own past. In the words of Floyd Dell, who was raised there and who later became an influential figure in the literary world first of Chicago and then New York, it was 'largely German and Jewish, with an 1848 European revolutionary foundation, and a liberal and socialist superstructure. There was also some native American mysticism in the picture, a mysticism which blossomed in the 30s and 40s, a curious religious expression of romantic libertarian ideas.' The town had 'the bravado of an old Mississippi river-port, and the liberal "cosmopolitan" atmosphere of a place that is in touch with European influences. It had its nose not too closely pressed against the grindstone of "practical" fact. It had an intelligentsia, who knew books and ideas. It even had some live authors.'[1] A curious mixture of small town prejudice and intellectual sophistication, Davenport proved both liberating and oppressive to those who challenged its conservative mores in terms of its radical tradition. The contradictions went deep, in its rebels no less than in its leading citizens.

Those writers which it produced, if scarcely fostered, people such as Floyd Dell, George Cram Cook and, perhaps most significantly, Susan Glaspell, never entirely lost their attachment to pioneer virtues, though they were disposed to translate these variously into a spiritual equality of opportunity (which at times they incautiously described as socialism), a radical anarchism (by which the individual chose to explore the frontiers of experience), or a Nietzschean egotism (which, particularly in the case of George Cram Cook, might be rooted in recognisably American notions of intellectual, moral and physical self-sufficiency but which pulled him constantly towards rather older models of the relationship between the self and its setting).

The fact is that during the first decades of the century, when these three writers were maturing, America itself was changing rapidly. Like so many other Americans, they moved from the small town to the large city and experienced there social and artistic influences which changed them profoundly. As much as any other figures they recognised this process as being of critical significance, as signalling, in particular, a renaissance in the arts of which they were at first simply reporters (all three writing for the newspapers) but eventually major figures. Inlanders, raised in the very heart of a nation which had prided itself for so long on its sturdy independence of

Europe, they found themselves eventually on the very edge of the continent, alert to the new developments from overseas but at the same time creating their own intensely American art.

Susan Glaspell was born in Davenport in 1876 (though, somewhat less plausibly, a later date – 1882 – has also been proposed). She came from pioneer stock, her family arriving with the first settlers in 1835. After graduating from Drake University, in Des Moines, she became a reporter on the Des Moines *Daily News*, but in her own mind was already a writer. Her first stories, several of which she wrote while still at university, were published in *Youth's Companion*, and in 1901 she abandoned newspaper work to return to Davenport and become a full-time writer, producing stories for such magazines as *Harper's Bazaar*.

For the most part trite and sentimental, these suggested little of the originality and power which were to mark her work in the theatre. Much the same could be said of many of her novels. The first, *The Glory of the Conquered*, which appeared in 1909, concerned the tragic love affair of an artist and a scientist. When he goes blind, infected by a laboratory organism, she struggles to master the techniques which will enable her to act as his eyes and thus forward his work. When he dies, before her scheme can be put into practice, she realises that the real memorial to him will be her own paintings which express precisely that sense of life to which he, too, had wished to bear witness. Glaspell's own unease with the book is apparent in what must surely be the most bizarre publisher's note ever to appear. In reprinting the novel, the English publisher prefaced it with a note which observes that: 'Although "The Glory of the Conquered" is, in the author's opinion, a less finished and mature work than "Fidelity", its reception in America – measured, at least, by sales – has been even more enthusiastic than that of some of her subsequent work. Without committing themselves either, on the one hand, to the author's or, on the other, to the public, judgement on this work, the Publishers feel that it is only fair to point out that it was Susan Glaspell's first novel.'[2] In one go, it seems, they succeeded in undermining both her first novel and her later books.

But the direction of Susan Glaspell's thought, and, indeed, life was in for a change. In 1909 she met first George Cram Cook and later Floyd Dell who had together started the Monist Club in Davenport. Both men were radical, though in different ways, and the Monist Club a forum for a grab bag of assorted ideas: both were also united in their conviction that things were changing, culturally and socially. Though scarcely free of their own romantic absurdities, they set out to rescue Susan from her sentimentalities and certainly her second novel, *The Visioning* (1911), touches on the issue of feminist socialism. But the critical change in her life came as a result of her love affair with Cook, a married man with two children. In a way such an affair was of a piece with her new views. The love which she had previously sanctified in her stories as the symbol of human selflessness and spiritual completion now acquired a radical tinge. Davenport society was shocked and, to judge by the frequency with which she herself dealt with the subject of adultery in novels and plays, she was not untouched by a sense of guilt. But the right, indeed in some sense the responsibility, to challenge convention and insist on a freedom of thought, emotion and action, was in tune with a society now finally turning its back on the old century. When the divorce came through she married Cook, in 1913, and they moved first to Greenwich Village and then Provincetown. Her third novel, ironically called *Fidelity* (1915), in many ways stood as a justification of her own actions, telling the story, as it does, of a woman who has an affair with a married man but whose fidelity is ultimately neither to marriage nor to her new relationship but to a sense of integrity which she will not surrender.

The marriage was Cook's third. The son of a wealthy Davenport family, he was, from their point of view, wildly eccentric. Not only did he develop radical views (in fact not wholly out of place in a town with a history of radical thought) but he turned his back on the family wealth in an attempt to be a subsistence farmer -- a Midwestern Thoreau. He was frequently drunk and a womaniser for much of his life. But he had an energy and an enthusiasm which was compelling and a talent for recognising the potential of others. Working as a reviewer for the *Chicago Evening Post* he observed and helped underwrite the Chicago Renaissance. In New York he and Susan Glaspell played midwife to the American theatre.

In some sense Cook seems to have been the fulfilment of his own romantic dreams. His diaries offer an account of a man who saw himself as a cross between Thoreau and Byron, itemising the crops on his farm but seeking to transform a prosaic reality with his imagination. An admirer of Nietzsche – an enthusiasm which he shared with Eugene O'Neill – he had moved from Harvard and Heidelberg to selling vegetables; Davenport was not amused. At thirty-two, his first wife left him after three years of quarrels and he seems to have reached the point of mental breakdown; indeed the fierce energy which drove him throughout his life was not always easily distinguishable from madness. A second marriage gave him a family but scarcely peace of mind. That came, at least in some limited degree, in his relationship with a woman whose own life was already being transformed by travel to Europe and by the new forces at large in American society.

When Susan Glaspell moved to Chicago it was fast becoming the literary capital of America. Still, then, hog butcher to the world, as Carl Sandburg hailed it in his poem called 'Chicago', it had the crude energy of a city on the make. It attracted talent from all over the Midwest and, coming together at a time when literary no less than social values were in a state of flux, such young writers saw themselves as part of a new spirit in American writing. For Edna Ferber, born in Kalamazoo, Michigan, the city seemed full of talent and Susan Glaspell was among the names she recited with a sense of awe. 'Carl Sandburg was writing his powerful lusty Chicago poems. Ben Hecht was living there, trying hard to be Rabelaisian ... Charlie MacArthur, brought up as a missionary's son, showing his rebellion by a series of puckish pranks; Floyd Dell, living his moon-calf days; Susan Glaspell, Llewellyn Jones, Sherwood Anderson; and Harriet Monroe with the face of a New England school teacher; Maxwell "Bogie" Bodenheim, striding along Michigan Avenue ... a chap called Ring Lardner ...'[3] Add to that list Theodore Dreiser, Sherwood Anderson, Edgar Lee Masters and Vachel Lindsay and claims for a Chicago Renaissance seem legitimate enough. Some of those figures were Chicago born and bred; others, like Cook and Glaspell, came from small-town America. Sherwood Anderson was from Camden, Ohio, Vachel Lindsay from Springfield, Illinois, Edgar Lee Masters from Garnett, Kansas, Dreiser from Terre Haute, Indiana, Ring Lardner from Niles, Michigan and Sandburg from Galesburg, Illinois. Some came from even further afield. Maurice Brown, who founded the Little Theatre, came from England and Francis Hackett, editor of the *Friday Literary Review* (a section of the *Chicago Evening Post*), which first appeared in 1909, from Ireland. But Harriet Monroe, whose *Poetry* magazine, founded in 1912, was a central feature of the Chicago Renaissance, was actually born in the city whose literary reputation she did so much to establish, and it was the second issue of that magazine which included a poem by John Reed (himself from Portland, Oregon), who was later to emerge as a crucial figure in New York cultural life and a friend and colleague of Cook and Glaspell.

Chicago developed its own version of Bohemian life and even its own version of the Latin Quarter where Thorstein Veblen lived and where Floyd Dell, himself editor of the *Friday Literary Review* after the departure of Francis Hackett, became a major influence. H. L. Mencken praised the city for all aspects of its new-found cultural vitality, including within his praise its new critical establishment. But in fact literary criticism seems to have concerned itself rather less with scrupulous analysis than with a romantic self-exploration. Thus Dell, in offering a book for review, advised, 'here is a book about China. Now don't send me an article about China but one about yourself.'[4] Cook obliged by offering criticism in which his own experiences were invoked as metaphor and moral exemplar. Thus, he observed that, 'There is a glow of civilized satisfaction ... in clearing up a rank, neglected piece of land, converting into serviceable firewood with a sharp axe the fallen trees which lie cluttering the earth, putting a well-whetted scythe through patches of tall weeds, raking the rubbish out of the grass and giving it to clean fire. And so is there a satisfaction in the work of clearing accumulated rubbish from an intellectual field.'[5] That process was going on in the culture at large. The populists had shaken the political assumptions of late nineteenth- and early twentieth-century America, as the muckrakers challenged the social and economic practices of big business. Political and sexual radicalism were on the agenda, at least for those who saw themselves as playing a central role in ushering in a new era in social and artistic affairs, even if that radicalism was often traced to its roots in national traditions rather than foreign theories: whosoever would be a man must be a non-conformist. In 1913 Dell defined both his own principles and those of Cook and Glaspell when he asserted, in an editorial essay on 'Literature and Life', that 'Science has its own purpose, and so has philosophy; but literature exists to encourage human beings to be human. The masters of prose fiction and of poetry in every age have been those who, while having the highest conception of order afforded by their generation, have nevertheless exalted the individual with his follies, his crimes, and his intractable aspirations above that conception of order. The poets have always preached the gospel of disorder. The novelists from Fielding to Galsworthy have spoken on behalf of the man at odds with society.'[6] That, essentially, remained Susan Glaspell's theme throughout her career, and although at that time she and Cook saw themselves primarily as novelists, Chicago was also changing the shape of drama. In 1900 a theatre was founded at Jane Addam's Hull House. In keeping with an institution whose origins lay in a social concern, it favoured plays which addressed public issues. It also placed an emphasis on Chicago writers (including Kenneth Goodman and Ben Hecht), but it was Maurice Browne's Little Theatre which most seized Susan Glaspell's imagination. The declared aim was to create and produce a poetic drama and to provoke a 'free discussion of life and the arts' which, provided that the notion of a poetic drama could be distinguished from verse drama, would have appealed to a writer who was drawn equally to the force of dramatic metaphor and to contemplation of life as an abstract force.

For Floyd Dell the signs that things were on the move were clear everywhere. The genteel tradition was a thing of the past; a new energy was apparent in the arts and more especially in poetry and theatre. As he explained in his autobiography:

> The year 1912 was really an extraordinary year, in America as well as Europe. It was the year of intense woman-suffragist activity. In the arts it marked a new era. Color was everywhere – even in neckties. The Lyric Year, published in New York, contained Edna St. Vincent Millay's 'Renascence'. In Chicago, Harriet Monroe founded Poetry. Vachel Lindsay suddenly came into his own with 'General William Booth Enters Into Heaven', and commenced to give back to his land in magnificent chanted poetry its own barbaric music. 'Hindle Wakes' startled New York, as it was later to startle

Chicago. The Irish Players came to America. It was then that plans
were made for the Post-Impressionist Show which revolutionized
American ideas of art. In Chicago, Maurice Browne started the
Little Theatre. One could go on with the evidence of a New Spirit
come suddenly to birth in America.[7]

Just as in New York the young Eugene O'Neill was to make repeated visits
to the Irish Players so, in Chicago, Glaspell and Cook were struck by the
implications for a native theatre of the visit of the Dublin company to the
Little Theatre: 'Quite possibly there would have been no Provincetown
Players had there not been Irish Players. What we saw done for Irish life he
wanted for American life – no stage conventions in the way of projecting
with the humility of true feeling.'[8]
   Chicago remained an important centre for a good many years after Cook,
Glaspell and Dell moved to New York but the exodus to the east was a
steady one. Edgar Lee Masters, Sherwood Anderson, Theodore Dreiser,
Ring Lardner and Ben Hecht all left between 1919 and 1924. *Poetry*
magazine continued but no longer with the same enthusiasm or effect. Even
the Little Theatre closed in 1917, though by then those it inspired had
already begun the creation of other more vital centres in New York.
   Indeed, by 1912 New York, too, was in a state of ferment. Politically, *The
Masses* and the *New Republic* were challenging values and assumptions
while Mabel Dodge had returned from Europe enthused by the Futurists
and determined to preside over a cultural revolution. A year later the
Armory Show exposed America to the excitement and innovations of
European modernism. 1913 was also the year of Walter Lippmann's *A
Preface to Politics* and of the Paterson strike pageant, a huge drama
organised by John Reed to support the striking miners of Paterson, New
Jersey. Reed himself was only one year out of Harvard when he reached
Greenwich Village which Max Eastman called the American Bohemia or
gipsy minded Latin Quarter. He expressed a radical strain in that Bohemia
but Greenwich Village represented more than this. In particular it came to
stand for the determination of women not to be trapped in the roles offered
to them. Sometimes such a concern had a radical edge; sometimes it was
studiously apolitical, claiming spiritual rather than social equality.
   Cook and Glaspell moved to New York in 1913, to a Greenwich Village
alive with every kind of literary and political faction. Apostles of free love,
communism, feminism, and anarchism sat in cafés along with artists and
writers. Though fiercely divided amongst themselves, they were united
against convention. A decade later they would have met in Paris; now they
created their Bohemia in lower Manhattan or, when the summer became
too oppressive, the seaside cottages on the extreme edge of Massachusetts
Bay, in Provincetown. But, to Susan Glaspell, whatever their views on art

or social organisation, they remained in some degree tied to a model of life which had its origins in other, more simple necessities. As she explained:

> We were supposed to be a sort of 'special' group – radical, wild.
> Bohemians, we have been called. But it seems to me we were a
> particularly simple people, who sought to arrange life for the thing
> we wanted to do, needing each other as protection against
> complexities, yet living as we did because of an instinct for the old,
> old things, to have a garden, and neighbors, to keep up the fire
> and let the cat in at night. None of us had much money, these were
> small houses we lived in: they had been fishermen's before they
> were ours. Most of us were from families who had other ideas – who
> wanted to make money, played bridge, voted the republican ticket,
> went to church, thinking one should be like every one else. And so,
> drawn together by the thing we really were, we were as a new
> family; we lent each other money, worried through illnesses, ate
> together when a cook had left, talked about our work. Each could
> be himself, that was perhaps the real thing we did for one another.[9]

This group was by no means homogeneous. It consisted of the aesthetes from Mabel Dodge's salon together with the more militantly revolutionary who advocated free love and wished to smash the existing social and political system; so Hutchins Hapgood was joined by Louise Bryant and John Reed. But somehow common cause was found not only in resisting the old but in creating the new.

In New York many of them met at the Liberal Club on Macdougal Street which was run by Henrietta Rudman as a meeting place for those of radical persuasion. From time to time they staged self-mocking skits and the popularity of these led to the formation of the Washington Square Players in a bookshop next door to the club. Their first production was Lord Dunsany's *The Glittering Gate*. In February, 1915, they moved to the Bandbox Theatre where they staged their first full season, a mixture of European and original American plays.

Jig Cook spoke the first word of the first production: 'I've had enough of this!' It was an appropriate announcement of the new mood, though when he and Susan wrote a play together which satirised the new vogue for Freudian analysis – *Suppressed Desires* – the Washington Square Players could find no space for it and as a result an impromptu performance was staged, in 1915, in the Hapgood house – along with *Constancy*, a barely concealed account of the love affair between John Reed and Mabel Dodge. The author was Neith Boyce and the designer, Robert Edmond Jones. So began the Provincetown Players, a group which effectively changed the direction of American drama. Indeed, in many ways it marked the birth of the American theatre in its modern form, more especially when the plays

(together with two more: *Change your Style* by Jig Cook and
Contemporaries by Wilber Steele) were repeated in the old wharf at
Provincetown, a building owned by Mary Vorse and specially converted as a
makeshift theatre. The following spring further new scripts were
forthcoming, among them a play by a young writer with a trunkful of
unproduced works – Eugene O'Neill. The play was *Bound East for Cardiff*
and Susan Glaspell, after hearing him read it aloud, commented that now
'we knew what we were for'. At a meeting held in September, 1916, they
decided to call the new group the Provincetown Players and, at O'Neill's
suggestion, called the theatre which they planned to open on Macdougal
Street in New York, The Playwrights' Theatre. The announcement of their
first New York season was in effect a manifesto.

> The present organisation is the outcome of a group of people
> interested in the theatre, who gathered spontaneously during two
> summers at Provincetown, Mass., for the purpose of writing,
> producing and acting their own plays. The impelling desire of the
> group was to establish a stage where playwrights of sincere, poetic,
> literary and dramatic purpose could see their plays in action and
> superintend their production without submitting to the commercial
> manager's interpretation of public taste. Equally, it was to afford an
> opportunity for actors, producers, scenic and costume-designers to
> experiment with a stage of extremely simple resources – it being the
> idea of the Players that elaborate settings are unnecessary to bring
> out the essential qualities of a good play.[10]

Floyd Dell welcomed the idea of the literary collaboration between Jig
Cook and Susan Glaspell since, as he later wrote, 'each had something the
other tremendously needed. Susan's humor, story-telling capacity and sheer
literary expertness', he assumed, 'conjoined with George's magnificent ideas
and brave truthfulness, should make a masterpiece. If Susan could put her
remarkable gifts at the service of truth instead of romantic illusion, if
George could have at his command words that raced and danced instead of
groped and stumbled, that would make a book.'[11] In fact most of Cook's
originality and energy went into the creation of the theatre, while Susan
Glaspell was less liberated by finding a co-author (*Suppressed Desires* was an
amusing satire of contemporary fads and little more), than by working in a
genre whose own assumptions were new to her and which was anyway in a
state of flux. Their own discovery of a talent as raw and original as that of
Eugene O'Neill, who wandered into their company at precisely the moment
when they were looking for new plays, meant that she had the inspiration of
working beside someone whose ideas were as original as her own. His
subsequent career and manifest importance to the development of American
drama has tended to eclipse the reputation of Susan Glaspell. However, not

merely was she seen at the time as a writer of comparable stature, in some ways her plays were more carefully structured (*Trifles* being a case in point) and more daringly original (*The Outside* and *The Verge* playing dangerous but original games with character, language and plot) than many of O'Neill's early efforts.

It remains true that Susan Glaspell is unlikely to have turned to the theatre without the influence of her husband but she brought to her new career a freshness of vision and a challenging aesthetic and social perspective absent from her novels and which Cook's own dramatic efforts never achieved. Following the success of their first season he arbitrarily announced a new play by his wife for the 1916 season. Apart from her collaboration over *Suppressed Desires* (1915), she had never written a play before and had none to offer; but within ten days *Trifles* was receiving its first run-through. Rehearsals began the next day. She has explained the process of writing the play in *The Road to the Temple*:

> So I went out on the wharf, sat alone on one of our wooden benches without a back, and looked a long time at that bare little stage. After a time the stage became a kitchen – a kitchen there all by itself. I saw just where the stove was, the table, and the steps going upstairs. Then the door at the back opened, and people all bundled up came in – two or three men, I wasn't sure which, but sure enough about the two women, who hung back, reluctant to enter that kitchen. When I was a newspaper reporter out in Iowa, I was sent down-state to do a murder trial, and I never forgot going into the kitchen of a woman locked up in town. I had meant to do it as a short story, but the stage took it for its own, so I hurried in from the wharf to write down what I had seen. Whenever I got stuck, I would run across the street to the old wharf, sit in that leaning little theater under which the sea sounded, until the play was ready to continue. Sometimes things written in my room would not form on the stage, and I must go home and cross them out. 'What playwrights need is a stage,' said Jig, 'their own stage.'[12]

In Provincetown they had that stage.

Trifles (1916) is deservedly Susan Glaspell's best-known play. Indeed, for many people it is the only Glaspell play with which they are familiar. Much reprinted and for many years a favourite with amateur companies, it was also an ideal play for the Provincetown Players. Its small cast and simple set and perhaps even more its hermetic atmosphere (unsurprising given the circumstances of its composition) suited the Wharf Theatre where it opened on August 8, 1916, with Susan Glaspell and George Cram Cook in the cast.

The play begins with a stage bereft of characters. The set, a gloomy disorganised kitchen, offers a compacted image of the lives of those who had lived there, its detailed realism representing a cipher to be decoded by the process of the play. Those who first enter this space are men. They carry authority, both in terms of their rank and their manner and they are precisely charged with 'reading' the text of the scene which confronts them. As Sheriff and County Attorney they have come to interpret, to explicate the tableau which confronts them. The women who accompany them are assumed to have no role outside their function as wives. They have come to collect a few clothes for the woman who, we learn, is held in jail for the suspected murder of her husband. To the neighbour who had first stumbled on the killing, they are prone to 'worrying over trifles'. Questions of meaning and significant action are presumed to be the preserve of men, as is the administration of justice and the conduct of business. In a few brief exchanges Glaspell establishes the nature of social power in this community as she does the conventions of social relationships. It is plain that women are granted no insight and no rational capacity as they are conceded no function beyond the merely domestic. They hesitate to communicate their models of social experience rather as the woman writer had historically accepted exclusion from the theatre as though her vision could have no public utility.

The 'action' takes place in the kitchen, the presumed preserve of women and as such is discounted by those who investigate the crime as being of no significance, containing no meaning, hinting at no experience of any relevance. It is, however, the very 'trifles' of domestic life which the men so casually dismiss that contain the real clues to the despair, the anxiety and the tension which in all probability explain the crime which so baffles them. It is not simply that supposedly trained observers fail to realise the significance of the details which confront them, but that their own male arrogance stands between them and understanding. Their myopia is a product of a more fundamental failure – a failure of human concern and emotional sensitivity. That failure is precisely at the root of the crime which they set out to investigate.

There is in fact very little action in the play in a conventional sense. The crime has already been committed, the discovery effected, the arrest completed. We are presented almost with a painterly tableau and as the play progresses our attention is slowly directed around the picture. For Susan Glaspell, character is action as she slowly creates the identities of two people who never appear – the murdered man and his wife. It is a device which she was later to use in both *Bernice* (1919) and *Alison's House* (1930). In *Trifles*, the same slow accumulation of detail, which leads the women to understand the motive for the crime, also constitutes Glaspell's dramatic strategy as she reconstitutes the self-destructive introspection of John Wright which had slowly overwhelmed the youthful vivacity of his wife. And buried within what appears to be a conventional detective story, which itself conceals an account of male–female relations, is a hint of another theme which dominates both her novels and her plays – the battle between a life instinct and a death instinct. John Wright's crime was to smother and eventually to destroy the vitality and emotional generosity of his wife. His refusal to instal a telephone is symptomatic of a withdrawal from communication which has left her solitary, with no companion but a caged bird – perhaps rather too obvious a symbol of her own plight. By degrees we come to learn that it was her very celebration of life – expressed through her singing – which Wright saw as implying a reproach to his own death-centred existence. Thus, in breaking the neck of her songbird he is simply re-enacting that breaking of her spirit to which his life had seemingly been dedicated. And that battle is clearly being restaged, in a less extreme form, by those who now attempt to penetrate the mystery which lies behind his murder, for although the men are far from being as misanthropic as John Wright, they, too, deny a human complexity to their wives, imprisoning them in a stereotype which is as spiritually debilitating as the mental prison within which he had incarcerated his wife.

The play is not, however, purely a feminist reaction against male insensitivity in a system which privileges such insensitivity nor yet an assault on a social organisation which confers power and social prestige on the basis of gender. For the fact is that the women, too, have failed one another. They, too, have allowed trifles to come between them and their human responsibilities: 'I wish I had come over sometimes when *she* was here', confesses Mrs Hale. 'I could've come. I stayed away because [. . .] it's down in a hollow and you don't see the road. I dunno what it is . . .'[13] Later she admits, 'I *wish* I'd come over here once in a while! That was a crime! That was a crime! Who's going to punish that . . . I might have known she needed help! I know how things can be – for women . . . We live close together and we live far apart. We all go through the same things – it's all just a different kind of the same thing.'[14] It is in large part a failure of sisterly solidarity of which she accuses herself, but, beyond that, it is a failure of understanding and compassion. She does consistently refer to the accused woman by her maiden name, thereby underscoring the fact that it was marriage which had deprived her of her selfhood, but she also acknowledges her own complicity in the process. Their rebellion against their husbands, as they both conspire to conceal the evidence which seems to point to the guilt of the accused woman, is thus both a rebellion against male authority – individually and socially sanctioned – and against their own previous failure of will. The link between these two aspects of authority is indeed deliberately underlined when the County Attorney observes that 'a sheriff's wife is married to the law'. Thus when Mrs Peters, wife of the Sheriff and herself previously nervous and cowed, herself takes the initiative, in effect choosing justice over law, the action is doubly significant.

Trifles is not merely a play which proposes that meaning may reside in the unconsidered trifles of experience; it is also a play about desperation, about the corner of experience into which women have been manœuvred, about the indifference of men and, in a disturbing way, about the extent to which human needs bow to other necessities – power, custom, self-concern. The intuitive knowledge of the women who are capable of solving the mystery both because of the acuteness of their attention and because they are able to inhabit that mystery and the lives which generated it, is contrasted with the logical ponderousness of the men, who observe but do not see, who seek to understand without the sympathy which generates understanding. The male world seems callous and Mrs Peters is a special victim of that. A pet kitten had been destroyed in front of her eyes, as John Wright, we assume, had wrung the neck of his wife's canary; she had lost a two-year-old child to the bleakness of a Dakota homestead and has to survive not only this but also condescension and disregard. It is men who determine the world in which the women are then required to live. But, remarkably it seems, they retain a grasp on moral realities as they acknowledge that shared experience which is the basis of the moral demand.

Not the least remarkable aspect of *Trifles* is the extent to which Susan Glaspell herself makes the slightest of dramatic forms carry such a burden of meaning. Understatement proves as effective a strategy for her as it was to be for Hemingway. Just as the principal characters never make an appearance, so the crucial revelations of the play are never fully voiced: reticence becomes a style as well as a subject. The joyless kitchen, bereft of warmth or life, underscores the absences which have destroyed the absent inhabitants. The coldness which has broken glass jars on the shelves invades the lives of characters who have failed to offer the companionship which alone might have offered consolation. *Trifles* was a modest but remarkable debut, more especially in the context of a national theatre which had consistently preferred melodrama to psychological truth.

The following year saw several new Glaspell plays: *Close the Book*, a comedy about social pretensions; *The People*, which develops an idealistic portrait of journalism, seeing it as being in the vanguard of social change, and, perhaps the most original of these early works, *The Outside*.

First performed in December, 1917, it was firmly rooted in the Provincetown which was to be their home until their departure for Greece in 1922. Set in an old abandoned life-saving station, which in reality had been renovated by Mabel Dodge and was later to be the home of Eugene O'Neill, it is an allegory of the battle between the life force and the death force. She and Cook may have offered a satire of the fashionable regard for Freud in *Suppressed Desires* but she was scarcely more immune to its influence than O'Neill was to prove in a work such as *The Great God Brown*. The very setting, as in so many of O'Neill's plays, is itself offered as a potent image containing the essence of the dramatic conflict. The life-saving station, significantly no longer functional, is located, as an elaborate stage direction indicates, on the outside of the shore of Cape Cod, at the point where the land curves round to create the natural harbour of Provincetown. In other words, in one direction lies the open sea – a place of risk, of shipwreck and death – while in the other lies a protective world in which life can flourish and be preserved. A similar contrast is apparent in the contention between the plants which struggle for survival in this exposed environment and the sand dunes which constantly threaten to overwhelm them. And that conflict can be glimpsed through the open doors of the building as the play begins.

It is into this disused life-saving station that a group of men have brought the body of a drowned man. Throughout the first few minutes of the play they struggle in vain to revive him, reluctant to acknowledge the futility of their actions, mindful, as they are, of the occasions in the past when this building had seen the recovery of many who were presumed dead. But now it seems to be given over to death, having abandoned not only its literal function but also its symbolic force. At first, then, it seems that death has been triumphant, but the very commitment of the men, and in particular of the Captain, serves to transform the life of one of those who had sought to immure herself in this remote house. Thus, in the end, they do, paradoxically, succeed in their efforts 'to put life in the dead'.[15]

Mrs Patrick has retreated to Provincetown after the loss of her husband – lost, it seems, not to death, but to faithlessness. Abandoned, she surrenders to misanthropy, taking a perverse pleasure in the slow smothering of life which she sees enacted around her as the sand slowly covers all signs of life. Her companion, Allie Mayo, feels similarly abandoned and betrayed by life, having lost her husband to the sea some twenty years earlier. Indeed, she has effectively been shocked into silence, or has chosen to abandon language as she has all interest in life. She has 'a prejudice against words'.[16] But the sight of the men's struggle to revive the drowned sailor, together with a remark which she overhears – one of the men implies that Mrs Patrick revels in the victory of death over life – tempts her back into the world, the semantic no less than the literal world of human relationships. Silent for so long, she can at first speak only in sentence fragments, unable to sustain the coherences of language any more than she had been able to bear the developments of experience. The grammar of her life has been dislocated. But now the recovery of her spirit is reflected in the restoration of her fluency as she challenges her own former despair in arguing with her employer. If she had retreated from language because of the facile consolations offered to her by those who failed to understand the profundity of her loss, she now reconstructs her life as she rebuilds her linguistic competence.

Mrs Patrick celebrates the sand which buries grass, trees and vines;

reawakened to life, Allie Mayo is drawn to the 'strange little things that reach out farthest', though the conversation which follows is admittedly more than a little arch, as they solemnly discuss metaphysics. Indeed an irony of Glaspell's text lies in the fact that it is at its most striking and original when she is dealing with a character who is unwilling to enter the linguistic world and only gradually reconstructs her selfhood rather than when she allows her full access to language and a confident vision of meaning. The silent Allie Mayo is disturbing; her stuttering attempts to feel her way back to life startlingly effective. When she recovers her articulateness it is to utter a series of abstract encomiums to life which are close kin to the vapid reassurances which had initially sent her spinning into silence. A patent symbolist, Glaspell has difficulty in generating a language which can adequately express abstractions without seeming hopelessly pretentious. The originality of the piece thus lies less in her romanticism, intensified by her monistic tendencies and her fascination with Nietzsche (which becomes a central concern later in *The Verge*), than in her radical approach to character, language and plot.

Mrs Patrick has responded to what she regards as the absurdity of existence, much as Camus' or Beckett's characters were to do, by hardening her heart to stone. By eroding the distinction between herself and the inanimate world she hopes to escape the irony of her position: 'Everything that can hurt me I want buried – buried deep. Spring is here [. . .] Spring – coming through the storm – to take me – take me to hurt me. That's why I couldn't bear – things that made me know I feel.'[17] Perhaps predictably, she is won back to the ironies of life, ironies which are composed equally of despair and exultance. It is a victory for the life force which, ironically, results in a reductive ending. The play's dramatic tensions are discharged in a flood of language whose abstractions diffuse the clarity of the play's own symbolic system as the two characters, at first in contention and then in harmony, substitute words for the actions which had distinguished the life savers at the beginning. Nonetheless, outside of O'Neill it is hard to think of anyone in the American theatre who would have been prepared to take the risks which Glaspell does in *The Outside*.

The feminist dimension of the play lies in the extent to which the two central characters have allowed their lives to be drained of meaning when abandoned by their husbands – through death or desertion. A central theme of the feminist drama of the 1970s and 80s, in Glaspell's hands it becomes a contemplation less of the need for her women characters to be independent and self-contained than of the necessity to embrace one's suffering and accept one's emotional self. Indeed the male life-savers have a simple determination lacking in the two women, whose story this nonetheless is as they stumble towards the realisation that their own relationship itself constitutes the beginning of the meaning which they fear but which coheres even as they contend.

It was plainly a theme which fascinated Glaspell; certainly she chose to return both to this setting and to many of the concerns of *The Outside* in the novel which she published in 1929, four years after Jig Cook's death – *Fugitive's Return*. Here, too, we have a character who is attracted to the Massachusetts' Bay Cape because of 'its difficulties, its hard-won triumphs. It moved her that so much should grow in the sand, taking strange, wind-formed shapes . . . This strip of land extending itself beyond other land, reaching far out to sea, was something like life itself. Rather lonely, brave, making its own place of safety, surrounded by what was not itself. She loved the way the wind bent the tall beach grass, and when she found bright flowers in the moss she had a more tender feeling than flowers had given before.' Here, too, we have a woman shocked into silence when her husband leaves her, a woman who finally becomes a symbol of the need to protect and celebrate life. Indeed, one character (not, as it happens, the one who withdraws into silence) has almost the same name as one of the principal figures in *The Outside* – Allie Myer (a more pointedly Jewish version of the name). The question asked is even much the same: 'Must one indeed earn one's right to emotion – earn it by having faced that which brings it, playing one's part in it, with effort, with awareness.'[18] The result is a reconciliation with experience which is essentially that with which her earlier play had ended, though now the action is transferred to Greece where Susan Glaspell had also lost her husband, though in her case to death. Where the play scores over the novel is that the latter allows her to indulge her sentimental vision at greater length. Once again the most impressive element is the voluntary aphasia which afflicts her central character but the impact of this is lost in the context of a fluent narrative voice. In the play, silence has its own compelling quality.

Glaspell was nothing if not experimental. Each play offered her an opportunity to explore different problems, to test her own abilities. Thus, though the one-act form was ideal for the purpose of the Provincetown Players, just as she had moved from short story to novel, so inevitably she moved to a full-length play, her first, *Bernice*, being produced in 1919. It focusses on the motives, emotional commitments and nature of a woman who never appears. Bernice has died and her family, including her philanderer husband, gather at her home. When the maid reveals that her death was a suicide her husband sees this as evidence of her concern for him and, stricken both by guilt and, paradoxically, by the belief that such a sacrifice is an indication of his worth, determines to change his life. When Bernice's best friend discovers that far from committing suicide her friend had in fact died of natural causes, she is at first disillusioned, by what she takes to be her wanton cruelty in instructing her husband to be deceived, but then eventually convinced that it is a deliberate attempt to redeem him. Somewhat unconvincing in its mannered dialogue and stereotypical characters, its interest lies in the skill with which she attempts to create a character who never appears and construct a play in which the tension derives not from action but from character.

Though well received, it is the play which seems to me to have suffered most from the passage of time. The roué husband is almost wholly unconvincing, with a shallowness of character which drains Bernice's action of meaning and significance; the legerdemain, whereby significant information is released to characters and audience, is a contrivance which elsewhere she handles with far greater skill. And, worse still, the absent Bernice never acquires the same reality and conviction as the desperate murderess of *Trifles* or even the solitary poet of her later play, *Alison's House*. What she was testing, however, was her ability to sustain a full length play, to generate a dramatic situation in which language alone could recreate relationships which we never see except as they are refracted through words which are themselves acknowledged to be deeply ambiguous and deceptive. The result was a curiously contrived and dramatically static work, albeit one in which the determining voice and actions are those of women who deliberately create the dramas within which men are obliged to act.

Susan Glaspell was a product of the Midwest and, though she spent many of the most important years of her life on the north-east coast or in Greece, that world remained crucial to her: 'Although my home has for some years been in the East ... almost everything I write has its roots in the Mid-West; I suppose because my own are there.'[19] As she later confessed, in a letter to Edmund Wilson written in 1945, 'The Middle West must have taken strong hold of me in my early years for I've never ceased trying to figure out why it is as it is.' Though repelled by its moralistic self-righteousness, its failure to allow the individual freedom to develop and experiment, she also acknowledged its importance to her and to the country. As she wrote of her last novel, *Judd Rankin's Daughter* (1945), 'here is my own past ... I came out of that kind of life. And as I do not agree with it, I wanted to be very fair to it; and that was not hard, for I love Judd Rankin and I think I understand him. He's America, the old-time America. He has so much to offer us.'[20] Just how much and how ambiguous that heritage is is expressed by *Inheritors* (1921), a play which James Agate, writing in the *Sunday Times*, ranked alongside *The Master Builder*. It is an assessment which it is hard to share. Compared to her other work the play is deeply conventional, offering the kind of expository writing which elsewhere she chose to avoid. On the other hand, it constitutes a very precise portrait of the tensions between her own dual commitment to a new radicalism and to the pioneer values of the world from which she came and as such it addressed an ambiguity which the critic Ludwig Lewisohn was not alone in detecting at the heart of the American experience.

The action begins, significantly, on the fourth of July, fourteen years after the Civil War. In a midwestern farmhouse whose pioneer origins are clear in everything from the home-made table and rugs to the toy boat on the floor – the house is set just back from the Mississippi – a pioneer settler identifies a primary moral failure of the Republic, its treatment of the Indian. She also describes the friendship between her son, Silas Morton, and Felix Fejevary, a refugee from the Hungarian War of Independence, a friendship which is turned into a practical form when Fejevary helps Morton to found a college on the hill overlooking the small settlement. They commit themselves to the future as they regard themselves as a product of the past, a link in a chain of being which has seen evolution sustained by the human spirit. The language in which this is expressed is sometimes distressingly laboured and occasionally absurd – 'from the first of life there have been adventurers – those of best brain and courage who wanted to be more than life had been ... from aspiration has come doing, and doing has shaped the thing with which to do – it gives our hand a history which should make us want to use it well.'[21] But this is a familiar Glaspell theme. When Silas remarks that 'we are what we are because through all that time there've been them that wanted to be more than life had been',[22] he expresses a conviction which recurs through many of her novels and plays but which scarcely gains force through reiteration.

The second act takes place forty years later when the dreams of the founders are at risk of being compromised. Felix Fejevary, son of the founder's friend and president of the board of trustees, takes pride in the role which his students have played as strike breakers, while applying for state funds to expand the institution. The price demanded is the expulsion of radical elements, especially a teacher who has pleaded the case of a conscientious objector. Felix's own son, Horace, is a racist determined to hound two Hindu students, apostles of a free India, ironically hoping to invoke Abraham Lincoln to underscore his patriotism. Unfortunately, what he finds in Lincoln is a justification for precisely that revolutionary stance advocated by the Indian students and of course embraced equally by his own grandfather. Indeed, here, as elsewhere in the play, the moral symmetry is all too pat.

It comes as no surprise to learn that the supposedly radical teacher, Professor Holden, finds his inspiration partly in an American tradition going back through Thoreau and Whitman, and partly in Greece, nor that it is a woman – the young granddaughter of Silas Morton – who is the centre of resistance and who is warned by Felix that 'there are women in our prisons' for proving as socially recalicitrant as he considers her to be. What has gone wrong is that the pursuit of wealth has replaced the pursuit of ideals; a country which once welcomed the stranger (the pioneers, we are told, would leave a window uncurtained so that the light would act as a beacon for those who might be lost) has become xenophobic (the Red Scare of 1919 reflected a profound isolationism which settled on the country following the First World War).

Here, as elsewhere (particularly in *The Verge*), idealism is the victim not only of bigotry, but of love which is seen as inhibiting those who might otherwise commit themselves more completely to the cause. So, Professor Holden finally advocates compromise because he cannot afford to place his invalid wife at risk. Virtues thus become vices under the pressure of those for whom conformity is a primary objective and it is tempting to see this concern as an expression of Susan Glaspell's own sense of the liberating and coercive power of an emotion which had threatened to suffocate her husband back in Iowa and which perhaps in her own case subordinated her own talents to his obsessions.

Here, as elsewhere, she derives a central image from the natural world. Madeline's father has devoted himself to improving the quality of his corn, greedily keeping the secret to himself and becoming paranoid in his suspicion of his neighbours. But the seed blows on the wind and thus his gains are shared by those around him. This seems patently offered as an image of an isolationist America, anxious to enjoy its privileges in isolation. By extension, it is also offered as an observation about a human obligation to lend one's talents to the cause of the generality. Perhaps in some sense it is even advanced as a justification of the writer. Beyond that, Glaspell may have found inspiration for the play in her husband's efforts to found a College Teachers' Union. In a series of articles he had expressed a concern at the power exercised by college trustees over professors, the threat to free thought and enquiry: 'Our professors', he objected, 'are not Freiherrs. Their humiliating dependence on the will of other men deprives them of their spiritual qualities which create discipleship. There was no board of financier trustees at Jena, to tell Haekel to soft-pedal his subversive evolutionary ideas, and dismiss him without trial if he declined.'[23] But in her hands this alarm becomes a key to more fundamental national dilemmas, a fact acknowledged by at least one of her critics. For Ludwig Lewisohn, *Inheritors* was

> the first American play in which a strong intellect and a ripe artistic nature grasped and set forth in human terms the central tradition and most burning problem of the national life quite justly and scrupulously, equally without acrimony and compromise. The American drama had not shown then and has scarcely shown since, anything comparable to the delineation of the three generations of

authentic American libertarians in 'Inheritors' nor anything
comparable to Miss Glaspell's dramatic projection of the decadence
of the great tradition of American idealism nor anything so stirring
in permanent dramatic force and fire as the beautifully credible fact
that once more in a mere girl, inheritor of the spirit of both the
pioneer and the continental revolutionary of 1848, there flamed up
an inner purity of soul that prompts her to resist the evil ways and
days upon which her civilization has fallen and go forth to certain
martyrdom rather than consent to the moral disintegration of both
her country and her kin. 'Inheritors', moreover, was more than a
stirring play; it was in its day and date, a deed of national import.[24]

The claim is an extreme one and difficult to sustain. That it should have
been made by a critic as astute as Lewisohn suggests the extent to which the
play addressed issues of genuine contemporary significance. Perceived as an
epic analysis of the decline of American idealism, it dramatised not only the
failure of pioneer values, but also the extent to which the fate of those
values now lay with a new generation. That it did so in a form less
challenging than many of her other works creates something of a tension
between a radicalism of subject and a conservatism of form which is never
resolved. Nevertheless, the sheer scale of the play, its attempts to identify
the roots of a national ambiguity of experience and thought, went beyond
anything else which she wrote.

But the same year which saw the relative conventionalities of *Inheritors*
also marked the production of a startlingly original work, one which, in its
inventiveness, rivalled anything produced by the young O'Neill. In *The
Verge* (1921), Susan Glaspell combined comedy and melodrama, symbolism
and expressionism, feminism and a critique of feminism, social criticism and
metaphysical enquiry. What begins as a play of witty social observation
quickly shifts its ground. The result is a work which is challenging in the
demands which it makes on producers and designers no less than on
audiences. At times its effects are pressed almost to the point of absurdity,
but few writers, before or since, would have attempted such a radical
revisioning of all aspects of theatre.

When the first act opens, the lights reveal a greenhouse surrounded with
snow, its glass covered with a tracery of frost. Inside is a strange plant,
dominating the stage, and this plant, together with another equally exotic
creation, becomes the symbolic centre of the play as a parallel is asserted
between mutation in the plant and human world. Behind *The Verge* it is not
difficult to see the influence of Strindberg and, more distantly, that of the
Monists for whom the human and the non-human bear the same imprint.

Not merely had Strindberg chosen to transform the stage into a huge
flower in *A Dream Play* ('When the castle burns, the flower bud on the roof

bursts into a gigantic chrysanthemum') but in various para-scientific experiments which he conducted he explored the relationship between the human and the plant world. He liked to think that he was projecting to a logical conclusion the views of those who, believing in the homogeneity of all matter, proclaimed themselves Monists. He chose to eliminate the frontiers separating matter from mind. And it is worth remembering not merely that Susan Glaspell was an admirer of Strindberg but that, back in Davenport, Iowa, she had met George Cram Cook at a meeting of the Monists, whose basic principle, as Glaspell defined it, was that 'God did not create man. Man rose in nature as one form of nature – even as sun and earth.'[25]

Thus a stage direction indicates that the frost which covers the greenhouse 'has made fresh patterns on the glass as if – as Plato would have it – the patterns inherent in abstract nature and behind all life had to come out not only in the creative heat within, but in the creative cold on the other side of the glass' – a direction as challenging to a designer as anything proposed by Eugene O'Neill. The vine which grows at the back of the greenhouse throbs with even greater meaning: 'You might see the form of a cross in it, if you happened to think it that way. The leaves of this vine are not the form that leaves have been. They are at once repellent and significant.'[26] In fact significance positively glows in a play which begins as the kind of comedy that she had written with Jig Cook, mocking the very pretensions to which they were themselves drawn, and ends as the most disturbing work she ever produced. The bizarre plant itself is called the Breath of Life while its companion is the Edge Vine, the blurring of the distinction between the plant and the human world being further underlined by the presence of a man called Edgeworthy.

The central character is a woman – Claire – who breeds plants which will transcend their origins, make some leap beyond the norm. It soon becomes plain that she plans much the same for herself, and what Claire sets herself to do in her own life Susan Glaspell tries to do with the form of the play. A comedy of manners, it reaches out towards something else. Glaspell wants to create a new dramatic hybrid just as Claire wants to escape the 'forms moulded for us'. Claire's description of her horticultural objectives are in effect Susan Glaspell's description of the processes of her own play: 'If it were all in pieces, we'd be shocked to aliveness – wouldn't we? There would be strange new comings together – mad new comings together'.[27] On the other hand she is equally aware of the necessity for form; madness, incoherence, the collapse of all structures, clearly carries its own risk. There is more than a streak of the conventional in Glaspell. It is very evident in her novels (as it was to be in a play such as *Alison's House*). Though her characters frequently challenge conventions, the conventions of the novel remain intact. If *The Verge* is a call to reach beyond the comfortable confines of character, plot and language, it is also a play which finally acknowledges the price exacted for such presumption. In a sense it is the price which the avant-garde is always called upon to pay – the risk of losing touch with one's audience. Not the least of the things it becomes necessary to transcend are the very forms which one has generated oneself. Thus, Claire remarks, 'It's hard to – get past what we've done. Our own dead things – block the way.'[28] The solution, in the case of Claire, seems to lie in insanity, a step beyond the norm which sends her spinning into the void. But the notion that invention, self-creation, the pressing back of boundaries may lead in the direction of madness was not only a familiar one, it was one for which she had a model close to home.

No one who lived with Jig Cook could doubt that a certain monomaniacal energy was the key to his power. He was certainly no less capable of being overwhelmed by an idea than O'Neill. Anyone reading his diary extracts in *The Road to the Temple* could not help but be struck by the obsessive nature of his imagination, the ferocity with which he tracked ideas or feelings to their lair. He quite plainly came to the brink of breakdown more than once and even as celebratory a volume as the hagiography with which Glaspell chose to mark his life and commemorate his death hints at tensions and drives which she could barely understand, let alone satisfy. Yet that was also the essence of his power. He did indeed go beyond the edge, and it is tempting to see in Claire a portrait of a man who was equally capable of severing the links between himself and conventionality in the pursuit of ambitions and meanings which he could only express indirectly, through the metaphor of theatre.

It is also tempting to see *The Verge* as Susan Glaspell's version of Jig Cook's 1911 novel, *The Chasm*. Even the titles seem to hint at a relationship. The theme of Cook's novel, as she herself described it, was the 'chasm ... between man and the higher race that may follow him', between 'the Socialist and the Nietzschean feeling about life'.[29] The Nietzschean figure in the book is a Russian nobleman; the socialist, a gardener. The former dreams of a race that may split off from men and become supermen: 'The instinct of the mass is to drag back and reabsorb all such aspiring life. In the past the mass has been successful. Somewhere, sometime – mankind will be overcome. Perhaps the intense effort to draw the wealth of the world into the power of a tiny social fraction may be a concentration of racial energy, destined to create a special environment, mold the new race and send a chosen people of nature across the chasm sundering species from species ... ' The image presented is of 'mankind as a female, big with the embryonic daughter race that shall replace us as the mistress of the earth'.[30] The socialist (possibly a portrait of the young Floyd Dell) is presented as a gardener, equally familiar with the world of plants and men. He insists on the need to transform not a part, but the whole of humanity.

Like Walt Whitman (and he is called Walt), he sees a vision of human unity.

In *The Verge* Susan Glaspell creates a portrait of a woman who sees herself as being in some sense pregnant with this new being. Herself a gardener, Claire displaces her efforts to achieve a breakthrough to a new sense of being onto the plant world, accepting no real distinction between species. She, too, is prepared to sacrifice others to bring this new being into existence; but here the playwright offers no socialist counterweight. The debate, in effect, is contained within the mind and sensibility of a central character who flirts with madness and even extinction in order to break out of the banality of forms. Like Cook, like O'Neill, like Dreiser and many of those drawn to Nietzsche, she was intoxicated by the notion of a radical restructuring of the sensibility, by the drive to attain a new level of being; but she was equally aware of the human cost. *The Verge* represents her attempt to debate this issue in a form which was itself novel. And novelty of form was an imperative to the modernist movement to which she was instinctively drawn, not least in the world of art from which she seems to have derived her strong pictorial sense, her stage sets frequently being offered as metaphors. She herself, in response to developments in art, wrote of the 'shock of new forms, and hence awareness of all form, the adventure of the great new chance for expressing what has not been formed'.[31] *The Verge* was a pure expression of this will.

Claire's husband wishes that she would restrict herself to creating flowers that were 'as good as possible of their kind'. It was a comment which Glaspell had heard before in relation both to the theatre and to the position of women. Indeed, his casual remark that, 'That's an awfully nice thing for a woman to do – raise flowers',[32] serves to underline another principal theme of the play – the necessity for and yet deeper danger of a woman seeking to transcend her social, and, indeed, biologic role. For it quickly becomes apparent that Claire makes no distinction between herself and the flowers with which she experiments. What once was perhaps a metaphor, an analogue for her own suppressed desires, becomes merely one dimension of an underlying metaphysical principle – the necessity to evolve, to breach the boundaries which only seem implacable because of a failure of imagination and will. In terms of art, that desire is expressed by Richard Demming, attracted to Claire in part because he recognises in her a reflection of his own desire to turn his back on artistic norms. His drawings offend Claire's husband precisely because they do not appear to conform to anything recognisable. They are 'lines that don't make anything'; in other words they fail to resemble anything beyond themselves. But even he falls short of the radical experimentation to which Claire commits herself in her life no less than her work.

Claire's first husband had been an artist, who disappointed her by the banality of form for which he settled. Her second was a pilot whom she married in an attempt to turn the literal into metaphor and when that, too, failed she saw the war as perversely offering the chance of new beginnings. With the old world smashed she had looked for a new one; instead the old patterns had reassembled themselves. Looking for mutation, sudden illogical leaps which displace being onto a different plane, she encounters instead a stubborn resistance symbolised by her husband's antiquated language and still more antiquated attitudes.

Despite the power of its invention, *The Verge* is not without its problems. Some passages dissolve into mere pretension, a frantic posturing by characters about whom we know little. Her daughter Elizabeth is unconvincing, her language often self-mocking, her social visions mere caricatures; and it is, moreover, one thing for Claire to feel contempt for her husband and daughter but quite another for Glaspell to do so. Yet suddenly the dialogue can flare with brilliant paradoxes and genuine wit, language becoming significant not only for its lexical meaning but for what it communicates about character and the nature of meaning itself. Indeed, just as the play could itself be seen as in part a defence of formalism – as Claire struggles to create for its own sake – so language itself becomes a subject. Words are prized away from their referents. It is almost as if, to Claire, the regularities of grammar, the coherences hinted at by linguistic structure, themselves imply a repressive order. Her language certainly begins to exhaust itself as she moves away from the conventional relationships which she seeks. Her syntax begins to break down. She is afraid that words will diminish what they set out to describe, that in defining they will limit. She aspires to something that is 'not shut up in saying', as logically she must if she wishes to escape the received, the accepted, the second-hand. When Tom Edgeworthy, who of all those who surround her most clearly understands her and her aspirations, suggests that 'things may be freed by expression. Come from the unrealized into the fabric of life', she insists that this is the essence of the problem in that this would in turn 'freeze into its pattern'.[33] What she wants is not definition but 'flow' and if this involves pain and anguish, which almost by definition can never find their way fully into words, then so be it. But so long as she speaks she is trapped. She has failed in her attempts to go beyond. Indeed the prison house of language is inescapable this side of insanity and she who wishes to avoid pattern finds herself falling into the formalities of language in the form of verse:

> My love, you're going away –
> Let me tell you how it is with me;
> I want to touch you – somehow touch you once before
>   I die –
> Let me tell you how it is with me.

> I do not want to work,
> I want to be;
> Do not want to make a rose or make a poem –
> Want to lie upon the earth and know.
> Stop doing that! – words going into patterns;[34]

Shocked, she moves towards a minimal articulateness. But even then she is ready to trade it for love in the hope that sheer passion will redeem her life. When that is denied there is only what passes for insanity as she rejects her sister 'always smothering it with the word for it', and subsequently both her husband and her daughter. Finally, she also rejects the man she loves whose crime it is to give a name to that love: 'Beauty is not something you say about beauty',[35] she reproves him. Love is one final snare, one final chain tying her to the familiar, the desired, the limiting. In a last effort to break free she kills the man she loves. The Breath of Life has made its leap into a new existence only to become a new repressive form. It was a subject which came close to home for a woman whose novels had centred on the nature of love and its consequences and who in her private life, no less than her art, had wrestled with the question of whether love should be seen as liberating or enslaving.

When she and Cook read Strindberg's *There Are Crimes and Crimes* they debated the virtues of insanity. To Cook, 'if the will of a man is able to reestablish its control over those abnormally intensified faculties – such a man possesses instruments of creation surpassing in power anything in the possession of the completely sane, well-balanced mind. To a mind once rendered acute to the perception of symbols the whole world turns marvellously into symbol.'[36] Nietzsche, likewise, he regarded as treading a necessary line on the very boundary of insanity: 'to fill the world with new, invigorating thought and passion – it was worth going mad for'.[37] But he was not unaware of the danger and in the self-dramatising bombast of his journal entry it is possible to hear more than an echo of *The Verge*: 'We must not evade our tests, though they are perhaps the most dangerous game we can play, and are propounded to us ourselves as witnesses and before no other judge. Not to be caught of a person, be it the most beloved – every person is a prison, and a corner ... Not to be caught of one's own emancipation, that voluptuous remoteness and strangeness of the bird mounting ever higher in order to see more beneath itself: the peril of the soarer.' In particular, he warned himself, 'Not to be caught of Frederick Nietzsche.' One must, he insisted, 'possess, not be possessed by, the opposite powers of self-expansion and self-obliteration',[38] precisely the dilemma of the central character in *The Verge*, a tension between what Cook regarded as the male and female aspects of the mind, between selfishness and selflessness. The dilemma of the idealist, embodied in the person of Claire, is precisely what he had described in his own journal (and in discussion with Glaspell): 'A true and strong idealist is a filament projected by the race out into its future path – as a moving amœba projects a fingerlike process and by it draws its whole self after. But the strain on the foremost point is great. The whole body pulls on it. If its hold on the new ground be weak, it is pulled back – the idealist ceases to be one. If its connection with the body be weak, the filament is torn and left alone, the body does not follow it. The only idealist who is of service is he whose grip on his own truth and on the world of men cannot be torn loose.'[39] At the time of the founding of the Monist Society he had asked, 'May there not be men who are such wild precursors of life's conquest of a new element? Who shall set bounds to this earthly life which had risen from soil to plant, from plant to animal, from water to air, from unconsciousness to consciousness, from mindlessness to mind, and from mind – whither?'[40] These questions are in essence those raised in a work which deals with a character who, like Nietzsche in Cook's mind, was 'insane with truth'. *The Verge* is a remarkable, if imperfect, work.

Before leaving for Greece in 1922, George Cram Cook wrote a valedictory for the Provincetown Players, although they were to continue under new management until 1927. The idea was to suspend productions for something over a year. In a public announcement of the fact he expressed some confidence about the future, but in the note with which he addressed his playwrights Cook introduced a rather sourer note.

> We have a frank word to say. Founded for you, committed to the production of your plays only with a steady flood of manuscripts almost submerging us, we have faced, notwithstanding, season after season, a discouraging lack of plays worth the doing. During our eight seasons we have produced ninety-three plays by forty-seven American playwrights. We have given two playwrights to America, Eugene O'Neill and Susan Glaspell: we could have given a dozen by now if the other ten had appeared. We have looked for them eagerly and we have not found those among you offering us a sustained stream of freely experimental work in new dramatic forms. We do not want plays cut to old theatric patterns but we have produced many mediocre plays because we had nothing better to offer. We have never cared about the public's reaction to theme and treatment but we have greatly cared about their production values to us. We have always faced so-called 'failure' as the inevitable price of many an experiment to be definitely 'for something' which would make it, even if it failed, a part of ultimate success.[41]

In fact he was never to return nor was Susan Glaspell to sustain her commitment to experiment. Her life with Cook was anything but easy. It could scarcely be otherwise with such an obsessive individual. From time to time she even thought of escaping her Greek exile, writing a desperate letter to Hutchins Hapgood who was then in Paris. But whatever it was that held them together was plainly powerful and after his death in 1924 and her return to Provincetown, Hapgood acknowledged that 'she had lost everything, not only her lover and companion, but the spiritual and artistic direction of her life'.[42] Certainly, after her return she contributed no further plays to the Provincetown and, indeed, with the single exception of *Alison's House* she never wrote another play (apart from a collaborative work called *The Comic Artist* which she wrote with Norman Matson). Whatever the nature of her relationship with Cook it seems clear that it was at the heart both of her private life and of the work which she produced for a theatre which he had played a central role in shaping.

The moral complexities of her originally adulterous affair with Jig Cook never really seem to have ceased fascinating her. Certainly it was a subject to which she repeatedly returned, examining fragile marriages (*Bernice, The Verge*), exploring the plight of the abandoned woman (*The Outside, Fugitive*) or offering a justification for the woman whose affair with a married man destroys a marriage: 'love was not a thing of right or wrong, it was the thing that had to have its way – life's great imperative'.[43] Her affair with Cook had left two children without a father (although the break with them was not final) and though pledged to asserting the authenticity of feeling over convention she never ceased offering implicit justifications for her action. In *The Road to the Temple*, the book with which she marked the death and celebrated the life of her husband, she insisted that 'love may be strong as death. Death you will face easily for love, for that somehow does itself. Even more than disgrace you will face for love. You will risk hurt and shame for those you love. You will violate your own sense of fairness and right. In a world that is falling around you love dwells as sure, as proud, as if life had come into being that this might be.'[44] *The Verge*, which she wrote during a period of some stress between herself and Cook, suggested otherwise – that if love represented freedom it could also carry its own coercions. But by the time she came to write her last play, six years after Cook's death, she was inclined to offer some kind of absolution to herself and others.

Alison's House, the play which brought her her greatest success, including a Pulitzer Prize, takes as one of its central motifs the need to follow the truth of one's feelings, identifying the price of failing to do so. Indeed, virtually the only kind of relationship in this play which is granted any authenticity is an extra-marital one. Very loosely based on the figure of Emily Dickinson, the play takes place in Susan Glaspell's home state of Iowa. Once again the central character is absent – the reclusive poet Alison Stanhope having died. The family are gathered to clear the house preparatory to its sale as Alison's sister, Agatha, is no longer capable of fending for herself. In the course of the play we learn not only that Alison had fallen in love with a married man, denying herself a relationship which might have transformed her life, but that her brother had made the same decision when tempted by a married woman. If that were not enough, the poet's niece also finds herself faced with the same dilemma, except that in her case she opts to leave town with the man she loves, thereby forcing him to abandon wife and children. Meanwhile, Alison's nephew is trapped in a marriage devoid of all meaning, in the process sacrificing his own ambition to be a poet. Held back by convention he has, in effect, sacrificed his talent and his life.

The action takes place literally at the turn of the century, on December 31, 1899. On the sudden death of Agatha, a previously unknown collection of Alison Stanhope's poems is discovered, poems which express the anguish which she felt in sacrificing her life to a stultifying morality. The family have to decide whether to destroy the poems or to release them to the world. It is in part a battle between the generations, as the young members of the family argue for a new world of openness, and in part a discussion of art and its responsibility to acknowledge life as it is rather than as it is represented to be. The world is plainly on the turn. There are echoes of *The Cherry Orchard* as the house is sold to a man who wishes to convert it into a resort hotel and who has no respect for its past; but it has little of the moral density of Chekhov's play, the would-be owner representing little more than a philistine pragmatism. This is because Glaspell's moral focus lies elsewhere. The playwright who presented herself as a New Woman, free of the restrictive morality and social constraints of the old world, seems intent on offering yet another justification for herself and her actions. As one of the characters observes, 'You can't run away with a married man – live with a man who has a wife and children and not be talked about.'[45] The decision over whether to preserve and publish the poems becomes only partly a family affair, a question of whether to allow the truth to leak out; more significantly, it is offered as a public gesture because 'Alison said it – for women'.[46] It becomes a decision which will acknowledge the rights of feeling over convention; and Susan Glaspell, too, says it for women, or at least for those who will no longer accept the terms of the contract as offered to them, albeit in a play whose logic leaves the terms of that contract largely unquestioned.

Alison's House is not a good play. In attacking social conventions it remains in thrall to theatrical convention. The adventurousness of her earlier work, her concern to press character to the point of disintegration, her sense of language as itself inhibiting access to feeling, gives way here to a conventional three-act play whose contrivances are painfully obvious. The reiterated pattern of would-be and actual adulterous affairs begins to seem like a pathological inherited condition rather than the focus for a debate about morality and passion. The concealed truth about Alison's life is coyly trailed through the play until its revelation serves maximum dramatic effect. The very setting – in the last hours of the century – presses symbolism in the direction of cliché, while her own penchant for sentimentality and melodrama – controlled earlier in her career by a startling originality of conception – is here given full licence. The result is a play which brought her popular success and exposed the extent to which she still felt it necessary to engage in a debate with her own past and with a morality which, if scarcely irrelevant, had lost a great deal of its immediacy. When she had first gone to New York such concerns had seemed central to the new freedoms then being claimed by women and by those newly liberated from Victorian pieties. By 1930, the issue no longer had the same force or relevance and the award of the Pulitzer Prize, if nothing else, was a clear enough indication of this fact.

Perhaps the most astute of Glaspell's critics was Ludwig Lewisohn who rightly chose to emphasise her reticence which he related to an innate puritanism:

> She is the Puritan struggling toward freedom, toward unaccustomed expression ... She is morbidly frugal in expression, but nakedly candid in substance ... She is a dramatist a little afraid of speech. Her dialogue is so spare that it often becomes arid. The bleak farmsteads of Iowa, the stagnant villages of New England touched her work with penury and chill. She wants to speak out and let her people speak out. But neither she nor they can conquer a sense that intimate and vigorous expression is a little shameless. To uncover one's soul seems, in these plays, almost like uncovering one's body. Behind Miss Glaspell's hardihood of thought hovered the fear and self-torment of the Puritan. She was never quite spontaneous and unconscious and free, never the unquestioning servant of her art. She brooded and tortured herself and weighed the issues of expression. Thus the fault of her early one-act tragedies was an insufficiency of actual speech. Somewhere in every drama words must ring out. One ached in her plays for something to release the dumbness, complete the crisis, and drive the tragic situation home. Yet those plays were, except for O'Neill's, the first American plays that belonged to dramatic literature and not to the false and tawdry artifice of the uncreative theatre.[47]

For all the insight of this criticism, he is surely wrong in suggesting the need for a greater explicitness. Susan Glaspell's work is at its weakest in those moments in which she does allow her characters eloquence, fluency and explicitness, since language is in many respects at the heart of their dilemma. The crucial problem which confronts them is how to emerge into the communality of language without being contained by it; how to express yourself in words shaped by other consciousnesses. Bernice's words are bequeathed to those who survive her. Their problem is to invest them with a meaning which can sustain their own lives. In *Inheritors* the rhetoric of the past has to be revivified by a new language of social responsibility. In *The Verge* language restrains a spirit which would free itself from the social contract implied by speech. Susan Glaspell does indeed weigh the issues of expression. They are the essence of her work. Neither was she unaware of the extent to which her own freedoms were circumscribed by a language which tied her to social and biologic function. Her plays both placed this concern at their centre and constituted a statement of her own independence. It is, however, no incapacity which leads her to create dramatic metaphors or to expose a tension between her characters and the language which they deploy but of which they remain profoundly suspicious. That is the essence of the irony which defines them. As a dramatist she acknowledged the need to 'gain control over the tunes of the speaking voice – the actual melodrama created by successive changes of pitch when we speak to one another', but she equally knew that silence or the stuttering incompletions of language under stress had its own force, its own meaning. There is undeniably a melodramatic streak in Glaspell's imagination, but, as with O'Neill, that element was also her strength as she sought to press her concerns, her language and her techniques to the point at which she could challenge social no less than dramatic conventions. Her heroines tend to be placed in extreme situations. Marriages collapse, insanity threatens, death is an imminent or immediate threat. When not silenced by male violence, by emotional stress or by death, they struggle to articulate their needs to men whose lives are structured around other necessities. The metaphors to which she turns reinforce a marginality which has its social no less than psychological dimension. As their titles suggest – *The Outside, The Verge* – she locates her characters at the edge; they scarcely ever stray away from that region in any of her major plays. In *Inheritors* it is a woman who is at the leading edge of radical thought; in *Alison's House* it is a woman who breaks the codes of society as it is a woman whose failure to do so generates an art which may set others free. That was the essence of her concern – to follow Ibsen's dictum and press back the boundary posts, and for a time it seemed that she might become an exemplary figure, both a major writer and actress. That she did not was a double loss.

She acted in a number of her own plays and when she stepped into the leading role of *Inheritors* Jacques Copeau, who saw the performance, pronounced her a 'truly great actress'. But, following the death of her husband, she seems to have abandoned any ambitions in that direction, as she did, eventually, her career as a dramatist. She did retain an interest in the theatre, participating as the Midwest Director of the Federal Theatre Project from 1936–8, but it was, for the most part, as a novelist that she concluded her career, her last book – *Judd Rankin's Daughter* – appearing in 1945. It was, however, as a dramatist that she came closest to realising her full potential. Without her there must be some doubt as to whether the Provincetown Players would ever have been established and certainly whether that crucial organisation would have been able to sustain itself as it did. She was, without doubt, one of its two greatest discoveries; and if her plays were imperfect then so, too, were O'Neill's and for much the same reason. In her work, as in her life, she never settled for anything less than total commitment. Sometimes that took her where few others were willing or ready to follow. She chanced more than most of her contemporaries and achieved more than many of them. She deserves more than a footnote in the history of drama. Susan Glaspell died of viral pneumonia on July 27, 1948 having written some of the most original plays ever to have come out of America.

NOTES

1 Floyd Dell, *Homecoming* (New York, 1933), p. 170.
2 Susan Glaspell, *The Glory of the Conquered* (London, 1925).
3 Clarence A. Andrews, *Chicago in Story: A Literary History* (Iowa City, 1982), pp. 140–2.
4 Bernard Duffey, *The Chicago Renaissance in American Letters* (East Lansing, 1956), p. 134.
5 Susan Glaspell, *The Road to the Temple* (New York, 1927), pp. 212–13.
6 Bernard Duffey, p. 175.
7 Floyd Dell, p. 218.
8 *Ibid.*, p. 208.
9 Susan Glaspell, *The Road to the Temple*, pp. 235–6.
10 Helen Deutsch and Stella Hanau, *The Provincetown: A Story of the Theatre* (New York, 1931), pp. 17–18.
11 Floyd Dell, p. 201.
12 Susan Glaspell, *The Road to the Temple*, pp. 255–66.
13 *Trifles*, p. 42.
14 *Ibid.*, p. 44.
15 *The Outside*, p. 48.
16 *Ibid.*, p. 51.
17 *Ibid.*, p. 54.
18 Susan Glaspell, *Fugitives Return* (New York, 1929), pp. 152, 157.
19 Marcia Noe, 'Susan Glaspell's Analysis of the Midwest Character', *Books at Iowa*, XXVII (1977), p. 5.
20 *Ibid.*, p. 14.
21 *Inheritors*, p. 116.
22 *Ibid.*, p. 117.

23 Ludwig Lewisohn, *Expression in America* (New York, 1932), pp. 242–3.
24 *Ibid.*, p. 395.
25 Susan Glaspell, *The Road to the Temple*, p. 199.
26 *The Verge*, p. 58.
27 *Ibid.*, p. 64.
28 *Ibid.*, p. 77.
29 Susan Glaspell, *The Road to the Temple*, p. 204.
30 *Ibid.*, p. 205–6.
31 *Ibid.*, p. 218.
32 *The Verge*, p. 65.
33 *Ibid.*, p. 86.
34 *Ibid.*, p. 88.
35 *Ibid.*, p. 98.
36 *The Road to the Temple*, p. 170.
37 *Ibid.*, p. 171.
38 *Ibid.*, p. 172.
39 *Ibid.*, p. 177.
40 *Ibid.*, p. 197.
41 Helen Deutsch and Stella Hanau, p. 92.
42 Hutchins Hapgood, *A Victorian in the Modern World* (New York, 1939), p. 431.
43 Susan Glaspell, *Fidelity* (New York, 1915), p. 191.
44 *The Road to the Temple*, p. 250.
45 Susan Glaspell, *Alison's House* (New York, 1930), p. 13.
46 *Ibid.*, p. 150.
47 Ludwig Lewisohn, pp. 393–4.

BIOGRAPHICAL RECORD

1876? Susan Glaspell's birth date is a matter of dispute. Somewhat implausibly the later date of 1882 has been proposed but this seems extremely unlikely given the fact that she was already contributing to the *Davenport Weekly Outlook* in 1896 and graduated from Drake University three years later. It seems probable, therefore, that she was born in Davenport, Iowa in 1876.

1896 First short story published in *Davenport Weekly Outlook*.

1899 Graduated from Drake University.

1899–1901 Worked as a reporter for the *Davenport Morning Republican, Davenport Weekly Outlook, Des Moines Daily News, Des Moines Capital*.

1901? Returned to Davenport to become freelance writer.

1907 Met George Cram Cook and Floyd Dell at the Monist Club in Davenport.

1909 First novel, *The Glory of the Conquered*, published.

1911 Second novel, *The Visioning*, published.

1913 Married George Cram Cook (his third marriage) and moved from Chicago to Greenwich Village and Provincetown.

1914 First performance by what was to become the Washington Square Players.

1915 First season of the Washington Square Players. *Suppressed Desires*, rejected by the Washington Square Players, performed at Hutchins Hapgood's house, thus marking the beginnings of what was to become the Provincetown Players. Third novel, *Fidelity*, published.

1916 The Playwrights' Theatre, the New York home of the Provincetown Players, established. Susan Glaspell's first play – *Trifles* – performed at the Wharf Theatre.

1917 *The People, Close the Book* and *The Outside* all performed at the Playwrights' Theatre.

1918 New theatre opened at 133 MacDougal Street after the first was closed for violation of fire regulations. *Women's Honor*

(In compiling the details of Susan Glaspell's biography, bibliography and production details I have relied on the pioneer work of Marcia Noe, Gerhard Bach and Arthur E. Waterman who, however, bear no responsibility for any errors I may have committed or judgements I have made.)

	and *Tickless Time* (like *Suppressed Desires*, written with George Cram Cook) both performed.
1919	Her first full-length play, *Bernice*, performed at the Provincetown Playhouse, with Glaspell in the role of Abbie.
1920	A collection of her plays published in Boston and New York.
1921	*Inheritors* and *The Verge* performed at the Provincetown Playhouse.
1922	*Chains of Dew* performed at the Provincetown Playhouse. Cook and Glaspell left for Greece.
1924	January 14, Cook died in Greece.
1925	Met and married Norman Matson. Edited an edition of Cook's poems under the title *Greek Coins*.
1927	*The Road to the Temple* published.
1928	*The Comic Artist*, a collaborative work written with Matson, performed at the Strand Theatre. Fourth novel, *Brook Evans*.
1929	Fifth novel, *Fugitive's Return*.
1930	*Alison's House*.
1931	Pulitzer Prize for *Alison's House*. *Ambrose Holt and Family* published.
1932	Norman Matson left her for young girl of nineteen.
1932–6	During these years Susan Glaspell suffered from depression, poor health and financial difficulties.
1936	Appointed head of the Midwest Play Bureau of the Federal Theatre.
1938	Resigned from Federal Theatre. She lived for a time in Chicago but subsequently returned to Provincetown.
1939	*The Morning is Near Us*, seventh novel.
1940	*Cherished and Shared of Old*, eighth novel.
1942	*Norma Ashe* published.
1945	*Judd Rankin's Daughter*, tenth and last novel.
1948	Susan Glaspell died of pneumonia and pleural embolism on July 27.

TRIFLES

First performed by the Provincetown Players at the Wharf Theatre, Provincetown, Mass., August 8, 1916, with the following cast:

GEORGE HENDERSON (County Attorney)	Robert Rogers
HENRY PETERS (Sheriff)	Robert Conville
LEWIS HALE, A neighboring farmer	George Cram Cook
MRS PETERS	Alice Hall
MRS HALE	Susan Glaspell

SCENE: *The kitchen is the now abandoned farmhouse of* JOHN WRIGHT, *a gloomy kitchen, and left without having been put in order – unwashed pans under the sink, a loaf of bread outside the bread-box, a dish-towel on the table – other signs of incompleted work. At the rear the outer door opens and the* SHERIFF *comes in followed by the* COUNTY ATTORNEY *and* HALE. *The* SHERIFF *and* HALE *are men in middle life, the* COUNTY ATTORNEY *is a young man; all are much bundled up and go at once to the stove. They are followed by the two women – the* SHERIFF'*s wife first; she is a slight wiry woman, a thin nervous face.* MRS HALE *is larger and would ordinarily be called more comfortable looking, but she is disturbed now and looks fearfully about as she enters. The women have come in slowly, and stand close together near the door.*

COUNTY ATTORNEY: (*rubbing his hands*) This feels good. Come up to the fire, ladies.

MRS PETERS: (*after taking a step forward*) I'm not – cold.

SHERIFF: (*unbuttoning his overcoat and stepping away from the stove as if to mark the beginning of official business*) Now, Mr Hale, before we move things about, you explain to Mr Henderson just what you saw when you came here yesterday morning.

COUNTY ATTORNEY: By the way, has anything been moved? Are things just as you left them yesterday?

SHERIFF: (*looking about*) It's just the same. When it dropped below zero last night I thought I'd better send Frank out this morning to make a fire for us – no use getting pneumonia with a big case on, but I told him not to touch anything except the stove – and you know Frank.

COUNTY ATTORNEY: Somebody should have been left here yesterday.

SHERIFF: Oh – yesterday. When I had to send Frank to Morris Center for that man who went crazy – I want you to know I had my hands full yesterday. I knew you could get back from Omaha by today and as long as I went over everything here myself –

COUNTY ATTORNEY: Well, Mr Hale, tell just what happened when you came here yesterday morning.

HALE: Harry and I had started to town with a load of potatoes. We came along the road from my place and as I got here I said, 'I'm going to see if I can't get John Wright to go in with me on a party telephone.' I spoke to Wright about it once before and he put me off, saying folks talked too much anyway, and all he asked was peace and quiet – I guess you know about how much he talked himself; but I thought maybe if I went to the house and talked about it before his wife, though I said to Harry that I didn't know as what his wife wanted made much difference to John –

COUNTY ATTORNEY: Let's talk about that later, Mr Hale. I do want to talk about that, but tell now just what happened when you got to the house.

HALE: I didn't hear or see anything; I knocked at the door, and still it was all quiet inside. I knew they must be up, it was past eight o'clock. So I knocked again, and I thought I heard somebody say, 'Come in.' I wasn't sure, I'm not sure yet, but I opened the door – this door (*indicating the door by which the two women are still standing*) and there in that rocker – (*pointing to it*) sat Mrs Wright.

(*They all look at the rocker.*)

COUNTY ATTORNEY: What – was she doing?

HALE: She was rockin' back and forth. She had her apron in her hand and was kind of – pleating it.

COUNTY ATTORNEY: And how did she – look?

HALE: Well, she looked queer.

COUNTY ATTORNEY: How do you mean – queer?

HALE: Well, as if she didn't know what she was going to do next. And kind of done up.

COUNTY ATTORNEY: How did she seem to feel about your coming?

HALE: Why, I don't think she minded – one way or other. She didn't pay much attention. I said, 'How do, Mrs Wright it's cold, ain't it?' And she said, 'Is it?' – and went on kind of pleating at her apron. Well, I was surprised; she didn't ask me to come up to the stove, or to set down, but just sat there, not even looking at me, so I said, 'I want to see John.' And then she – laughed. I guess you would call it a laugh. I thought of Harry and the team outside, so I said a little sharp: 'Can't I see John?' 'No', she says, kind o' dull like. 'Ain't he home?' says I. 'Yes', says she, 'he's home'. 'Then why can't I see him?' I asked her, out of patience. ''Cause he's dead', says she. '*Dead?*' says I. She just nodded her head, not getting a bit excited, but rockin' back and forth. 'Why – where is he?' says I, not knowing what to say. She just pointed upstairs – like that (*himself pointing to the room above*) I got up, with the idea of going up there. I walked from there to here – then I says, 'Why, what did he die of?' 'He died of a rope round his neck', says she, and just went on pleatin' at her apron. Well, I went out and called Harry. I thought I might – need help. We went upstairs and there he was lyin' –

COUNTY ATTORNEY: I think I'd rather have you go into that upstairs, where you can point it all out. Just go on now with the rest of the story.

HALE: Well, my first thought was to get that rope off. It looked ... (*stops, his face twitches*) ... but Harry, he went up to him, and he said, 'No, he's dead all right, and we'd better not touch anything.' So we went back down stairs. She was still sitting that same way. 'Has anybody been notified?' I asked. 'No', says she unconcerned. 'Who did this, Mrs Wright?' said Harry. He said it business-like – and she stopped pleatin' of her apron. 'I don't know', she says. 'You don't *know*?' says Harry. 'No', says she. 'Weren't you sleepin' in the bed with him?' says Harry. 'Yes', says she, 'but I was on the inside'. 'Somebody slipped a rope round his neck and strangled him and you didn't wake up?' says Harry. 'I didn't wake up', she said after him. We must 'a looked as if we didn't see how that could be, for after a minute she said, 'I sleep sound'. Harry was going to ask her more questions but I said maybe we ought to let her tell her story first to the coroner, or the sheriff, so Harry went fast as he could to Rivers' place, where there's a telephone.

COUNTY ATTORNEY: And what did Mrs Wright do when she knew that you had gone for the coroner?

HALE: She moved from that chair to this one over here (*pointing to a small chair in the corner*) and just sat there with her hands held together and looking down. I got a feeling that I ought to make some conversation, so I said I had come in to see if John wanted to put in a telephone, and at that she started to laugh, and then she stopped and looked at me – scared. (*the* COUNTY ATTORNEY, *who has had his notebook out, makes a note*) I dunno, maybe it wasn't scared. I wouldn't like to say it was. Soon Harry got back, and then Dr Lloyd came, and you, Mr Peters, and so I guess that's all I know that you don't.

COUNTY ATTORNEY: (*looking around*) I guess we'll go upstairs first – and then out to the barn and around there. (*to the* SHERIFF) You're convinced that there was nothing important here – nothing that would point to any motive.

SHERIFF: Nothing here but kitchen things.

> (*The* COUNTY ATTORNEY, *after again looking around the kitchen, opens the door of a cupboard closet. He gets up on a chair and looks on a shelf. Pulls his hand away, sticky.*)

COUNTY ATTORNEY: Here's a nice mess.

> (*The women draw nearer.*)

MRS PETERS: (*to the other woman*) Oh, her fruit; it did freeze. (*to the* LAWYER) She worried about that when it turned so cold. She said the fire'd go out and her jars would break.

SHERIFF: Well, can you beat the women! Held for murder and worryin' about her preserves.

COUNTY ATTORNEY: I guess before we're through she may have something more serious than preserves to worry about.

HALE: Well, women are used to worrying over trifles.

> (*The two women move a little closer together.*)

COUNTY ATTORNEY: (*with the gallantry of a young politician*) And yet, for all their worries, what would we do without the ladies? (*the women do not unbend. He goes to the sink, takes a dipperful of water from the pail and pouring it into a basin, washes his hands. Starts to wipe them on the roller-towel, turns it for a cleaner place*) Dirty towels! (*kicks his foot against the pans under the sink*) Not much of a housekeeper, would you say, ladies?

MRS HALE: (*stiffly*) There's a great deal of work to be done on a farm.

COUNTY ATTORNEY: To be sure. And yet (*with a little bow to her*) I know there are some Dickson county farmhouses which do not have such roller towels.

> (*He gives it a pull to expose its length again.*)

MRS HALE: Those towels get dirty awful quick. Men's hands aren't always as clean as they might be.

COUNTY ATTORNEY: Ah, loyal to your sex, I see. But you and Mrs Wright were neighbors. I suppose you were friends, too.

MRS HALE: (*shaking her head*) I've not seen much of her of late years. I've not been in this house – it's more than a year.

COUNTY ATTORNEY: And why was that? You didn't like her?

MRS HALE: I liked her all well enough. Farmers' wives have their hands full, Mr Henderson. And then –

COUNTY ATTORNEY: Yes –?

MRS HALE: (*looking about*) It never seemed a very cheerful place.

COUNTY ATTORNEY: No – it's not cheerful. I shouldn't say she had the homemaking instinct.

MRS HALE: Well, I don't know as Wright had, either.

COUNTY ATTORNEY: You mean that they didn't get on very well?

MRS HALE: No, I don't mean anything. But I don't think a place'd be any cheerfuller for John Wright's being in it.

COUNTY ATTORNEY: I'd like to talk more of that a little later. I want to get the lay of things upstairs now.

(*He goes to the left, where three steps lead to a stair door.*)

SHERIFF: I suppose anything Mrs Peters does'll be all right. She was to take in some clothes for her, you know, and a few little things. We left in such a hurry yesterday.

COUNTY ATTORNEY: Yes, but I would like to see what you take, Mrs Peters, and keep an eye out for anything that might be of use to us.

MRS PETERS: Yes, Mr Henderson.

(*The women listen to the men's steps on the stairs, then look about the kitchen.*)

MRS HALE: I'd hate to have men coming into my kitchen, snooping around and criticising.

(*She arranges the pans under sink which the* LAWYER *had shoved out of place.*)

MRS PETERS: Of course it's no more than their duty.

MRS HALE: Duty's all right, but I guess that deputy sheriff that came out to make the fire might have got a little of this on. (*gives the roller towel a pull*) Wish I'd thought of that sooner. Seems mean to talk about her for not having things slicked up when she had to come away in such a hurry.

MRS PETERS: (*who has gone to a small table in the left rear corner of the room, and lifted one end of a towel that covers a pan*) She had bread set.
(*Stands still.*)

MRS HALE: (*eyes fixed on a loaf of bread beside the bread-box, which is on a low shelf at the other side of the room. Moves slowly toward it*) She was going to put this in there. (*picks up loaf, then abruptly drops it. In a manner of returning to familiar things*) It's a shame about her fruit. I wonder if it's all gone. (*gets up on the chair and looks*) I think there's some here that's all right, Mrs Peters. Yes – here; (*holding it toward the window*) this is cherries, too. (*looking again*) I declare I believe that's the only one. (*gets down, bottle in her hand. Goes to the sink and wipes it off on the outside*) She'll feel awful bad after all her hard work in the hot weather. I remember the afternoon I put up my cherries last summer.
(*She puts the bottle on the big kitchen table, center of the room. With a sigh, is about to sit down in the rocking-chair. Before she is seated realizes what chair it is; with a slow look at it, steps back. The chair which she has touched rocks back and forth.*)

MRS PETERS: Well, I must get those things from the front room closet. (*she goes to the door at the right, but after looking into the other room, steps back*) You coming with me, Mrs Hale? You could help me carry them.

(*They go in the other room; reappear,* MRS PETERS *carrying a dress and skirt,* MRS HALE *following with a pair of shoes.*)

MRS PETERS: My, it's cold in there.

(*She puts the clothes on the big table, and hurries to the stove.*)

MRS HALE: (*examining the skirt*) Wright was close. I think maybe that's why she kept so much to herself. She didn't even belong to the Ladies Aid. I suppose she felt she couldn't do her part, and then you don't enjoy things when you feel shabby. She used to wear pretty clothes and be lively, when she was Minnie Foster, one of the town girls singing in the choir. But that – oh, that was thirty years ago. This all you was to take in?

MRS PETERS: She said she wanted an apron. Funny thing to want, for there isn't much to get you dirty in jail, goodness knows. But I suppose just to make her feel more natural. She said they was in the top drawer in this cupboard. Yes, here. And then her little shawl that always hung behind the door. (*opens stair door and looks*) Yes, here it is.

(*Quickly shuts door leading upstairs.*)

MRS HALE: (*abruptly moving toward her*) Mrs Peters?

MRS PETERS: Yes, Mrs Hale?

MRS HALE: Do you think she did it?

MRS PETERS: (*in a frightened voice*) Oh, I don't know.

MRS HALE: Well, I don't think she did. Asking for an apron and her little shawl. Worrying about her fruit.

MRS PETERS: (*starts to speak, glances up, where footsteps are heard in the room above. In a low voice*) Mr Peters says it looks bad for her. Mr Henderson is awful sarcastic in a speech and he'll make fun of her sayin' she didn't wake up.

MRS HALE: Well, I guess John Wright didn't wake when they was slipping that rope under his neck.

MRS PETERS: No, it's strange. It must have been done awful crafty and still. They say it was such a – funny way to kill a man, rigging it all up like that.

MRS HALE: That's just what Mr Hale said. There was a gun in the house. He says that's what he can't understand.

MRS PETERS: Mr Henderson said coming out that what was needed for the case was a motive; something to show anger, or – sudden feeling.

MRS HALE: (*who is standing by the table*) Well, I don't see any signs of anger around here. (*she puts her hand on the dish towel which lies on the table, stands looking down at table, one half of which is clean, the other half messy*) It's wiped to here. (*makes a move as if to finish work, then turns and looks at loaf of bread outside the breadbox. Drops towel. In that voice of coming back to familiar things.*) Wonder how they are finding things upstairs. I hope she had it a little more red-up up there. You know, it seems kind of *sneaking*. Locking her up in town and then coming out here and trying to get her own house to turn against her!

MRS PETERS: But Mrs Hale, the law is the law.

MRS HALE: I s'pose 'tis. (*unbuttoning her coat*) Better loosen up your things, Mrs Peters. You won't feel them when you go out.

---

red-up: orderly; tidied or cleaned up.

(MRS PETERS *takes off her fur tippet, goes to hang it on hook at back of room, stands looking at the under part of the small corner table.*)

MRS PETERS: She was piecing a quilt.

(*She brings the large sewing basket and they look at the bright pieces.*)
MRS HALE: It's log cabin pattern. Pretty, isn't it? I wonder if she was goin' to quilt it or just knot it?

(*Footsteps have been heard coming down the stairs. The* SHERIFF *enters followed by* HALE *and the* COUNTY ATTORNEY.)

SHERIFF: They wonder if she was going to quilt it or just knot it!

(*The men laugh, the women look abashed.*)

COUNTY ATTORNEY: (*rubbing his hands over the stove*) Frank's fire didn't do much up there, did it? Well, let's go out to the barn and get that cleared up.

(*The men go outside.*)

MRS HALE: (*resentfully*) I don't know as there's anything so strange, our takin' up our time with little things while we're waiting for them to get the evidence. (*she sits down at the big table smoothing out a block with decision*) I don't see as it's anything to laugh about.

MRS PETERS: (*apologetically*) Of course they've got awful important things on their minds.

(*Pulls up a chair and joins* MRS HALE *at the table.*)

MRS HALE: (*examining another block*) Mrs Peters, look at this one. Here, this is the one she was working on, and look at the sewing! All the rest of it has been so nice and even. And look at this! It's all over the place! Why, it looks as if she didn't know what she was about!

(*After she has said this they look at each other, then start to glance back at the door. After an instant* MRS HALE *has pulled at a knot and ripped the sewing.*)

MRS PETERS: Oh, what are you doing, Mrs Hale?

MRS HALE: (*mildly*) Just pulling out a stitch or two that's not sewed very good. (*threading a needle*) Bad sewing always made me fidgety.

MRS PETERS: (*nervously*) I don't think we ought to touch things.

MRS HALE: I'll just finish up this end. (*suddenly stopping and leaning forward*) Mrs Peters?

MRS PETERS: Yes, Mrs Hale?

MRS HALE: What do you suppose she was so nervous about?

MRS PETERS: Oh – I don't know. I don't know as she was nervous. I sometimes sew awful queer when I'm just tired. (MRS HALE *starts to say something, looks at* MRS PETERS, *then goes on sewing*) Well I must get these things wrapped up. They may be through sooner than we think. (*putting apron and other things together*) I wonder where I can find a piece of paper, and string.

MRS HALE: In that cupboard, maybe.

MRS PETERS: (*looking in cupboard*) Why, here's a bird-cage. (*holds it up*) Did she have a bird, Mrs Hale?

MRS HALE: Why, I don't know whether she did or not – I've not been here for so

---

tippet: garment covering the shoulders, and sometimes the neck as well

long. There was a man around last year selling canaries cheap, but I don't
know as she took one; maybe she did. She used to sing real pretty herself.

MRS PETERS: (*glancing around*) Seems funny to think of a bird here. But she must
have had one, or why would she have a cage? I wonder what happened to it.

MRS HALE: I s'pose maybe the cat got it.

MRS PETERS: No, she didn't have a cat. She's got that feeling some people have
about cats – being afraid of them. My cat got in her room and she was real
upset and asked me to take it out.

MRS HALE: My sister Bessie was like that. Queer, ain't it?

MRS PETERS: (*examining the cage*) Why, look at this door. It's broke. One hinge is
pulled apart.

MRS HALE: (*looking too*) Looks as if someone must have been rough with it.

MRS PETERS: Why, yes.
> (*She brings the cage forward and puts it on the table.*)

MRS HALE: I wish if they're going to find any evidence they'd be about it. I don't
like this place.

MRS PETERS: But I'm awful glad you came with me, Mrs Hale. It would be
lonesome for me sitting here alone.

MRS HALE: It would, wouldn't it? (*dropping her sewing*) But I tell you what I do
wish, Mrs Peters. I wish I had come over sometimes when *she* was here. I –
(*looking around the room*) – wish I had.

MRS PETERS: But of course you were awful busy, Mrs Hale – your house and your
children.

MRS HALE: I could've come. I stayed away because it weren't cheerful – and that's
why I ought to have come. I – I've never liked this place. Maybe because it's
down in a hollow and you don't see the road. I dunno what it is, but it's a
lonesome place and always was. I wish I had come over to see Minnie Foster
sometimes. I can see now – (*shakes her head*)

MRS PETERS: Well, you mustn't reproach yourself, Mrs Hale. Somehow we just
don't see how it is with other folks until – something comes up.

MRS HALE: Not having children makes less work – but it makes a quiet house, and
Wright out to work all day, and no company when he did come in. Did you
know John Wright, Mrs Peters?

MRS PETERS: Not to know him; I've seen him in town. They say he was a good
man.

MRS HALE: Yes – good; he didn't drink, and kept his word as well as most, I
guess, and paid his debts. But he was a hard man, Mrs Peters. Just to pass the
time of day with him – (*shivers*) Like a raw wind that gets to the bone. (*pauses,
her eye falling on the cage*) I should think she would 'a wanted a bird. But what
do you suppose went with it?

MRS PETERS: I don't know, unless it got sick and died.
> (*She reaches over and swings the broken door, swings it again, both
> women watch it.*)

MRS HALE: You weren't raised round here, were you? (MRS PETERS *shakes her
head*) You didn't know – her?

MRS PETERS: Not till they brought her yesterday.

MRS HALE: She – come to think of it, she was kind of like a bird herself – real sweet and pretty, but kind of timid and – fluttery. How – she – did – change. (*silence; then as if struck by a happy thought and relieved to get back to everyday things*) Tell you what, Mrs Peters, why don't you take the quilt in with you? It might take up her mind.

MRS PETERS: Why, I think that's a real nice idea, Mrs Hale. There couldn't possibly be any objection to it, could there? Now, just what would I take? I wonder if her patches are in here – and her things.

    (*They look in the sewing basket.*)

MRS HALE: Here's some red. I expect this has got sewing things in it. (*brings out a fancy box*) What a pretty box. Looks like something somebody would give you. Maybe her scissors are in here. (*Opens box. Suddenly puts her hand to her nose*) Why – (MRS PETERS *bends nearer, then turns her face away*) There's something wrapped up in this piece of silk.

MRS PETERS: Why, this isn't her scissors.

MRS HALE: (*lifting the silk*) Oh, Mrs Peters – it's –

    (MRS PETERS *bends closer.*)

MRS PETERS: It's the bird.

MRS HALE: (*jumping up*) But, Mrs Peters – look at it! It's neck! Look at its neck! It's all – other side *to.*

MRS PETERS: Somebody – wrung – its – neck.

    (*Their eyes meet. A look of growing comprehension, of horror. Steps are heard outside. MRS HALE slips box under quilt pieces, and sinks into her chair. Enter SHERIFF and COUNTY ATTORNEY. MRS PETERS rises.*)

COUNTY ATTORNEY: (*as one turning from serious things to little pleasantries*) Well ladies, have you decided whether she was going to quilt it or knot it?

MRS PETERS: We think she was going to – knot it.

COUNTY ATTORNEY: Well, that's interesting, I'm sure. (*seeing the birdcage*) Has the bird flown?

MRS HALE: (*putting more quilt pieces over the box*) We think the – cat got it.

COUNTY ATTORNEY: (*preoccupied*) Is there a cat?

    (MRS HALE *glances in a quick covert way at* MRS PETERS.)

MRS PETERS: Well, not *now.* They're superstitious, you know. They leave.

COUNTY ATTORNEY: (*to SHERIFF PETERS, continuing an interrupted conversation*) No sign at all of anyone having come from the outside. Their own rope. Now let's go up again and go over it piece by piece. (*they start upstairs*) It would have to have been someone who knew just the –

    (MRS PETERS *sits down. The two women sit there not looking at one another, but as if peering into something and at the same time holding back. When they talk now it is in the manner of feeling their way over strange ground, as if afraid of what they are saying, but as if they can not help saying it.*)

MRS HALE: She liked the bird. She was going to bury it in that pretty box.

MRS PETERS: (*in a whisper*) When I was a girl – my kitten – there was a boy took a hatchet, and before my eyes – and before I could get there – (*covers her face an instant*) If they hadn't held me back I would have – (*catches herself, looks upstairs where steps are heard, falters weakly*) – hurt him.

MRS HALE: (*with a slow look around her*) I wonder how it would seem never to have had any children around. (*pause*) No, Wright wouldn't like the bird – a thing that sang. She used to sing. He killed that, too.

MRS PETERS: (*moving uneasily*) We don't know who killed the bird.

MRS HALE: I knew John Wright.

MRS PETERS: It was an awful thing was done in this house that night, Mrs Hale. Killing a man while he slept, slipping a rope around his neck that choked the life out of him.

MRS HALE: His neck. Choked the life out of him.

(*Her hand goes out and rests on the bird-cage.*)

MRS PETERS: (*with rising voice*) We don't know who killed him. We don't *know*.

MRS HALE: (*her own feeling not interrupted*) If there'd been years and years of nothing, then a bird to sing to you, it would be awful – still, after the bird was still.

MRS PETERS: (*something within her speaking*) I know what stillness is. When we homesteaded in Dakota, and my first baby died – after he was two years old, and me with no other then –

MRS HALE: (*moving*) How soon do you suppose they'll be through, looking for the evidence?

MRS PETERS: I know what stillness is. (*pulling herself back*). The law has got to punish crime, Mrs Hale.

MRS HALE: (*not as if answering that*) I wish you'd seen Minnie Foster when she wore a white dress with blue ribbons and stood up there in the choir and sang. (*a look around the room*) Oh, I *wish* I'd come over here once in a while! That was a crime! That was a crime! Who's going to punish that?

MRS PETERS: (*looking upstairs*) We mustn't – take on.

MRS HALE: I might have known she needed help! I know how things can be – for women. I tell you, it's queer, Mrs Peters. We live close together and we live far apart. We all go through the same things – it's all just a different kind of the same thing. (*brushes her eyes, noticing the bottle of fruit, reaches out for it*) If I was you, I wouldn't tell her her fruit was gone. Tell her it *ain't*. Tell her it's all right. Take this in to prove it to her. She – she may never know whether it was broke or not.

MRS PETERS: (*takes the bottle, looks about for something to wrap it in; takes petticoat from the clothes brought from the other room, very nervously begins winding this around the bottle. In a false voice*) My, it's a good thing the men couldn't hear us. Wouldn't they just laugh! Getting all stirred up over a little thing like a – dead canary. As if that could have anything to do with – with – wouldn't they *laugh!*

(*The men are heard coming down stairs.*)

MRS HALE: (*under her breath*) Maybe they would – maybe they wouldn't.

COUNTY ATTORNEY: No, Peters, it's all perfectly clear except a reason for doing it. But you know juries when it comes to women. If there was some definite thing. Something to show – something to make a story about – a thing that would connect up with this strange way of doing it –

(*The women's eyes meet for an instant. Enter* HALE *from outer door.*)

HALE: Well, I've got the team around. Pretty cold out there.

COUNTY ATTORNEY: I'm going to stay here a while by myself. (*to the* SHERIFF) You can send Frank out for me, can't you? I want to go over everything. I'm not satisfied that we can't do better.

SHERIFF: Do you want to see what Mrs Peters is going to take in?

(*The* LAWYER *goes to the table, picks up the apron, laughs.*)

COUNTY ATTORNEY: Oh, I guess they're not very dangerous things the ladies have picked out. (*Moves a few things about, disturbing the quilt pieces which cover the box. Steps back*) No, Mrs Peters doesn't need supervising. For that matter, a sheriff's wife is married to the law. Ever think of it that way, Mrs Peters?

MRS PETERS: Not – just that way.

SHERIFF: (*chuckling*) Married to the law. (*moves toward the other room*) I just want you to come in here a minute, George. We ought to take a look at these windows.

COUNTY ATTORNEY: (*scoffingly*) Oh, windows!

SHERIFF: We'll be right out, Mr Hale.

(HALE *goes outside. The* SHERIFF *follows the* COUNTY ATTORNEY *into the other room. Then* MRS HALE *rises, hands tight together, looking intensely at* MRS PETERS, *whose eyes make a slow turn, finally meeting* MRS HALE's. *A moment* MRS HALE *holds her, then her own eyes point the way to where the box is concealed. Suddenly* MRS PETERS *throws back quilt pieces and tries to put the box in the bag she is wearing. It is too big. She opens box, starts to take bird out, cannot touch it, goes to pieces, stands there helpless. Sound of a knob turning in the other room.* MRS HALE *snatches the box and puts it in the pocket of her big coat. Enter* COUNTY ATTORNEY *and* SHERIFF.)

COUNTY ATTORNEY: (*facetiously*) Well, Henry, at least we found out that she was not going to quilt it. She was going to – what is it you call it, ladies?

MRS HALE: (*her hand against her pocket*) We call it – knot it, Mr Henderson.

(CURTAIN)

THE OUTSIDE

First performed by the Provincetown Players at the Playwrights' Theatre, December 28, 1917, with the following cast:

CAPTAIN (of 'The Bars' Life-Saving Station)	Abram Gillette
BRADFORD (a Life-Saver)	Hutchinson Collins
TONY (a Portuguese Life-Saver)	Louis Ell
MRS PATRICK (who lives in the abandoned Station)	Ida Rauh
ALLIE MAYO (who works for her)	Susan Glaspell

SCENE: *A room in a house which was once a life-saving station. Since ceasing to be that it has taken on no other character, except that of a place which no one cares either to preserve or change. It is painted the life-saving grey, but has not the life-saving freshness. This is one end of what was the big boat room, and at the ceiling is seen a part of the frame work from which the boat once swung. About two thirds of the back wall is open, because of the big sliding door, of the type of barn door, and through this open door are seen the sand dunes, and beyond them the woods. At one point the line where woods and dunes meet stands out clearly and there are indicated the rude things, vines, bushes, which form the outer uneven rim of the woods – the only things that grow in the sand. At another point a sand-hill is menacing the woods. This old life-saving station is at a point where the sea curves, so through the open door the sea also is seen. (The station is located on the outside shore of Cape Cod, at the point, near the tip of the Cape, where it makes that final curve which forms the Provincetown Harbor.) The dunes are hills and strange forms of sand on which, in places, grows the stiff beach grass – struggle; dogged growing against odds. At right of the big sliding door is a drift of sand and the top of buried beach grass is seen on this. There is a door left, and at right of big sliding door is a slanting wall. Door in this is ajar at rise of curtain, and through this door BRADFORD and TONY, life-savers, are seen bending over a man's body, attempting to restore respiration. The captain of the life-savers comes into view outside the big open door, at left; he appears to have been hurrying, peers in, sees the men, goes quickly to them.*

CAPTAIN: I'll take this now, boys.

BRADFORD: No need for anybody to take it, Capt'n. He was dead when we picked him up.

CAPTAIN: Dannie Sears was dead when we picked him up. But we brought him back. I'll go on awhile.
> (*The two men who have been bending over the body rise, stretch to relax, and come into the room.*)

BRADFORD: (*pushing back his arms and putting his hands on his chest*) Work, – tryin' to put life in the dead.

CAPTAIN: Where'd you find him, Joe?

BRADFORD: In front of this house. Not forty feet out.

CAPTAIN: What'd you bring him up here for?
> (*He speaks in an abstracted way, as if the working part of his mind is on something else, and in the muffled voice of one bending over.*)

BRADFORD: (*with a sheepish little laugh*) Force of habit, I guess. We brought so many of 'em back up here. (*looks around the room*) And then it was kind of unfriendly down where he was – the wind spittin' the sea onto you till he'd have no way of knowin' he was ashore.

TONY: Lucky I was not sooner or later as I walk by from my watch.

BRADFORD: You have accommodating ways, Tony. No sooner or later. I wouldn't say it of many Portagees. But the sea (*calling it in to the* CAPTAIN) is friendly as a kitten alongside the women that live *here*. Allie Mayo – they're *both* crazy – had that door open (*moving his head toward the big sliding door*) sweepin'

Portagees: local name for members of the large Portuguese fishing community in Provincetown.

out, and when we come along she backs off and stands lookin' at us, *lookin'* –
Lord, I just wanted to get him somewhere else. So I kicked this door open
with my foot (*jerking his hand toward the room where the* CAPTAIN *is seen
bending over the man*) and got him *away*. (*under his voice*) If he did have any
notion of comin' back to life, he wouldn't a come if he'd seen her. (*more
genially*) I wouldn't.

CAPTAIN: You know who he is, Joe?

BRADFORD: I never saw him before.

CAPTAIN: Mitchell telephoned from High Head that a dory came ashore there.

BRADFORD: Last night wasn't the *best* night for a dory. (*to* TONY, *boastfully*) Not
that I couldn't 'a' stayed in one. Some men can stay in a dory and some can't.
(*going to the inner door*) That boy's dead, Capt'n.

CAPTAIN: Then I'm not doing him any harm.

BRADFORD: (*going over and shaking the frame where the boat once swung*) This
the first time you ever been in this place, ain't it, Tony?

TONY: I never was here before.

BRADFORD: Well, *I* was here before. (*a laugh*) And the old man – (*nodding
toward the* CAPTAIN) he lived here for twenty-seven years. Lord, the things
that happened *here*. There've been dead ones carried through *that* door.
(*pointing to the outside door*) Lord – the ones *I've* carried. I carried in Bill
Collins, and Lou Harvey and – huh! 'sall over now. You ain't seen no *wrecks*.
Don't ever think you have. I was here the night the Jennie Snow was out
there. (*pointing to the sea*) There was a *wreck*. We got the boat that stood here
(*again shaking the frame*) down that bank. (*goes to the door and looks out*)
Lord, how'd we ever do it? The sand has put his place on the blink all right.
And then when it gets too God-for-saken for a life-savin' station, a lady takes
it for a summer residence – and then spends the winter. She's a cheerful one.

TONY: A woman – she makes things pretty. This not like a place where a woman
live. On the floor there is nothing – on the wall there is nothing. Things –
(*trying to express it with his hands*) do not hang on other things.

BRADFORD: (*imitating* TONY's *gesture*) No – things do not hang on other things.
In my opinion the woman's crazy – sittin' over there on the sand – (*a gesture
towards the dunes*) what's she *lookin'* at? There ain't nothin' to *see*. And I
know the woman that works for her's crazy – Allie Mayo. She's a
Provincetown girl. She was all right once, but –

> (MRS PATRICK *comes in from the hall at the right. She is a 'city
> woman', a sophisticated person who has been caught into something as
> unlike the old life as the dunes are unlike a meadow. At the moment
> she is excited and angry.*)

MRS PATRICK: You have no right here. This isn't the life-saving station any more.
Just because it used to be – I don't see why you should think – This is my
house! And – I want my house to myself!

CAPTAIN: (*putting his head through the door. One arm of the man he is working
with is raised, and the hand reaches through the doorway*) Well I must say,

---

dory: small boat with flat bottom used in sea-fishing.

lady, I would think that any house could be a life-saving station when the sea
had sent a man to it.

MRS PATRICK: (*who has turned away so she cannot see the hand*) I don't want him
here! I – (*defiant, yet choking*) I must have my house to myself!

CAPTAIN: You'll get your house to yourself when I've made up my mind there's no
more life in this man. A good many lives have been saved in this house, Mrs
Patrick – I believe that's your name – and if there's any chance of bringing one
more back from the dead, the fact that you own the house ain't goin' to make
a damn bit of difference to me!

MRS PATRICK: (*in a thin wild way*) I must have my house to myself.

CAPTAIN: Hell with such a woman!

(*Moves the man he is working with and slams the door shut. As the
CAPTAIN says, 'And if there's any chance of bringing one more back
from the dead', ALLIE MAYO has appeared outside the wide door
which gives on to the dunes, a bleak woman, who at first seems little
more than a part of the sand before which she stands. But as she listens
to this conflict one suspects in her that peculiar intensity of twisted
things which grow in unfavoring places.*)

MRS PATRICK: I – I don't want them here! I must –

(*But suddenly she retreats, and is gone.*)

BRADFORD: Well, I couldn't say, Allie Mayo, that you work for any too
kind-hearted a lady. What's the matter with the woman? Does she want folks
to die? Appears to break her all up to see somebody trying to save a life. What
d'you work for such a fish for? A crazy fish – that's what I call the woman. I've
seen her – day after day – settin' over there where the dunes meet the woods,
just sittin' there, lookin'. (*suddenly thinking of it*) I believe she *likes* to see the
sand slippin' down on the woods. Pleases her to see somethin' gettin' buried, I
guess.

(*ALLIE MAYO, who has stepped inside the door and moved half
across the room, toward the corridor at the right, is arrested by this last
– stands a moment as if seeing through something, then slowly on, and
out.*)

BRADFORD: Some coffee'd taste good. But coffee, in this house? Oh, no. It might
make somebody feel better. (*opening the door that was slammed shut*) Want
me now, Capt'n?

CAPTAIN: No.

BRADFORD: Oh, that boy's dead, Capt'n.

CAPTAIN: (*snarling*) Dannie Sears was dead, too. Shut that door. I don't want to
hear that woman's voice again, ever.

(*Closing the door and sitting on a bench built into that corner between
the big sliding door and the room where the CAPTAIN is.*)

BRADFORD: They're a cheerful pair of women – livin' in this cheerful place – a
place that life savers had to turn over to the sand – huh! This Patrick woman
used to be all right. She and her husband was summer folks over in town. They
used to picnic over here on the outside. It was Joe Dyer – he's always talkin' to
summer folks – told 'em the government was goin' to build the new station and
sell this one by sealed bids. I heard them talkin' about it. They was sittin' right

down there on the beach, eatin' their supper. They was goin' to put in a
fire-place and they was goin' to paint it bright colors, and have parties over
here – summer folk notions. Their bid won it – who'd want it? – a buried house
you couldn't move.

TONY: I see no bright colors.

BRADFORD: Don't you? How astonishin'! You must be color blind. And I guess
we're the first party. (*laughs*) I was in Bill Joseph's grocery store, one day last
November, when in she comes – Mrs Patrick, from New York. 'I've come to
take the old life-saving station', says she. 'I'm going to sleep over there
tonight!' Huh! Bill is used to queer ways – he deals with summer folks, but that
got *him*. November – an empty house, a buried house, you might say, off here
on the outside shore – way across the sand from man or beast. He got it out of
her, not by what she said, but by the way she looked at what he said, that her
husband had died, and she was runnin' off to hide herself, I guess. A person'd
feel sorry for her if she weren't so stand-offish, and so doggon *mean*. But mean
folks have got minds of their own. She slept here that night. Bill had men
hauling things till after dark – bed, stove, coal. And then she wanted
somebody to work for her. 'Somebody', says she, 'that doesn't say an
unnecessary word!' Well, then Bill come to the back of the store, I said,
'Looks to me as if Allie Mayo was the party she's lookin' for.' Allie Mayo has
got a prejudice against words. Or maybe she likes 'em so well she's savin' of
'em. She's not spoke an unnecessary word for twenty years. She's got her
reasons. Women whose men go to sea ain't always talkative.
   (*The* CAPTAIN *comes out. He closes door behind him and stands
   there beside it. He looks tired and disappointed. Both look at him.
   Pause.*)

CAPTAIN: Wonder who he was.

BRADFORD: Young. Guess he's not been much at sea.

CAPTAIN: I hate to leave even the dead in this house. But we can get right back for
him. (*a look around*) The old place used to be more friendly. (*moves to outer
door, hesitates, hating to leave like this*) Well, Joe, we brought a good many of
them back here:

BRADFORD: Dannie Sears is tendin' bar in Boston now.
   (*The three men go; as they are going around the drift of sand* ALLIE
   MAYO *comes in carrying a pot of coffee; sees them leaving, puts
   down the coffee pot, looks at the door the* CAPTAIN *has closed,
   moves toward it, as if drawn.* MRS PATRICK *follows her in.*)

MRS PATRICK: They've gone?
   (MRS MAYO *nods, facing the closed door.*)

MRS PATRICK: And they're leaving – him? (*again the other woman nods*) Then
he's –? (MRS MAYO *just stands there*) They have no right – just because it
used to be their place –! I want my house to myself!
   (*Snatches her coat and scarf from a hook and starts through the big
   door toward the dunes.*)

ALLIE MAYO: Wait.
   (*When she has said it she sinks into that corner seat – as if
   overwhelmed by what she has done. The other woman is held.*)

ALLIE MAYO: (*to herself.*) If I could say that, I can say more. (*looking at woman she has arrested, but speaking more to herself*) That boy in there – his face – uncovered something – (*her open hand on her chest. But she waits, as if she cannot go on; when she speaks it is in labored way – slow, monotonous, as if snowed in by silent years*) For twenty years, I did what you are doing. And I can tell you – it's not the way. (*her voice has fallen to a whisper; she stops, looking ahead at something remote and veiled*) We had been married – two years. (*a start, as of sudden pain. Says it again, as if to make herself say it*) Married – two years. He had a chance to go north on a whaler. Times hard. He had to go. A year and a half – it was to be. A year and a half. Two years we'd been married.
> (*She sits silent, moving a little back and forth.*)

The day he went away. (*not spoken, but breathed from pain*) The days after he was gone.

I heard at first. Last letter said farther north – not another chance to write till on the way home. (*a wait*)

Six months. Another, I did not hear. (*long wait*) Nobody ever heard. (*after it seems she is held there, and will not go on*) I used to talk as much as any girl in Provincetown. Jim used to tease me about my talking. But they'd come in to talk to me. They'd say – 'You may hear *yet.*' They'd talk about what must have happened. And one day a woman who'd been my friend all my life said – 'Suppose he was to walk *in!*' I got up and drove her from my kitchen – and from that time till this I've not said a word I didn't have to say. (*she has become almost wild in telling this. That passes. In a whisper*) The ice that caught Jim – caught me. (*a moment as if held in ice. Comes from it. To* MRS PATRICK *simply*) It's not the way. (*a sudden change*) You're not the only woman in the world whose husband is dead!

MRS PATRICK: (*with a cry of the hurt*) Dead? My husband's not *dead.*

ALLIE MAYO: He's *not?* (*slowly understands*) Oh.
> (*The woman in the door is crying. Suddenly picks up her coat which has fallen to the floor and steps outside.*)

ALLIE MAYO: (*almost failing to do it*) Wait.

MRS PATRICK: Wait? Don't you think you've said enough? They told me you didn't say an unnecessary word!

ALLIE MAYO: I don't.

MRS PATRICK: And you can see, I should think, that you've bungled into things you know nothing about!
> (*As she speaks, and crying under her breath, she pushes the sand by the door down on the half buried grass – though not as if knowing what she is doing.*)

ALLIE MAYO: (*slowly*) When you keep still for twenty years you know – things you didn't know you knew. I know why you're doing that. (*she looks up at her, startled*) Don't bury the only thing that will grow. Let it grow.
> (*The woman outside still crying under her breath turns abruptly and starts toward the line where dunes and woods meet.*)

ALLIE MAYO: I know where you're going! (MRS PATRICK *turns but not as if she wants to*) What you'll try to do. Over there. (*pointing to the line of woods*)

Bury it. The life in you. Bury it – watching the sand bury the woods. But I'll tell you something! *They* fight too. The woods! They fight for life the way that Captain fought for life in there!

(*Pointing to the closed door.*)

MRS PATRICK: (*with a strange exultation*) And lose the way he lost in there!

ALLIE MAYO: (*sure, sombre*) They don't lose.

MRS PATRICK: Don't *lose*? (*triumphant*) I have walked on the tops of buried trees!

ALLIE MAYO: (*slow, sombre, yet large*) And vines will grow over the sand that covers the trees, and hold it. And other trees will grow over the buried trees.

MRS PATRICK: I've watched the sand slip down on the vines that reach out farthest.

ALLIE MAYO: Another vine will reach that spot. (*under her breath, tenderly*) Strange little things that reach out farthest!

MRS PATRICK: And will be buried soonest!

ALLIE MAYO: And hold the sand for things behind them. They save a wood that guards a town.

MRS PATRICK: I care nothing about a wood to guard a town. This is the outside – these dunes where only beach grass grows, this outer shore where men can't live. The Outside. You who were born here and who die here have named it that.

ALLIE MAYO: Yes, we named it that, and we had reason. He died here (*reaches her hand toward the closed door*) and many a one before him. But many another reached the harbor! (*slowly raises her arm, bends it to make the form of the Cape. Touches the outside of her bent arm*) The Outside. But an arm that bends to make a harbor – where men are safe.

MRS PATRICK: I'm outside the harbor – on the dunes, land not life.

ALLIE MAYO: Dunes meet woods and woods hold dunes from a town that's shore to a harbor.

MRS PATRICK: This is the Outside. Sand (*picking some of it up in her hand and letting it fall on the beach grass*) Sand that *covers* – hills of sand that move and cover.

ALLIE MAYO: Woods. Woods to hold the moving hills from Provincetown. Provincetown – where they turn when boats can't live at sea. Did you ever see the sails come round here when the sky is dark? A line of them – swift to the harbor – where their children live. Go back! (*pointing*) Back to your edge of the woods that's the *edge of the dunes*.

MRS PATRICK: The edge of life. Where life trails off to dwarfed things not worth a name.

(*Suddenly sits down in the doorway.*)

ALLIE MAYO: Not worth a name. And – meeting the Outside!

(*Big with the sense of the wonder of life.*)

MRS PATRICK: (*lifting sand and letting it drift through her hand.*) They're what the sand will let them be. They take strange shapes like shapes of blown sand.

ALLIE MAYO: Meeting the Outside. (*moving nearer; speaking more personally*) I know why you came here. To this house that had been given up; on this shore where only savers of life try to live. I know what holds you on these dunes, and

draws you over there. But other things are true beside the things you want to
see.

MRS PATRICK: How do you know they are? Where have you been for twenty
years?

ALLIE MAYO: Outside. Twenty years. That's why I know how brave *they* are
(*indicating the edge of the woods. Suddenly different*) You'll not find peace
there again! Go back and watch them *fight!*

MRS PATRICK: (*swiftly rising*) You're a cruel woman – a hard, insolent woman! I
knew what I was doing! What do you know about it? About me? I didn't *go* to
the Outside. I was left there. I'm only – trying to get along. Everything that
can hurt me I want buried – buried deep. Spring is here. This morning I *knew*
it. Spring – coming through the storm – to take me – take me to hurt me.
That's why I couldn't bear – (*she looks at the closed door*) things that made me
know I feel. You haven't felt for so long you don't know what it means! But I
tell you, Spring is here! And now you'd take *that* from me – (*looking now
toward the edge of the woods*) the thing that made me know they would be
buried in my heart – those things I can't *live* and know I feel. You're more
cruel than the sea! 'But other things are true beside the things you want to
see!' Outside. Springs will come when I will not know that it is spring. (*as if
resentful of not more deeply believing what she says*) What would there be for
me but the Outside? What was there for you? What did you ever find after you
lost the thing you wanted?

ALLIE MAYO: I found – what I find now I know. The edge of life – to hold life
behind me –

     (*A slight gesture toward* MRS PATRICK.)

MRS PATRICK: (*stepping back*) You call what you are life? (*laughs*) Bleak as those
ugly things that grow in the sand!

ALLIE MAYO: (*under her breath, as one who speaks tenderly of beauty*) Ugly!

MRS PATRICK: (*passionately*) I have *known* life. I have known *life*. You're like
this Cape. A line of land way out to sea – land not life.

ALLIE MAYO: A harbor far at sea. (*raises her arm, curves it in as if around
something she loves*) Land that encloses and gives shelter from storm.

MRS PATRICK: (*facing the sea, as if affirming what will hold all else out*) Outside
sea. Outer shore. Dunes – land not life.

ALLIE MAYO: Outside sea – outer shore, dark with the wood that once was ships –
dunes, strange land not life – woods, town and harbor. The line! Stunted
straggly line that meets the Outside face to face – and fights for what itself can
never be. Lonely line. Brave growing.

MRS PATRICK: It loses.

ALLIE MAYO: It wins.

MRS PATRICK: The farthest life is buried.

ALLIE MAYO: And life grows over buried life! (*lifted into thàt; then, as one who
states a simple truth with feeling*) It will. And Springs will come when you will
want to know that it is Spring.

     (*The* CAPTAIN *and* BRADFORD *appear behind the drift of sand.
They have a stretcher. To get away from them* MRS PATRICK *steps
farther into the room;* ALLIE MAYO *shrinks into her corner. The*

*men come in, open the closed door and go in the room where they left
the dead man. A moment later they are seen outside the big open door,
bearing the man away.* MRS PATRICK *watches them from sight.*)

MRS PATRICK: (*bitter, exultant*) Savers of life! (*to* ALLIE MAYO) You savers of
life! 'Meeting the Outside!' Meeting – (*but she cannot say it mockingly again;
in saying it, something of what it means has broken through, rises. Herself lost,
feeling her way into the wonder of life*) Meeting the Outside!

(*It grows in her as* CURTAIN *lowers slowly.*)

THE VERGE

First performed at the Provincetown Playhouse on November 14, 1921.

PERSONS OF THE PLAY

ANTHONY	
HARRY ARCHER	Claire's husband
HATTIE	The maid
CLAIRE	
DICK	Richard Demming
TOM EDGEWORTHY	
ELIZABETH	Claire's daughter
ADELAIDE	Claire's sister
DR EMMONS	

ACT I

The Curtain lifts on a place that is dark, save for a shaft of light from below which comes up through an open trap-door in the floor. This slants up and strikes the long leaves and the huge brilliant blossom of a strange plant whose twisted stem projects from right front. Nothing is seen except this plant and its shadow. A violent wind is heard. A moment later a buzzer. It buzzes once long and three short. Silence. Again the buzzer. Then from below – his shadow blocking the light, comes ANTHONY, a rugged man past middle life; – he emerges from the stairway into the darkness of the room. Is dimly seen taking up a phone.

ANTHONY: Yes, Miss Claire? – I'll see. (*he brings a thermometer to the stairway for light, looks sharply, then returns to the phone*) It's down to forty-nine. The plants are in danger – (*with great relief and approval*) Oh, that's fine! (*hangs up the receiver*) Fine!

> (*He goes back down the stairway, closing the trap-door upon himself, and the curtain is drawn upon darkness and wind. It opens a moment later on the greenhouse in the sunshine of a snowy morning. The snow piled outside is at times blown through the air. The frost has made patterns on the glass as if – as Plato would have it – the patterns inherent in abstract nature and behind all life had to come out, not only in the creative heat within, but in the creative cold on the other side of the glass. And the wind makes patterns of sound around the glass house.*
>
> *The back wall is low; the glass roof slopes sharply up. There is an ouside door, a little toward the right. From outside two steps lead down to it. At left a glass partition and a door into the inner room. One sees a little way into this room. At right there is no dividing wall save large plants and vines, a narrow aisle between shelves of plants leads off.*
>
> *This is not a greenhouse where plants are being displayed, nor the usual workshop for the growing of them, but a place for experiment with plants, a laboratory.*
>
> *At the back grows a strange vine. It is arresting rather than beautiful. It creeps along the low wall, and one branch gets a little way up the glass. You might see the form of a cross in it, if you happened to think it that way. The leaves of this vine are not the form that leaves have been. They are at once repellent and significant.*
>
> *ANTHONY is at work preparing soil – mixing, sifting. As the wind tries the door he goes anxiously to the thermometer, nods as if reassured and returns to his work. The buzzer sounds. He starts to answer the telephone, remembers something, halts and listens sharply. It does not buzz once long and three short. Then he returns to his work. The buzzer goes on and on in impatient jerks which mount in anger. Several times ANTHONY is almost compelled by this insistence, but the thing that holds him back is stronger. At last, after a*

particularly mad splutter, to which ANTHONY *longs to make retort, the buzzer gives it up.* ANTHONY *goes on preparing soil.*
A moment later the glass door swings violently in, snow blowing in, and also MR HARRY ARCHER, *wrapped in a rug.*)

ANTHONY: Oh, please close the door, sir.

HARRY: Do you think I'm not trying to? (*he holds it open to say this*)

ANTHONY: But please *do*. This stormy air is not good for the plants.

HARRY: I suppose it's just the thing for me! Now, what do you mean, Anthony, by not answering the phone when I buzz for you?

ANTHONY: Miss Claire – Mrs Archer told me not to.

HARRY: Told you not to answer me?

ANTHONY: Not you especially – nobody but her.

HARRY: Well, I like her nerve – and yours.

ANTHONY: You see, she thought it took my mind from my work to be interrupted when I'm out here. And so it does. So she buzzes once long and – Well, she buzzes her way, and all other buzzing –

HARRY: May buzz.

ANTHONY: (*nodding gravely*) She thought it would be better for the flowers.

HARRY: I am not a flower – true, but I too need a little attention – and a little heat. Will you please tell me why the house is frigid?

ANTHONY: Miss Claire ordered all the heat turned out here. (*patiently explaining it to* MISS CLAIRE's *speechless husband*) You see the roses need a great deal of heat.

HARRY: (*reading the thermometer*) The roses have seventy-three I have forty-five.

ANTHONY: Yes, the roses need seventy-three.

HARRY: Anthony, this is an outrage!

ANTHONY: I think it is myself; when you consider what we paid for the heating plant – but as long as it is defective – Why, Miss Claire would never have done what she has if she hadn't looked out for her plants in just such ways as this. Have you forgotten that Breath of Life is about to flower?

HARRY: And where's my breakfast about to flower? – that's what I want to know.

ANTHONY: Why, Miss Claire got up at five o'clock to order the heat turned off from the house.

HARRY: I see you admire her vigilance.

ANTHONY: Oh, I do. (*fervently*) I do. Harm was near, and that woke her up.

HARRY: And what about the harm to – (*tapping his chest*) Do roses get pneumonia?

ANTHONY: Oh, yes – yes, indeed they do. Why, Mr Archer, look at Miss Claire herself. Hasn't she given her heat to the roses?

HARRY: (*pulling the rug around him, preparing for the blizzard*) She has the fire within.

ANTHONY: (*delighted*) Now isn't that true! How well you said it. (*with a glare for this appreciation,* HARRY *opens the door. It blows away from him*) Please do close the door!

HARRY: (*furiously*) You think it is the aim of my life to hold it open?

ANTHONY: (*getting hold of it*) Growing things need an even temperature. (*while saying this he gets the man out into the snow*)

> (ANTHONY *consults the thermometer, not as pleased this time as he was before. He then looks minutely at two of the plants – one is a rose, the other a flower without a name because it has not long enough been a flower. Peers into the hearts of them. Then from a drawer under a shelf, takes two paper bags, puts one over each of these flowers, closing them down at the bottom. Again the door blows wildly in, also* HATTIE, *a maid with a basket.*)

ANTHONY: What do you mean – blowing in here like this? Mrs Archer has ordered –

HATTIE: Mr Archer has ordered breakfast served here. (*she uncovers the basket and takes out an electric toaster*)

ANTHONY: *Breakfast* – here? *Eat* – here? Where plants grow?

HATTIE: The plants won't poison him, will they? (*at a loss to know what to do with things, she puts the toaster under the stange vine at the back, whose leaves lift up against the glass which has frost leaves on the outer side*)

ANTHONY: (*snatching it away*) You – you think you can *cook eggs* under the Edge Vine?

HATTIE: I guess Mr Archer's eggs are as important as a vine. I guess my work's as important as yours.

ANTHONY: There's a million people like you – and like Mr Archer. In all the world there is only one Edge Vine.

HATTIE: Well, maybe one's enough. It don't look like nothin', anyhow.

ANTHONY: And you've not got the wit to know that that's why it's the Edge Vine.

HATTIE: You want to look out, Anthony. You talk nutty. Everybody says so.

ANTHONY: Miss Claire don't say so.

HATTIE: No, because she's –

ANTHONY: You talk too much!

> (*Door opens, admitting* HARRY; *after looking around for the best place to eat breakfast, moves a box of earth from the table.*)

HARRY: Just give me a hand, will you, Hattie?

> (*They bring it to the open space and he and* HATTIE *arrange breakfast things,* HATTIE *with triumphant glances at the distressed* ANTHONY)

ANTHONY: (*deciding he must act*) Mr Archer, this is not the place to eat breakfast!

HARRY: Dead wrong, old boy. The place that has heat is the place to eat breakfast. (*to* HATTIE) Tell the other gentlemen – I heard Mr Demming up, and Mr Edgeworthy, if he appears, that as long as it is such a pleasant morning, we're having breakfast outside. To the conservatory for coffee.

> (HATTIE *giggles, is leaving.*)

And let's see, have we got everything? (*takes the one shaker, shakes a little pepper on his hand. Looks in vain for the other shaker*) And tell Mr Demming to bring the salt.

ANTHONY: But Miss Claire will be very angry.

HARRY: I am very angry. Did I choose to eat my breakfast at the other end of a blizzard?

ANTHONY: (*an exclamation of horror at the thermometer*) The temperature is falling. I must report. (*he punches the buzzer, takes up the phone*) Miss Claire? It is Anthony. A terrible thing has happened. Mr Archer – what? Yes, a terrible thing. – Yes, it is about Mr Archer. – No – no, not dead. But here. He is here. Yes, he is well, he seems well, but he is eating his breakfast. Yes, he is having breakfast served out here – for himself, and the other gentlemen are to come too. – Well, he seemed to be annoyed because the heat had been turned off from the house. But the door keeps opening – this stormy wind blowing right over the plants. The temperature has already fallen. – Yes, yes. I thought you would want to come.

> (ANTHONY *opens the trap-door and goes below.* HARRY *looks disapprovingly down into this openness at his feet, returns to his breakfast.* ANTHONY *comes up, bearing a box.*)

HARRY: (*turning his face away*) Phew! What a smell.

ANTHONY: Yes. Fertilizer has to smell.

HARRY: Well, it doesn't have to smell up my breakfast!

ANTHONY: (*with a patient sense of order*) The smell belongs here. (*he and the smell go to the inner room*)

> (*The outer door opens just enough to admit* CLAIRE – *is quickly closed. With* CLAIRE *in a room another kind of aliveness is there.*)

CLAIRE: What are you doing here?

HARRY: Getting breakfast. (*all the while doing so*)

CLAIRE: I'll not have you in my place!

HARRY: If you take all the heat then you have to take me.

CLAIRE: I'll show you how I have to take you. (*with her hands begins scooping upon him the soil* ANTHONY *has prepared*)

HARRY: (*jumping up, laughing, pinning down her arms, putting his arms around her*) Claire – be decent. What harm do I do here?

CLAIRE: You pull down the temperature.

HARRY: Not after I'm in.

CLAIRE: And you told Tom and Dick to come and make it uneven.

HARRY: Tom and Dick are our guests We can't eat where it's warm and leave them to eat where it's cold.

CLAIRE: I don't see why not.

HARRY: You only see what you want to see.

CLAIRE: That's not true. I wish it were. No; no, I don't either. (*she is disturbed – that troubled thing which rises from within, from deep, and takes* CLAIRE. *She turns to the Edge Vine, examines. Regretfully to* ANTHONY, *who has come in with a plant*) It's turning back, isn't it?

ANTHONY: Can you be sure yet, Miss Claire?

CLAIRE: Oh yes – it's had its chance. It doesn't want to be – what hasn't been.

HARRY: (*who has turned at this note in her voice. Speaks kindly*) Don't take it so seriously, Claire. (CLAIRE *laughs*)

CLAIRE: No, I suppose not. But it *does* matter – and why should I pretend it doesn't, just because I've failed with it?

HARRY: Well, I don't want to see it get you – it's not important enough for that.
CLAIRE: (*in her brooding way*) Anything is important enough for that – if it's important at all. (*to the vine*) I thought you were out, but you're – going back home.
ANTHONY: But you're doing it this time, Miss Claire. When Breath of Life opens – and we see its heart –
> (CLAIRE *looks toward the inner room. Because of intervening plants they do not see what is seen from the front – a plant like caught motion, and of a greater transparency than plants have had. Its leaves, like waves that curl, close around a heart that is not seen. This plant stands by itself in what, because of the arrangement of things about it, is a hidden place. But nothing is between it and the light.*)
CLAIRE: Yes, if the heart has (*a little laugh*) held its own, then Breath of Life is alive in its otherness. But Edge Vine is running back to what it broke out of.
HARRY: Come, have some coffee, Claire.
> (ANTHONY *returns to the inner room, the outer door opens.* DICK *is hurled in.*)
CLAIRE: (*going to the door, as he gasps for breath before closing it*) How dare you make my temperature uneven! (*she shuts the door and leans against it*)
DICK: Is that what I do?
> (*A laugh, a look between them, which is held into significance.*)
HARRY: (*who is not facing them*) Where's the salt?
DICK: Oh, I fell down in the snow. I must have left the salt where I fell. I'll go back and look for it.
CLAIRE: And change the temperature? We don't need salt.
HARRY: You don't need salt, Claire. But we eat eggs.
CLAIRE: I must tell you I don't like the idea of any food being eaten here, where things have their own way to go. Please eat as little as possible, and as quickly.
HARRY: A hostess calculated to put one at one's ease.
CLAIRE: (*with no ill-nature*) I care nothing about your ease. Or about Dick's ease.
DICK: And no doubt that's what makes you so fascinating a hostess.
CLAIRE: Was I a fascinating hostess last night, Dick? (*softly sings*) 'Oh, night of love – ' (*from the Barcorole of 'Tales of Hoffman'*)
HARRY: We've got to have salt.
> (*He starts for the door.* CLAIRE *slips in ahead of him, locks it, takes the key. He marches off, right.*)
CLAIRE: (*calling after him*) That end's always locked.
DICK: Claire darling, I wish you wouldn't say those startling things. You do get away with it, but I confess it gives me a shock – and really, it's unwise.
CLAIRE: Haven't you learned that the best place to hide is in the truth? (*as* HARRY *returns*) Why won't you believe me, Harry, when I tell you the truth – about doors being locked?
HARRY: Claire, it's selfish of you to keep us from eating salt just because you don't eat salt.
CLAIRE: (*with one of her swift changes*) Oh, Harry! Try your egg without salt. Please – please try it without salt! (*an intensity which seems all out of proportion to the subject*)

HARRY: An egg demands salt.

CLAIRE: 'An egg demands salt.' Do you know, Harry, why you are such an unseasoned person? 'An egg demands salt.'

HARRY: Well, it doesn't always get it.

CLAIRE: But your spirit gets no lift from the salt withheld.

HARRY: Not an inch of lift. (*going back to his breakfast*)

CLAIRE: And pleased – so pleased with itself, for getting no lift. Sure, it is just the right kind of spirit – because it gets no lift. (*more brightly*) But, Dick, you must have tried your egg without salt.

DICK: I'll try it now. (*he goes to the breakfast table*)

CLAIRE: You must have tried and tried things. Isn't that the way one leaves the normal and gets into the byways of perversion?

HARRY: Claire.

DICK: (*pushing back his egg*) If so, I prefer to wait for the salt.

HARRY: Claire, there is a *limit*.

CLAIRE: Precisely what I had in mind. To perversion too there is a limit. So – the fortifications are unassailable. If one ever does get out, I suppose it is – quite unexpectedly, and perhaps – a bit terribly.

HARRY: Get out where?

CLAIRE: (*with a bright smile*) Where you, darling, will never go.

HARRY: And from which you, darling, had better beat it.

CLAIRE: I wish I could. (*to herself*) No – no I don't either

> (*Again this troubled thing turns her to the plant. She puts by themselves the two which* ANTHONY *covered with paper bags. Is about to remove these papers.* HARRY *strikes a match.*)

CLAIRE: (*turning sharply*) You can't smoke here. The plants are not used to it.

HARRY: Then I should think smoking would be just the thing for them.

CLAIRE: There is design.

HARRY: (*to* DICK) Am I supposed to be answered? I never can be quite sure at what moment I am answered.

> (*They both watch* CLAIRE, *who has uncovered the plants and is looking intently into the flowers. From a drawer she takes some tools. Very carefully gives the rose pollen to an unfamiliar flower – rather wistfully unfamiliar, which stands above on a small shelf near the door of the inner room.*)

DICK: What is this you're doing, Claire?

CLAIRE: Pollenizing. Crossing for fragrance.

DICK: It's all rather mysterious, isn't it?

HARRY: And Claire doesn't make it any less so.

CLAIRE: Can I make life any less mysterious?

HARRY:If you know what you are doing, why can't you tell Dick?

DICK: Never mind. After all, why should I be told? (*he turns away*)

> (*At that she wants to tell him. Helpless, as one who cannot get across a stream, starts uncertainly.*)

CLAIRE: I want to give fragrance to Breath of Life (*faces the room beyond the wall of glass*) – the flower I have created that is outside what flowers have been. What has gone out should bring fragrance from what it has left. But no definite fragrance, no limiting enclosing thing. I call the fragrance I am trying to create Reminiscence. (*her hand on the pot of the wistful little flower she has just given pollen*) Reminiscent of the rose, the violet, arbutus – but a new thing – itself. Breath of Life may be lonely out in what hasn't been. Perhaps some day I can give it reminiscence.

DICK: I see, Claire.

CLAIRE: I wonder if you do.

HARRY: Now, Claire, you're going to be gay to-day, aren't you? These are Tom's last couple of days with us.

CLAIRE: That doesn't make me especially gay.

HARRY: Well, you want him to remember you as yourself, don't you?

CLAIRE: I would like him to. Oh – I would like him to!

HARRY: Then be amusing. That's really you, isn't it, Dick?

DICK: Not quite all of her – I should say.

CLAIRE: (*gaily*) Careful, Dick. Aren't you indiscreet? Harry will be suspecting that I am your latest strumpet.

HARRY: Claire! What language you use! A person knowing you only by certain moments could never be made to believe you are a refined woman.

CLAIRE: True, isn't it, Dick?

HARRY: It would be a good deal of a lark to let them listen in at times – then tell them that here is the flower of New England!

CLAIRE: Well, if this is the flower of New England, then the half has never been told.

DICK: About New England?

CLAIRE: I thought I meant that. Perhaps I meant – about me.

HARRY: (*going on with his own entertainment*) Explain that this is what came of the men who made the laws that made New England, that here is the flower of those gentlemen of culture who –

DICK: Moulded the American mind!

CLAIRE: Oh! (*it is pain*)

HARRY: Now what's the matter?

CLAIRE: I want to get away from them!

HARRY: Rest easy, little one – you do.

CLAIRE: I'm not so sure – that I do. But it *can* be done! We need not be held in forms moulded for us. There is outness – and otherness.

HARRY: Now, Claire – I didn't mean to start anything serious.

CLAIRE: No; you never mean to do that. I want to break it up! I tell you, I want to break it up! If it were all in pieces, we'd be (*a little laugh*) shocked to aliveness (*to DICK*) – wouldn't we? There would be strange new comings together – mad new comings together, and we would know what it is to be born, and then we might know – that we are. Smash it. (*her hand is near an egg.*) As you'd smash an egg. (*she pushes the egg over the edge of the table and leans over and looks, as over a precipice*)

---

arbutus: genus of evergreen trees and shrubs.

HARRY: (*with a sigh*) Well, all you've smashed is the egg, and all that amounts to is that now Tom gets no egg. So that's that.
CLAIRE: (*with difficulty, drawing herself back from the fascination of the precipice*) You think I can't smash anything? You think life can't break up, and go outside what it was? Because you've gone dead in the form in which you found yourself, you think that's all there is to the whole adventure? And that is called sanity. And made a virtue – to lock one in. You never worked with things that grow! Things that take a sporting chance – go mad – that sanity mayn't lock them in – from life untouched – from life – that waits. (*she turns toward the inner room*) Breath of Life. (*she goes in there*)
HARRY: Oh, I wish Claire wouldn't be strange like that. (*helplessly*) What is it? What's the matter?
DICK: It's merely the excess of a particularly rich temperament.
HARRY: But it's growing on her. I sometimes wonder if all this (*indicating the place around him*) is a good thing. It would be all right if she'd just do what she did in the beginning – make the flowers as good as possible of their kind. That's an awfully nice thing for a woman to do – raise flowers. But there's something about this – changing things into other things – putting things together and making queer new things – this –
DICK: Creating?
HARRY: Give it any name you want it to have – it's unsettling for a woman. They say Claire's a shark at it, but what's the good of it, if it gets her? What *is* the good of it, anyway? Suppose we can produce new things. Lord – look at the one ones we've got. (*looks outside; turns back*) Heavens, what a noise the wind does make around this place. (*but now it is not all the wind, but* TOM EDGEWORTHY, *who is trying to let himself in at the locked door, their backs are to him*) I want my *egg*. You can't eat an egg without salt. I must say I don't get Claire lately. I'd like to have Charlie Emmons see her – he's fixed up a lot of people shot to pieces in the war. Claire needs something to tone her nerves *up*. You think it would irritate her?
DICK: She'd probably get no little entertainment out of it.
HARRY: Yes, dog-gone her, she would. (TOM *now takes more heroic measures to make himself heard at the door*) Funny – how the wind can fool you. Now by not looking around I could imagine – why, I could imagine anything. Funny, isn't it, about imagination? And Claire says I haven't got any!
DICK: It would make an amusing drawing – what the wind makes you think is there. (*first makes forms with his hands, then levelling the soil prepared by* ANTHONY, *traces lines with his finger*) Yes, really – quite jolly.
        (TOM, *after a moment of peering in at them, smiles, goes away.*)
HARRY: You're another one of the queer ducks, aren't you? Come now – give me the dirt. Have you queer ones really got anything – or do you just put it over on us that you have? (DICK *smiles, draws on*) Not saying anything, eh? Well, I guess you're wise there. If you keep mum – how are we going to prove there's nothing there?
DICK: I don't keep mum. I draw.
HARRY: Lines that don't make anything – how can they tell you anything? Well, all

I ask is, don't make Claire queer. Claire's a first water good sport – really, so
don't encourage her to be queer.

DICK: Trouble is, if you're queer enough to be amusing, it might – open the door to
queerness.

HARRY: Now don't say things like that to Claire.

DICK: I don't have to.

HARRY: Then *you* think she's queer, do you? Queer as you are, you think she's
queer. I would like to have Dr Emmons come out. (*after a moment of silently
watching* DICK, *who is having a good time with his drawing*) You know,
frankly, I doubt if you're a good influence for Claire. (DICK *lifts his head ever
so slightly*) Oh, I don't worry a bit about – things a husband might worry
about. I suppose an intellectual woman – and for all Claire's hate of her
ancestors, she's got the bug herself. Why, she has times of boring into things
until she doesn't know you're there. What do you think I caught her doing the
other day? Reading Latin. Well – a woman that reads Latin needn't worry a
husband much.

DICK: They said a good deal in Latin.

HARRY: But I was saying, I suppose a woman who lives a good deal in her mind
never does have much – well, what you might call passion. (*uses the word as if
it shouldn't be used. Brows knitted, is looking ahead, does not see* DICK's *face.
Turning to him with a laugh*) I suppose you know pretty much all there is to
know about women?

DICK: Perhaps one or two details have escaped me.

HARRY: Well, for that matter, you might know all there is to know about women
and not know much about Claire. But now about (*does not want to say passion
again*) – oh, feeling – Claire has a certain – well, a certain –

DICK: Irony?

HARRY: Which is really more – more –

DICK: More fetching, perhaps.

HARRY: Yes! Than the thing itself. But of course – you wouldn't have much of a
thing that you have irony about.

DICK: Oh – wouldn't you! I mean – a man might.

HARRY: I'd like to talk to Edgeworth about Claire. But it's not easy to talk to Tom
about Claire – or to Claire about Tom.

DICK: (*alert*) They're very old friends, aren't they?

HARRY: Why – yes, they are. Though they've not been together much of late
years, Edgeworthy always going to the ends of the earth to – meditate about
something. I must say I don't get it. If you have a place – that's the place for
you to be. And he did have a place – best kind of family connections, and it
was a very good business his father left him. Publishing business – in good
shape, too, when old Edgeworthy died. I wouldn't call Tom a great success in
life – but Claire does listen to what he says.

DICK: Yes, I've noticed that.

HARRY: So, I'd like to get him to tell her to quit this queer business of making
things grow that never grew before.

DICK: But are you sure that's what he would tell her? Isn't he in the same business
himself?

HARRY: Why, he doesn't raise anything.
> (TOM *is again at the door.*)

DICK: Anyway, I think he might have some idea that we can't very well reach each other.

HARRY: Damn nonsense. What have we got intelligence for?

DICK: To let each other alone, I suppose. Only we haven't enough to do it.
> (TOM *is now knocking on the door with a revolver. HARRY half turns, decides to be too intelligent to turn.*)

HARRY: Don't tell me I'm getting nerves. But the way some of you people talk is enough to make even an aviator jumpy. Can't reach each other! Then we're fools. If I'm here and you're there, why can't we reach each other?

DICK: Because I am I and you are you.

HARRY: No wonder your drawing's queer. A man who can't reach another man –
> (TOM *here reaches them by pointing the revolver in the air and firing it. DICK digs his hand into the dirt. HARRY jumps to one side, fearfully looks around. TOM, with a pleased smile to see he at last has their attention, moves the handle to indicate he would be glad to come in.*)

HARRY: Why – it's Tom! What the – ? (*going to the door*) He's locked out. And Claire's got the key. (*goes to the inner door, tries it*) And she's locked in! (*trying to see her in there*) Claire! Claire! (*returning to the outer door*) Claire's got the key – and I can't get to Claire. (*makes a futile attempt at getting the door open without a key, goes back to inner door – peers, pounds*) Claire! Are you there? Didn't you hear the revolver? Has she gone down the cellar? (*tries the trap-door*) Bolted! Well, I love the way she keeps people locked out!

DICK: And in.

HARRY: (*getting angry, shouting at the trap-door*) Didn't you hear the revolver? (*going to TOM*) Awfully sorry, old man, but – (*in astonishment to DICK*) He can't hear me. (TOM, *knocking with the revolver to get their attention, makes a gesture of inquiry with it*) No – no – no! Is he asking if he shall shoot himself? (*shaking his head violently*) Oh, no – no! Um – *um!*

DICK: Hardly seems a man would shoot himself because he can't get to his breakfast.

HARRY: I'm coming to believe people would do anything! (TOM *is making another inquiry with the revolver*) *No!* not here. Don't shoot yourself. (*trying hard to get the word through*) *Shoot* yourself. I mean – don't. (*petulantly to DICK*) It's ridiculous that you can't make a man understand you when he looks right at you like that. (*turning back to TOM*) Read my lips. Lips. I'm saying – Oh damn. Where is Claire? All right – I'll explain it with motions. We wanted the salt ... (*going over it to himself*) and Claire wouldn't let us go out for it on account of the temperature. Salt. Temperature. (*takes his egg-cup to the door, violent motion of shaking in salt*) But – no (*shakes his head*) No salt. (*he then takes the thermometer, a flower pot, holds them up to* TOM) On account of the temperature. Tem-per-a – (TOM *is not getting it*) Oh – well, what can you do when a man don't *get* a thing? (TOM *seems to be preparing the revolver for action. HARRY pounds on the inner door*) Claire! Do you want Tom to shoot himself?

(*As he looks in there, the trap-door lifts, and* CLAIRE *comes half-way up.*)

CLAIRE: Why, what is Tom doing out there, with a revolver?

HARRY: He is about to shoot himself because you've locked him out from his breakfast.

CLAIRE: He must know more interesting ways of destroying himself. (*bowing to* TOM) Good morning. (*from his side of the glass* TOM *bows and smiles back*) Isn't it strange – our being in here – and he being out there?

HARRY: Claire, have you no ideas of hospitality? Let him in!

CLAIRE: In? Perhaps that isn't hospitality.

HARRY: Well, whatever hospitality is, what is out there is snow – and wind – and our guest – who was asked to come here for his breakfast. To think a man has to *say* such things.

CLAIRE: I'm going to let him in. Though I like his looks out there. (*she takes the key from her pocket*)

HARRY: Thank heaven the door's coming open. Somebody can go for salt, and we can have our eggs.

CLAIRE: And open the door again – to let the salt in? No. If you insist on salt, tell Tom now to go back and get it. It's a stormy morning and there'll be just one opening of the door.

HARRY: How can we tell him what we can't make him hear? And why does he think we're holding this conversation instead of letting him in?

CLAIRE: It would be interesting to know. I wonder if he'll tell us?

HARRY: Claire! Is this any time to wonder anything?

CLAIRE: Give up the idea of salt for your egg and I'll let him in. (*holds up the key to* TOM *to indicate that for her part she is quite ready to let him in*)

HARRY: I want my egg!

CLAIRE: Then ask him to bring the salt. It's quite simple.

(HARRY *goes through another pantomime with the egg-cup and the missing shaker.* CLAIRE, *still standing half-way down cellar, sneezes.* HARRY, *growing all the while less amiable, explains with thermometer and flower-pot that there can only be one opening of the door.* TOM *looks interested, but unenlightened. But suddenly he smiles, nods, vanishes.*)

HARRY: Well, thank heaven (*exhausted*) that's over.

CLAIRE: (*sitting on the top step*) It was all so queer. He locked out on his side of the door. You locked in on yours. Looking right at each other and –

HARRY: (*in mockery*) And me trying to tell him to kindly fetch the salt!

CLAIRE: Yes.

HARRY: (*to* DICK) Well, I didn't do so bad a job, did I? Quite an idea, explaining our situation with the thermometer and the flower-pot. That was really an apology for keeping him out there. Heaven knows – some explanation was in order. (*he is watching, and sees* TOM *coming*) Now there he is, Claire. And probably pretty well fed up with the weather.

(CLAIRE *goes to the door, stops before it. She and* TOM *look at each other through the glass. Then she lets him in.*)

TOM: And now I am in. For a time it seemed I was not to be in. But after I got the idea that you were keeping me out there to see if I could get the idea – it would be too humiliating for a wall of glass to keep one from understanding. (*taking it from his pocket*) So there's the other thermometer. Where do you want it? (CLAIRE *takes it*)

CLAIRE: And where's the pepper?

TOM: (*putting it on the table*) And here's the pepper.

HARRY: Pepper?

TOM: When Claire sneezed I knew –

CLAIRE: Yes, I knew if I sneezed you would bring the pepper.

TOM: Funny how one always remembers the salt, but the pepper gets overlooked in preparations. And what is an egg without pepper?

HARRY: (*nastily*) There's your egg, Edgeworth. (*pointing to it on the floor*) Claire decided it would be a good idea to smash everything, so she began with your egg.

TOM: (*looking at his egg*) The idea of smashing everything is really more intriguing than an egg.

HARRY: Nice that you feel that way about it.

CLAIRE: (*giving* TOM *his coffee*) You want to hear something amusing? I married Harry because I thought he would smash something.

HARRY: Well, that was an error in judgment.

CLAIRE: I'm such a naive trusting person (HARRY *laughs* – CLAIRE *gives him a surprised look, continues simply*). Such a guileless soul that I thought flying would do something to a man. But it didn't take us out. We just took it in.

TOM: It's only our own spirit can take us out.

HARRY: Whatever you mean by out.

CLAIRE: (*after looking intently at* TOM, *and considering it*) But our own spirit is not something on the loose. Mine isn't. It has something to do with what I do. To fly. To be free in air. To look from above on the world of all my days. Be where man has never been! Yes – wouldn't you think the spirit could get the idea? The earth grows smaller. I am leaving. What are they – running around down there? Why do they run around down there? Houses? Houses are funny lines and down-going slants – houses are vanishing slants. I am alone. Can I breathe this rarer air? Shall I go higher? Shall I go too high? I am loose. I am out. But no; man flew, and returned to earth the man who left it.

HARRY: And jolly well likely not to have returned at all if he'd had those flighty notions while operating a machine.

CLAIRE: Oh, Harry! (*not lightly asked*) Can't you see it would be better not to have returned than to return the man who left it?

HARRY: I have some regard for human life.

CLAIRE: Why, no – I am the one who has the regard for human life. (*more lightly*) That was why I swiftly divorced my stick-in-the-mud artist and married – the man of flight. But I merely passed from a stick-in-the-mud artist to a –

DICK: Stick-in-the-air aviator?

HARRY: Speaking of your stick-in-the-mud artist, as you romantically call your first blunder, isn't his daughter – and yours – due here to-day?

CLAIRE: I knew something was disturbing me. Elizabeth. A daughter is being delivered unto me this morning. I have a feeling it will be more painful than the original delivery. She has been, as they quaintly say, educated; prepared for her place in life.

HARRY: And fortunately Claire has a sister who is willing to give her young niece that place.

CLAIRE: The idea of giving anyone a place in life.

HARRY: Yes! The very idea!

CLAIRE: Yes! (*as often, the mocking thing gives true expression to what lies sombrely in her*) The war. There was another gorgeous chance.

HARRY: Chance for what? I call you, Claire. I ask you to say what you mean.

CLAIRE: I don't know – precisely. If I did – there'd be no use saying it. (*at HARRY's impatient exclamation she turns to* TOM)

TOM: (*nodding*) The only thing left worth saying is the thing we can't say.

HARRY: Help!

CLAIRE: Yes. But the war didn't help. Oh, it was a stunning chance! But fast as we could – scuttled right back to the trim little thing we'd been shocked out of.

HARRY: You bet we did – showing our good sense.

CLAIRE: Showing our incapacity – for madness.

HARRY: Oh, come now, Claire – snap out of it. You're not really trying to say that capacity for madness is a good thing to *have*?

CLAIRE: (*in simple surprise*) Why yes, of course.

DICK: But I should say the war did leave enough madness to give you a gleam of hope.

CLAIRE: Not the madness that – breaks through. And it was – a stunning chance! Mankind massed to kill. We have failed. We are through. We will destroy. Break this up – it can't go farther. In the air above – in the sea below – it is to kill! All we had thought we were – we aren't. We were shut in with what wasn't so. Is there one ounce of energy has not gone to this killing? Is there one love not torn in two? Throw it in! Now? Ready? Break up. Push. Harder. Break up. And then – and then – But we didn't say – 'And then – ' The spirit didn't take the tip.

HARRY: Claire! Come now (*looking to the others for help*) – let's talk of something else.

CLAIRE: Plants do it. The big leap – it's called. Explode their species – because something in them knows they've gone as far as they can go. Something in them knows they're shut in to just that. So – go mad – that life may not be prisoned. Break themselves up into crazy things – into lesser things, and from the pieces – may come one sliver of life with vitality to find the future. How beautiful. How brave.

TOM: (*as if he would call her from too far – or would let her know he has gone with her*) Claire!

CLAIRE: (*her eyes turning to him*) Why should we mind lying under the earth? We who have no such initiative – no proud madness? Why think it death to lie under life so flexible – so ruthless and ever-renewing?

ANTHONY: (*from the door of the inner room*) Miss Claire?

I call you: poker term, used when matching another player's bet, thus requiring them to show their hand. Here used in the sense of 'put your cards on the table': i.e., be explicit.

CLAIRE: (*after an instant*) Yes? (*she goes with him, as they disappear his voice heard*, 'show me now ... want those violets bedded')

HARRY: Oh, this has got to *stop*. I've got to – put a stop to it some way. Why, Claire used to be the best sport a man ever played around with. I can't stand it to see her getting hysterical.

TOM: That was not hysterical.

HARRY: What was it then – I want to know?

TOM: It was – a look.

HARRY: Oh, I might have known I'd get no help from either of you. Even you, Edgeworthy – much as she thinks of you – and fine sort as I've no doubt you are, you're doing Claire no good – encouraging her in these queer ways.

TOM: I couldn't change Claire if I would.

HARRY: And wouldn't if you could.

TOM: No. But you don't have to worry about me. I'm going away in a day or two. And I shall not be back.

HARRY: Trouble with you is, it makes little difference whether you're here or away. Just the fact of your existence does encourage Claire in this – this way she's going.

TOM: (*with a smile*) But you wouldn't ask me to go so far as to stop my existence? Though I would do that for Claire – if it were the way to help her.

HARRY: By Jove, you say that as if you meant it.

TOM: Do you think I would say anything about Claire I didn't mean?

HARRY: You think a lot of her, don't you? (TOM *nods*) You don't mean (*a laugh letting him say it*) – that you're – in love with Claire!

TOM: In love? Oh, that's much too easy. Certainly I do love Claire.

HARRY: Well, you're a cool one!

TOM: Let her be herself. Can't you see she's troubled?

HARRY: Well, what is there to trouble Claire? Now I ask you. It seems to me she has everything.

TOM: She's left so – open. Too exposed. (*as* HARRY *moves impatiently*) Please don't be annoyed with me. I'm doing my best at saying it. You see Claire isn't hardened into one of those forms she talks about. She's too – aware. Always pulled toward what could be – tormented by the lost adventure.

HARRY: Well, there's danger in all that. Of course there's danger.

TOM: But you can't help that.

HARRY: Claire was the best fun a woman could be. Is yet – at times.

TOM: Let her be – at times. As much as she can and will. She does need that. Don't keep her from it by making her feel you're holding her in it. Above all, don't try to stop what she's doing here. If she can do it with plants, perhaps she won't have to do it with herself.

HARRY: Do what?

TOM: (*low, after a pause*) Break up what exists. Open the door to destruction in the hope of – a door on the far side of destruction.

HARRY: Well, you give me the willies. (*moves around in irritation, troubled. To* ANTHONY, *who is passing through with a sprayer*) Anthony, have any arrangements been made about Miss Claire's daughter?

ANTHONY: I haven't heard of any arrangements.

HARRY: Well, she'll have to have some heat in her room. We can't all live out here.

ANTHONY: Indeed you cannot. It is not good for the plants.

HARRY: I'm going where I can *smoke*. (*goes out*)

DICK: (*lightly, but fascinated by the idea*) You think there is a door on the – hinter side of destruction?

TOM: How can one tell – where a door may be? One thing I want to say to you – for it is about you. (*regards DICK and not with his usual impersonal contemplation*) I don't think Claire should have – any door closed to her. (*pause*) You know, I think, what I mean. And perhaps you can guess how it hurts to say it. Whether it's – mere escape within, – rather shameful escape within, or the wild hope of that door through, it's – (*suddenly all human*) Be good to her! (*after a difficult moment, smiles*) Going away for ever is like dying, so one can say things.

DICK: Why do you do it – go away for ever?

TOM: I haven't succeeded here.

DICK: But you've tried the going away before.

TOM: Never knowing I would not come back. So that wasn't going away. My hope is that this will be like looking at life from outside life.

DICK: But then you'll not be in it.

TOM: I haven't been able to look at it while in it.

DICK: Isn't it more important to be in it than to look at it?

TOM: Not what I mean by look.

DICK: It's hard for me to conceive of – loving Claire and going away from her for ever.

TOM: Perhaps it's harder to do than to conceive of.

DICK: Then why do it?

TOM: It's my only way of keeping her.

DICK: I'm afraid I'm like Harry now. I don't get you.

TOM: I suppose not. Your way is different. (*with calm, with sadness – not with malice*) But I shall have her longer. And from deeper.

DICK: I know that.

TOM: Though I miss much. Much. (*the buzzer.* TOM *looks around to see if anyone is coming to answer it, then goes to the phone*) Yes? ... I'll see if I can get her. (*to* DICK) Claire's daughter has arrived. (*looking in the inner room – returns to phone*) I don't see her. (*catching a glimpse of* ANTHONY *off right*) Oh, Anthony, where's Miss Claire? Her daughter has arrived.

ANTHONY: She's working at something very important in her experiments.

DICK: But isn't her daughter one of her experiments?

ANTHONY: (*after a baffled moment*) Her daughter is finished.

TOM: (*at the phone*) Sorry – but I can't get to Claire. She appears to have gone below. (ANTHONY *closes the trap-door*) I did speak to Anthony, but he says that Claire is working at one of her experiments and that her daughter is finished. I don't know how to make her hear – I took the revolver back to the house. Anyway you will remember Claire doesn't answer the revolver. I hate to reach Claire when she doesn't want to be reached. Why, of course – a daughter is very important, but oh, that's too bad. (*putting down the receiver*)

He says the girl's feelings are hurt. Isn't that annoying? (*gingerly pounds on the trap-door. Then with the other hand. Waits.* ANTHONY *has a gentle smile for the gentle tapping – nods approval as* TOM *returns to the phone*) She doesn't come up. Indeed I did – with both fists – Sorry.

ANTHONY: Please, you won't try again to disturb Miss Claire, will you?

DICK: Her daughter is here, Anthony. She hasn't seen her daughter for a year.

ANTHONY: Well, if she got along without a mother for a year – (*goes back to his work*)

DICK: (*smiling after* ANTHONY) Plants are queer. Perhaps it's safer to do it with pencil (*regards* TOM) – or with pure thought. Things that grow in the earth –

TOM: (*nodding*) I suppose because we grew in the earth.

DICK: I'm always shocked to find myself in agreement with Harry, but I too am worried about Claire – and this. (*looking at the plants*)

TOM: It's her best chance.

DICK: Don't you hate to go away to India – for ever – leaving Claire's future uncertain?

TOM: You're cruel now. And you knew that you were being cruel.

DICK: Yes, I like the lines of your face when you suffer.

TOM: The lines of yours when you're causing suffering – I don't like them.

DICK: Perhaps that's your limitation.

TOM: I grant you it may be. (*They are silent*) I had an odd feeling that you and I sat here once before, long ago, and that we were plants. And you were a beautiful plant, and I – I was a very ugly plant. I confess it surprised me – finding myself so ugly a plant.

> (*A young girl is seen outside.* HARRY *gets the door open for her and brings* ELIZABETH *in.*)

HARRY: There's heat here. And two of your mother's friends. Mr Demming – Richard Demming – the artist – and I think you and Mr Edgeworthy are old friends.

> (ELIZABETH *comes forward. She is the creditable young American – well built, poised, 'cultivated', so sound an expression of the usual as to be able to meet the world with assurance – assurance which training has made rather graceful. She is about seventeen – and mature. You feel solid things behind her.*)

TOM: I knew you when you were a baby. You used to kick a great deal then.

ELIZABETH: (*laughing, with ease*) And scream, I haven't a doubt. But I've stopped that. One does, doesn't one? And it was you who gave me the idol.

TOM: Proselytizing, I'm afraid.

ELIZABETH: I beg – ? Oh – yes (*laughing cordially*) I see. (*she doesn't*) I dressed the idol up in my doll's clothes. They fitted perfectly – the idol was just the size of my doll Ailine. But mother didn't like the idol that way, and tore the clothes getting them off. (*to* HARRY, *after looking around*) Is mother here?

HARRY: (*crossly*) Yes, she's here. Of course she's here. And she must know you're here. (*after looking in the inner room he goes to the trap-door and makes a great noise*)

ELIZABETH: Oh – please. Really – it doesn't make the least difference.

HARRY: Well, all I can say is, your manners are better than your mother's.

ELIZABETH: But you see I don't do anything interesting, so I have to have good manners. (*lightly, but leaving the impression there is a certain superiority in not doing anything interesting. Turning cordially to* DICK) My father was an artist.

DICK: Yes, I know.

ELIZABETH: He was a portrait painter. Do you do portraits?

DICK: Well, not the kind people buy.

ELIZABETH: They bought father's.

DICK: Yes, I know he did that kind.

HARRY: (*still irritated*) Why, you don't do portraits.

DICK: I did one of you the other day. You thought it was a milk-can.

ELIZABETH: (*laughing delightedly*) No? Not really? Did you think – How *could* you think – (*as* HARRY *does not join the laugh*) Oh, I beg your pardon. I – Does mother grow beautiful roses now?

HARRY: No, she does not.

> (*The trap-door begins to move.* CLAIRE's *head appears.*)

ELIZABETH: Mother! It's been so long – (*she tries to overcome the difficulties and embrace her mother*)

CLAIRE: (*protecting a box she has*) Careful, Elizabeth. We mustn't upset the lice.

ELIZABETH: (*retreating*) Lice? (*but quickly equal even to lice*) Oh – yes. You take it – them – off plants, don't you?

CLAIRE: I'm putting them on certain plants.

ELIZABETH: (*weakly*) Oh, I thought you took them off.

CLAIRE: (*calling*) Anthony! (*he comes*) The lice. (*he takes them from her*)

> (CLAIRE, *who has not fully ascended, looks at* ELIZABETH, *hesitates, then suddenly starts back down the stairs.*)

HARRY: (*outraged*) Claire! (*slowly she re-ascends – sits on the top step. After a long pause in which he has waited for* CLAIRE *to open a conversation with her daughter.*) Well, and what have you been doing at school all this time?

ELIZABETH: Oh – studying.

CLAIRE: Studying what?

ELIZABETH: Why – the things one studies, mother.

CLAIRE: Oh! The things one studies. (*looks down cellar again*)

DICK: (*after another wait*) And what have you been doing besides studying?

ELIZABETH: Oh – the things one does. Tennis and skating and dancing and –

CLAIRE: The things one does.

ELIZABETH: Yes. All the things. The – the things one does. Though I haven't been in school these last few months, you know. Miss Lane took us to Europe.

TOM: And how did you like Europe?

ELIZABETH: (*capably*) Oh, I thought it was awfully amusing. All the girls were quite mad about Europe. Of course, I'm glad I'm an American.

CLAIRE: Why?

ELIZABETH: (*laughing*) Why – mother! Of course one is glad one is an American. All the girls –

CLAIRE: (*turning away*) O – h! (*a moan under the breath*)

ELIZABETH: Why, mother – aren't you well?

HARRY: Your mother has been working pretty hard at all this.

ELIZABETH: Oh, I do so want to know all about it? Perhaps I can help you! I think it's just awfully amusing that you're doing something. One does nowadays, doesn't one? – if you know what I mean. It was the war, wasn't it, made it the thing to do something?

DICK: (*slyly*) And you thought, Claire, that the war was lost.

ELIZABETH: The *war ? Lost !* (*her capable laugh*) Fancy our losing a war! Miss Lane says we should give *thanks*. She says we should each do some expressive thing – you know what I mean? And that this is the *keynote* of the age. Of course, one's own kind of thing. Like mother – growing flowers.

CLAIRE: You think that is one's own kind of thing?

ELIZABETH: Why, of course I do, mother. And so does Miss Lane. All the girls –

CLAIRE: (*shaking her head as if to get something out*) S–hoo.

ELIZABETH: What is it, mother?

CLAIRE: A fly shut up in my ear – 'All the girls!'

ELIZABETH: (*laughing*) Mother was always so amusing. So *different* – if you know what I mean. Vacations I've lived mostly with Aunt Adelaide, you know.

CLAIRE: My sister who is fitted to rear children.

HARRY: Well, somebody has to do it.

ELIZABETH: And I do love Aunt Adelaide, but I think its going to be awfully amusing to be around with mother now – and help her with her work. Help do some useful beautiful thing.

CLAIRE: I am not doing any useful beautiful thing.

ELIZABETH: Oh, but you are, mother. Of course you are. Miss Lane says so. She says it is your splendid heritage gives you this impulse to do a beautiful thing for the race. She says you are doing in your way what the great teachers and preachers behind you did in theirs.

CLAIRE: (*who is good for little more*) Well, all I can say is, Miss Lane is stung.

ELIZABETH: Mother! What a thing to say of Miss *Lane*. (*from this slipping into more of a little girl manner*) Oh, she gave me a spiel one day about living up to the men I come from.

(CLAIRE *turns and regards her daughter.*)

CLAIRE: You'll do it, Elizabeth.

ELIZABETH: Well, I don't know. Quite a job, I'll say. Of course, I'd have to do it in my way. I'm not going to teach or preach or be a stuffy person. But now that – (*she here becomes the product of a superior school*) values have shifted and such sensitive new things have been liberated in the world –

CLAIRE: (*low*) Don't use those words.

ELIZABETH: Why – why not?

CLAIRE: Because you don't know what they mean.

ELIZABETH: Why, of course I know what they mean!

CLAIRE: (*turning away*) You're – stepping on the plants.

HARRY: (*hastily*) Your mother has been working awfully hard at all this.

ELIZABETH: Well, now that I'm here you'll let me help you, won't you, mother?

CLAIRE: (*trying for control*) You needn't – bother.

ELIZABETH: But I *want* to. Help add to the wealth of the world.

CLAIRE: Will you please get it out of your head that I am adding to the wealth of the world!

ELIZABETH: But, mother – of course you are. To produce a new and better kind of plant –
CLAIRE: They may be new. I don't give a damn whether they're better.
ELIZABETH: But – but what are they then?
CLAIRE: (*as if choked out of her*) They're different.
ELIZABETH: (*thinks a minute, then laughs triumphantly*) But what's the use of making them different if they aren't better?
HARRY: A good square question, Claire. Why don't you answer it?
CLAIRE: I don't have to answer it.
HARRY: Why not give the girl a fair show? You never have, you know. Since she's interested, why not tell her what it is you're doing?
CLAIRE: She is not interested.
ELIZABETH: But I am, mother. Indeed I am. I do want awfully to understand what you are doing, and help you.
CLAIRE: You can't help me, Elizabeth.
HARRY: Why not let her try?
CLAIRE: Why do you ask me to do that? This is my own thing. Why do you make me feel I should – (*goes to* ELIZABETH) I will be good to you, Elizabeth. We'll go around together. I haven't done it, but – you'll see. We'll do gay things. I'll have a lot of beaus around for you. Anything else. Not – this is – Not this.
ELIZABETH: As you like, mother, of course. I just would have been so glad to – to share the thing that interests you. (*hurt borne with good breeding and a smile*)
HARRY: Claire! (*which says, 'How can you?'*)
CLAIRE: (*who is looking at* ELIZABETH) Yes, I will try.
TOM: *I* don't think so. As Claire says – anything else.
ELIZABETH: Why, of course – I don't at all want to intrude.
HARRY: It'll do Claire good to take someone in. To get down to brass tacks and actually say what she's driving at.
CLAIRE: Oh – *Harry.* But yes – I will try. (*does try, but no words come. Laughs*) When you come to say it it's not – One would rather not nail it to a cross of words – (*laughs again*) with brass tacks.
HARRY: (*affectionately*) But I want to see you put things into words, Claire, and realize just where you are.
CLAIRE: (*oddly*) You think that's a – good idea?
ELIZABETH: (*in her manner of holding the world capably in her hands*) Now let's talk of something else. I hadn't the least idea of making mother feel badly.
CLAIRE: (*desperately*) No, we'll go on. Though I don't know – where we'll end. I can't answer for that. These plants – (*beginning flounderingly*) Perhaps they are less beautiful – less sound – than the plants from which they diverged. But they have found – otherness. (*laughs a little shrilly*) If you know – what I mean.
TOM: Claire – stop this! (*To* HARRY) This is wrong.
CLAIRE: (*excitedly*) No; I'm going on. They have been shocked out of what they were – into something they were not; they've broken from the forms in which they found themselves. They are alien. Outside. That's it, outside; if you – know what I mean.

ELIZABETH: (*not shocked from what she is*) But of course, the object of it all is to make them better plants. Otherwise, what would be the sense of doing it?

CLAIRE: (*not reached by* ELIZABETH) Out there – (*giving it with her hands*) lies all that's not been touched – lies life that waits. Back here – the old pattern, done again, again and again. So long done it doesn't even know itself for a pattern – in immensity. But this – has invaded. Crept a little way into – what wasn't. Strange lines in life unused. And when you make a pattern new you know a pattern's made with life. And then you know that anything may be – if only you know how to reach it. (*this has taken form, not easily, but with great struggle between feeling and words*)

HARRY: (*cordially*) Now I begin to get you, Claire. I never knew before why you called it the Edge Vine.

CLAIRE: I should destroy the Edge Vine. It isn't – over the edge. It's running, back to – 'all the girls'. It's a little afraid of Miss Lane. (*looking sombrely at it*) You are out, but you are not alive.

ELIZABETH: Why, it looks all right, mother.

CLAIRE: Didn't carry life with it from the life it left. Dick – you know what I mean. At least you ought to. (*her ruthless way of not letting anyone's feelings stand in the way of truth*) Then destroy it for me! It's hard to do it – with the hands that made it.

DICK: But what's the point in destroying it, Claire?

CLAIRE: (*impatiently*) I've told you. It cannot create.

DICK: But you say you can go on producing it, and it's interesting in form.

CLAIRE: And you think I'll stop with that? Be shut in – with different life – that can't creep on? (*after trying to put destroying hands upon it*) It's hard to – get past what we've done. Our own dead things – block the way.

TOM: But you're doing it this next time, Claire. (*nodding to the inner room.*) In there!

CLAIRE: (*turning to that room*) I'm not sure.

TOM: But you told me Breath of Life has already produced itself. Doesn't that show it has brought life from the life it left?

CLAIRE: But timidly, rather – wistfully. A little homesick. If it is less sure this time, then it is going back to – Miss Lane. But if the pattern's clearer now, then it has made friends of life that waits. I'll know to-morrow.

ELIZABETH: You know, something tells me this is *wrong*.

CLAIRE: The hymn-singing ancestors are tuning up.

ELIZABETH: I don't know what you mean by that, mother but –

CLAIRE: But we will now sing, 'Nearer, my God, to Thee: Nearer to – '

ELIZABETH: (*laughingly breaking in*) Well, I don't care. Of course you can make fun at me, but something does tell me this is wrong. To do what – what –

DICK: What God did?

ELIZABETH: Well – yes. Unless you do it to make them better – to do it just to *do* it – that doesn't seem right to me.

CLAIRE: (*roughly*) 'Right to you!' And that's all you know of adventure – and of anguish. Do you know it is you – world of which you're so true a flower – makes me have to leave? You're there to hold the door shut! Because you're young and of a gayer world, you think I can't *see* them – those old men? Do

you know why you're so sure of yourself? Because you can't *feel*. Can't feel –
the limitless – out there – a sea just over the hill. I will not stay with you!
(*buries her hands in the earth around the Edge Vine. But suddenly steps back
from it as she had from ELIZABETH*) And I will not stay with *you* ! (*grasps it
as we grasp what we would kill, is trying to pull it up. They all step forward in
horror.* ANTHONY *is drawn in by this harm to the plant*)

ANTHONY: Miss Claire! Miss Claire! The work of years!

CLAIRE: May only make a prison! (*struggling with HARRY, who is trying to stop
her*) You think I too will die on the edge? (*she has thrown him away, is now
struggling with the vine*) Why did I make you? To get past you! (*as she twists it*)
Oh yes, I know you have thorns! The Edge Vine should have thorns. (*with a
long tremendous pull for deep roots, she has it up. As she holds the torn roots*)
Oh, I have loved you so! You took me where I hadn't been.

ELIZABETH: (*who has been looking on with a certain practical horror*) Well, I'd
say it would be better not to go there!

CLAIRE: Now I know what you are for! (*flings her arm back to strike ELIZABETH
with the Edge Vine*)

HARRY: (*wresting it from her*) Claire! Are you mad?

CLAIRE: No, I'm not mad. I'm – too sane! (*pointing to ELIZABETH – and the
words come from mighty roots*) To think that object ever moved my belly and
sucked my breast! (ELIZABETH *hides her face as if struck*)

HARRY: (*going to ELIZABETH, turning to CLAIRE*) This is atrocious! You're
cruel.

> (*He leads ELIZABETH to the door and out. After an irresolute
> moment in which he looks from CLAIRE to TOM, DICK follows.
> ANTHONY cannot bear to go. He stoops to take the Edge Vine from
> the floor. CLAIRE's gesture stops him. He goes into the inner room.*)

CLAIRE: (*kicking the Edge Vine out of her way, drawing deep breaths, smiling*)
O–h. How good I feel! Light! (*a movement as if she could fly*) Read me
something, Tom dear. Or say something pleasant – about God. But be very
careful what you say about him! I have a feeling – he's not far off.

CURTAIN

ACT II

Late afternoon of the following day. CLAIRE *is alone in the tower – a tower which is
thought to be round but does not complete the circle. The back is curved, then jagged
lines break from that, and the front is a queer bulging window – in a curve that leans.
The whole structure is as if given a twist by some terrific force – like something wrong.
It is lighted by an old-fashioned watchman's lantern hanging from the ceiling; the
innumerable pricks and slits in the metal throw a marvellous pattern on the curved
wall – like some masonry that hasn't been.*
*There are no windows at back, and there is no door save an opening in the floor. The
delicately distorted rail of a spiral staircase winds up from below.* CLAIRE *is seen
through the huge ominous window as if shut into the tower. She is lying on a seat at
the back looking at a book of drawings. To do this she has left the door of her lantern
a little open – and her own face is clearly seen.*

A door is heard opening below; laughing voices, CLAIRE *listens, not pleased.*

ADELAIDE: (*voice coming up*) Dear – dear, why do they make such twisting steps.
HARRY: Take your time, most up now. (HARRY's *head appears, he looks back.*) Making it all right?
ADELAIDE: I can't tell yet. (*laughingly*) No, I don't think so.
HARRY: (*reaching back a hand for her*) The last lap – is the bad lap.
　　　　(ADELAIDE *is up, and occupied with getting her breath.*)
HARRY: Since you wouldn't come down, Claire, we thought we'd come up.
ADELAIDE: (*as* CLAIRE *does not greet her*) I'm sorry to intrude, but I have to see you, Claire. There are things to be arranged. (CLAIRE *volunteering nothing about arrangements,* ADELAIDE *surveys the tower. An unsympathetic eye goes from the curves to the lines which diverge. Then she looks from the window*) Well, at least you have a view.
HARRY: This is the first time you've been up here?
ADELAIDE: Yes, in the five years you've had the house I was never asked up here before.
CLAIRE: (*amiably enough*) You weren't asked up here now.
ADELAIDE: Harry asked me.
CLAIRE: It isn't Harry's tower. But never mind – since you don't like it – it's all right.
ADELAIDE: (*her eyes again rebuking the irregularities of the tower*) No, I confess I do not care for it. A round tower should go on being round.
HARRY: Claire calls this the thwarted tower. She bought the house because of it. (*going over and sitting by her, his hand on her ankle*) Didn't you, old girl? She says she'd like to have known the architect.
ADELAIDE: Probably a tiresome person too incompetent to make a perfect tower.
CLAIRE: Well, now he's disposed of, what next?
ADELAIDE: (*sitting down in a manner of capably opening a conference*) Next, Elizabeth, and you, Claire. Just what is the matter with Elizabeth?
CLAIRE: (*whose voice is cool, even, as if herself is not really engaged by this*) Nothing is the matter with her. She is a tower that is a tower.
ADELAIDE: Well, is that anything against her?
CLAIRE: She's just like one of her father's portraits. They never interested me. Nor does she. (*looks at the drawings which do interest her*)
ADELAIDE: A mother cannot cast off her own child simply because she does not interest her!
CLAIRE: (*an instant raising cool eyes to* ADELAIDE) Why can't she?
ADELAIDE: Because it would be monstrous!
CLAIRE: And why can't she be monstrous – if she has to be?
ADELAIDE: You don't have to be. That's where I'm out of patience with you Claire. You are really a particularly intelligent, competent person, and it's time for you to call a halt to this nonsense and be the woman you were meant to be!
CLAIRE: (*holding the book up to see another way*) What inside dope have you on what I was meant to be?
ADELAIDE: I know what you came from.

CLAIRE: Well, isn't it about time somebody got loose from that? What I came from made you, so –

ADELAIDE: (*stiffly*) I see.

CLAIRE: So – you being such a tower of strength, why need I too be imprisoned in what I came from?

ADELAIDE: It isn't being imprisoned. Right there is where you make your mistake, Claire. Who's in a tower – in an unsuccessful tower? Not I. I go about in the world – free, busy, happy. Among people, I have no time to think of myself.

CLAIRE: No.

ADELAIDE: No. My family. The things that interest them; from morning till night it's –

CLAIRE: Yes, I know you have a large family, Adelaide; five and Elizabeth makes six.

ADELAIDE: We'll speak of Elizabeth later. But if you would just get out of yourself and enter into other people's lives –

CLAIRE: Then I would become just like you. And we should all be just alike in order to assure one another that we're all just right. But since you and Harry and Elizabeth and ten million other people bolster each other up, why do you especially need me?

ADELAIDE: (*not unkindly*) We don't need you as much as you need us.

CLAIRE: (*a wry face*) I never liked what I needed.

HARRY: I am convinced I am the worst thing in the world for you, Claire.

CLAIRE: (*with a smile for his tactics, but shaking her head*) I'm afraid you're not. I don't know – perhaps you are.

ADELAIDE: Well, what is it you want, Claire?

CLAIRE: (*simply*) You wouldn't know if I told you.

ADELAIDE: That's rather arrogant.

HARRY: Yes, take a chance, Claire. I have been known to get an idea – and Adelaide quite frequently gets one.

CLAIRE: (*the first resentment she has shown*) You two feel very superior, don't you?

ADELAIDE: I don't think we are the ones who are feeling superior.

CLAIRE: Oh, yes, you are. Very superior to what you think is my feeling of superiority, comparing my – isolation with your 'heart of humanity'. Soon we will speak of the beauty of common experiences, of the – Oh, I could say it all before we come to it.

HARRY: Adelaide came up here to help you, Claire.

CLAIRE: Adelaide came up here to lock me in. Well, she can't do it.

ADELAIDE: (*gently*) But can't you see that one may do that to one's self?

CLAIRE: (*thinks of this, looks suddenly tired – then smiles*) Well, at least I've changed the keys.

HARRY: 'Locked in.' Bunkum. Get that our of your head, Claire. Who's locked in? Nobody that I know of, we're all free Americans. Free as air.

ADELAIDE: I wish you'd come and hear one of Mr Morley's sermons, Claire. You're very old-fashioned if you think sermons are what they used to be.

CLAIRE: (*with interest*) And do they still sing 'Nearer, my God, to Thee'?

ADELAIDE: They do, and a noble old hymn it is. It would do you no harm at all to sing it.

CLAIRE: (*eagerly*) Sing it to me, Adelaide. I'd like to hear you sing it.

ADELAIDE: It would be sacrilege to sing it to you in this mood.

CLAIRE: (*falling back*) Oh, I don't know. I'm not so sure God would agree with you. That would be one on you, wouldn't it?

ADELAIDE: It's easy to feel one's self set apart!

CLAIRE: No, it isn't.

ADELAIDE: (*beginning anew*) It's a new age, Claire. Spiritual values –

CLAIRE: Spiritual values! (*in her brooding way*) So you have pulled that up. (*with cunning*) Don't think I don't know what it is you do.

ADELAIDE: Well, what do I do? I'm sure I have no idea what you're talking about.

HARRY: (*affectionately, as* CLAIRE *is looking with intentness at what he does not see*) What does she do, Claire?

CLAIRE: It's rather clever, what she does. Snatching the phrase – (*a movement as if pulling something up*) standing it up between her and – the life that's there. And by saying it enough – 'We have life! We have life! We have life!' Very good come-back at one who would really be – 'Just so! *We* are that. Right this way, please – ' That, I suppose is what we mean by needing each other. All join in the chorus, 'This is it! This is it! This is it!' And anyone who won't join is to be – visited by relatives. (*regarding* ADELAIDE *with curiosity*) Do you really think that anything is going on in you?

ADELAIDE: (*stiffly*) I am not one to hold myself up as a perfect example of what the human race may be.

CLAIRE: (*brightly*) Well, that's good.

HARRY: Claire!

CLAIRE: Humility's a *real* thing – not just a fine name for laziness.

HARRY: Well, Lord A'mighty, you can't call Adelaide lazy.

CLAIRE: She stays in one place because she hasn't the energy to go anywhere else.

ADELAIDE: (*as if the last word in absurdity has been said*) *I* haven't energy?

CLAIRE: (*mildly*) You haven't any energy at all, Adelaide. That's why you keep so busy.

ADELAIDE: *Well* – Claire's nerves are in a worse state than I had realized.

CLAIRE: So perhaps we'd better look at Blake's drawings. (*takes up the book*)

ADELAIDE: It would be all right for me to look at Blake's drawings. You'd better look at the Sistine Madonna. (*affectionately, after she has watched* CLAIRE's *face a moment*) What is it, Claire? Why do you shut yourself out from us?

CLAIRE: I told you. Because I do not want to be shut in with you.

ADELAIDE: All of this is not very pleasant for Harry.

HARRY: I want Claire to be *gay*.

CLAIRE: Funny – you should want that. (*speaks unwillingly, a curious, wistful*

Blake's drawings ... Sistine Madonna: William Blake (1757–1827), romantic poet and visionary artist, rejected conventional realism and experimented with techniques and materials for painting and printing. He based many of his engraved figures on those of Michelangelo (1475–1564), whose frescoes on the Sistine Chapel ceiling comprise one of the greatest works of High Renaissance art.

unwillingness) Did you ever say a preposterous thing, then go trailing after the thing you've said and find it wasn't so preposterous? Here is the circle we are in. (*describes a big circle*) Being gay. It shoots little darts through the circle, and a minute later – gaiety all gone, and you looking through that little hole the gaiety left.

ADELAIDE: (*going to her, as she is still looking through that little hole*) Claire, dear, I wish I could make you feel how much I care for you. (*simply, with real feeling*) You can call me all the names you like – dull, commonplace, lazy – that *is* a new idea, I confess, but the rest of our family's gone now, and the love that used to be there between us all – the only place for it now is between you and me. You were so much loved, Claire. You oughtn't to try and get away from a world in which you are so much loved. (*to HARRY*) Mother – father – all of us, always loved Claire best. We always loved Claire's queer gaiety. Now you've got to hand it to us for that, as the children say.

CLAIRE: (*moved, but eyes shining with a queer bright loneliness*) But never one of you – once – looked with me through the little pricks the gaiety made – never one of you – once, looked with me at the queer light that came in through the pricks.

ADELAIDE: And can't you see, dear, that it's better for us we didn't? And that it would be better for you now if you would just resolutely look somewhere else? You must see yourself that you haven't the poise of people who are held – well, within the circle, if you choose to put it that way. There's something about being in that main body, having one's roots in the big common experiences, gives a calm which you have missed. That's why I want you to take Elizabeth, forget yourself, and –

CLAIRE: I do want calm. But mine would have to be a calm I – worked my way to. A calm all prepared for me – would stink.

ADELAIDE: (*less sympathetically*) I know you have to be yourself, Claire. But I don't admit you have a right to hurt other people.

HARRY: I think Claire and I had better take a nice long trip.

ADELAIDE: Now why don't you?

CLAIRE: I am taking a trip.

ADELAIDE: Well, Harry isn't, and he'd like to go and wants you to go with him. Go to Paris and get yourself some awfully good-looking clothes – and have one grand fling at the gay world. You really love that, Claire, and you've been awfully dull lately. I think that's the whole trouble.

HARRY: I think so too.

ADELAIDE: This sober business of growing plants –

CLAIRE: Not sober – it's mad.

ADELAIDE: All the more reason for quitting it.

CLAIRE: But madness that is the only chance for sanity.

ADELAIDE: Come, come, now – let's not juggle words.

CLAIRE: (*springing up*) How dare you say that to me, Adelaide. You who are such a liar and thief and whore with words!

ADELAIDE: (*facing her, furious*) How *dare* you –

HARRY: Of course not, Claire. You have the most preposterous way of using words.

CLAIRE: I respect words.

ADELAIDE: Well, you'll please respect me enough not to dare use certain words to me!

CLAIRE: Yes, I do dare. I'm tired of what you do – you and all of you. Life – experience – values – calm – sensitive words which raise their heads as indications. And you *pull them up* – to decorate your stagnant little minds – and think that makes you – And because you have pulled that word from the life that grew it you won't let one who's honest, and aware, and troubled, try to reach through to – to what she doesn't know is there. (*she is moved, excited, as if a cruel thing has been done*) Why did you come here?

ADELAIDE: To try and help you. But I begin to fear I can't do it. It's pretty egotistical to claim that what so many people are, is wrong.

> (CLAIRE, *after looking intently at* ADELAIDE, *slowly, smiling a little, describes a circle. With deftly used hands makes a quick vicious break in the circle which is there in the air.*

HARRY: (*going to her, taking her hands*) It's getting close to dinner-time. You were thinking of something else, Claire, when I told you Charlie Emmons was coming to dinner to-night. (*answering her look*) Sure – he is a neurologist, and I want him to see you. I'm perfectly honest with you – cards all on the table, you know that. I'm hoping if you like him – and he's the best scout in the world, that he can help you. (*talking hurriedly against the stillness which follows her look from him to* ADELAIDE, *where she sees between them an 'understanding' about her*) Sure you need help, Claire. Your nerves are a little on the blink – from all you've been doing. No use making a mystery of it – or a tragedy. Emmons is a cracker-jack, and naturally I want you to get a move on yourself and be happy again.

CLAIRE: (*who has gone over to the window*) And this neurologist can make me happy?

HARRY: Can make you well – and then you'll be happy.

ADELAIDE: (*in the voice of now fixing it all up*) And I had just an idea about Elizabeth. Instead of working with mere plants, why not think of Elizabeth as a plant and –

> (CLAIRE, *who has been looking out of the window, now throws open one of the panes that swings out – or seems to, and calls down in great excitement.*)

CLAIRE: Tom! *Tom!* Quick! Up here! I'm in trouble!

HARRY: (*going to the window*) That's a rotten thing to do, Claire! You've frightened him.

CLAIRE: Yes, how fast he can run. He was deep in thought and I stabbed right through.

HARRY: Well, he'll be none too pleased when he gets up here and finds there was no reason for the stabbing!

> (*They wait for his footsteps,* HARRY *annoyed,* ADELAIDE *offended, but stealing worried looks at* CLAIRE, *who is looking fixedly at the place in the floor where* TOM *will appear. – Running footsteps.*)

TOM: (*his voice getting there before he does*) Yes, Claire – yes – yes – (*as his head appears*) What is it?

CLAIRE: (*at once presenting him and answering his question*) My sister.

TOM: (*gasping*) Oh, – why – is that all? I mean – how do you do? Pardon, I (*panting*) came up – rather hurriedly.

HARRY: If you want to slap Claire, Tom, I for one have no objection.

CLAIRE: Adelaide has the most interesting idea, Tom. She proposes that I take Elizabeth and roll her in the gutter. Just let her lie there until she breaks up into –

ADELAIDE: *Claire!* I don't see how – even in fun – pretty vulgar fun – you can speak in those terms of a pure young girl. I'm beginning to think I had better take Elizabeth.

CLAIRE: Oh, I've thought that all along.

ADELAIDE: And I'm also beginning to suspect that – oddity may be just a way of shifting responsibility.

CLAIRE: (*cordially interested in this possibility*) Now you know – that might be.

ADELAIDE: A mother who does not love her own child! You are an unnatural woman, Claire.

CLAIRE: Well, at least it saves me from being a natural one.

ADELAIDE: Oh – I know, you think you have a geat deal! But let me tell you, you've missed a great deal! You've never known the faintest stirring of a mother's love.

CLAIRE: That's not true.

HARRY: No. Claire loved our boy.

CLAIRE: I'm glad he didn't live.

HARRY: (*low*) Claire!

CLAIRE: I loved him. Why should I want him to live?

HARRY: Come, dear, I'm sorry I spoke of him – when you're not feeling well.

CLAIRE: I'm feeling all right. Just because I'm seeing something, it doesn't mean I'm sick.

HARRY: Well, let's go down now. About dinner-time. I shouldn't wonder if Emmons were here. (*as* ADELAIDE *is starting down stairs*) Coming, Claire?

CLAIRE: No.

HARRY: But it's time to go down for dinner.

CLAIRE: I'm not hungry.

HARRY: But we have a guest. Two guests – Adelaide's staying too.

CLAIRE: Then you're not alone.

HARRY: But I invited Dr Emmons to meet you.

CLAIRE: (*her smile flashing*) Tell him I am violent to-night.

HARRY: Dearest – how can you joke about such things!

CLAIRE: So you do think they're serious?

HARRY: (*irritated*) No, I do not! But I want you to come down for dinner!

ADELAIDE: Come, come, Claire; you know quite well this is not the sort of thing one does.

CLAIRE: Why go on saying one doesn't, when you are seeing one does (*to* TOM) Will you stay with me a while? I want to purify the tower.

(ADELAIDE *begins to disappear*)

HARRY: Fine time to choose for a *tête-à-tête*. (*as he is leaving*) I'd think more of you, Edgeworthy, if you refused to humour Claire in her ill-breeding.

ADELAIDE: (*her severe voice coming from below*) It is not what she was taught.

CLAIRE: No, it's not what I was taught. (*laughing rather timidly*) And perhaps you'd rather have your dinner?

TOM: No.

CLAIRE: We'll get something later. I want to talk to you. (*but she does not – laughs*) Absurd that I should feel bashful with you. Why am I so awkward with words when I go to talk to you?

TOM: The words know they're not needed.

CLAIRE: No, they're not needed. There's something underneath – an open way – down below the way that words can go. (*rather desperately*) It is there, isn't it?

TOM: Oh, yes, it is there.

CLAIRE: Then why do we never – go it?

TOM: If we went it, it would not be there.

CLAIRE: Is that true? How terrible, if that is true.

TOM: Not terrible, wonderful – that it should – of itself – be there.

CLAIRE: (*with the simplicity that can say anything*) I want to go it, Tom, I'm lonely up on top here. Is it that I have more faith than you, or is it only that I'm greedier? You see, you don't know (*her reckless laugh*) what you're missing. You don't know how I could love you.

TOM: Don't, Claire; that isn't – how it is – between you and me.

CLAIRE: But why can't it be – every way – between you and me?

TOM: Because we'd lose – the open way. (*the quality of his denial shows how strong is his feeling for her*) With anyone else – not with you.

CLAIRE: But you are the only one I want. The only one – all of me wants.

TOM: I know; but that's the way it is.

CLAIRE: You're cruel.

TOM: Oh, Claire, I'm trying so hard to – save it for us. Isn't it our beauty and our safeguard that underneath our separate lives, no matter where we may be, with what other, there is this open way between us? That's so much more than anything we could bring to being.

CLAIRE: Perhaps. But – it's different with me. I'm not – all spirit.

TOM: (*his hand on her*) Dear!

CLAIRE: No, don't touch me – since (*moving*) you're going away to-morrow? (*he nods*) For – always? (*his head just moves assent*) India is just another country. But there are undiscovered countries.

TOM: Yes, but we are so feeble we have to reach our country through the actual country lying nearest. Don't you do that yourself, Claire? Reach your country through the plants' country?

CLAIRE: My country? You mean – outside?

TOM: No, I don't think it that way.

CLAIRE: Oh, yes, you do.

TOM: Your country is the inside, Claire. The innermost. You are disturbed because you lie too close upon the heart of life.

CLAIRE: (*restlessly*) I don't know; you can think it one way – or another. No way says it, and that's good – at least it's not shut up in saying. (*she is looking at her enclosing hand, as if something is shut up there*)

TOM: But also, you know, things may be freed by expression. Come from the unrealized into the fabric of life.

CLAIRE: Yes, but why does the fabric of life have to – freeze into its pattern? It should (*doing it with her hands*) flow. (*then turning like an unsatisfied child to him*) But I wanted to talk to you.

TOM: You are talking to me. Tell me about your flower that never was before – your Breath of Life.

CLAIRE: I'll know to-morrow. You'll not go until I know?

TOM: I'll try to stay.

CLAIRE: It seems to me, if it has – then I have, integrity in – (*smiles, it is as if the smile lets her say it*) otherness. I don't want to die on the edge!

TOM: Not you!

CLAIRE: Many do. It's what makes them too smug in allness – those dead things on the edge, died, distorted – trying to get through. Oh – don't think I don't see – The Edge Vine! (*a pause, then swiftly*) Do you know what I mean? Or do you think I'm just a fool, or crazy?

TOM: I think I know what you mean, and you know I don't think you are a fool, or crazy.

CLAIRE: Stabbed to awareness – no matter where it takes you, isn't that more than a safe place to stay? (*telling him very simply despite the pattern of pain in her voice*) Anguish may be a thread – making patterns that haven't been. A thread – blue and burning.

TOM: (*to take her from what even he fears for her*) But you were telling me about the flower you breathed to life. What is your Breath of Life?

CLAIRE: (*an instant playing*) It's a secret. A secret? – it's a trick. Distilled from the most fragile flowers there are. It's only air – pausing – playing; except, far in, one stab of red, its quivering heart – that asks a question. But here's the trick – I bred the air – form to strength. The strength shut up behind us I've sent – far out. (*troubled*) I'll know tomorrow. And I have another gift for Breath of Life; some day – though days of work lie in between – some day I'll give it reminiscence. Fragrance that is – no one thing in here but – reminiscent. (*silence, she raises wet eyes*) We need the haunting beauty from the life we've left. I need that. (*he takes her hands and breathes her name*) Let me reach my country with you. I'm not a plant. After all, they don't – accept me. Who does – accept me? Will you?

TOM: My dear – dear, dear, Claire – you move me so! You stand alone in a clearness that breaks my heart. (*her hands move up his arms. He takes them to hold them from where they would go – though he can hardly do it*) But you've asked what you yourself could answer best. We'd only stop in the country where everyone stops.

CLAIRE: We might come through – to radiance.

TOM: Radiance is an enclosing place.

CLAIRE: Perhaps radiance lighting forms undreamed. (*her reckless laugh*) I'd be willing to – take a chance, I'd rather lose than never know.

TOM: No, Claire. Knowing you from underneath, I know you couldn't bear to lose.

CLAIRE: Wouldn't men say you were a fool!

TOM: They would.

CLAIRE: And perhaps you are. (*he smiles a little*) I feel so desperate, because if only I could – show you what I am, you might see I could have without losing. But I'm a stammering thing with you.

TOM: You do show me what you are.

CLAIRE: I've known a few moments that were life. Why don't they help me now? One was in the air. I was up with Harry – flying – high. It was about four months before David was born – the doctor was furious – pregnant women are supposed to keep to earth. We were going fast – I *was* flying – I had left the earth. And then – within me, movement, for the first time – stirred to life far in air – movement within. The man unborn, he too, would fly. And so – I always loved him. He was movement – and wonder. In his short life were many flights. I never told anyone about the last one. His little bed was by the window – he wasn't four years old. It was night, but him not asleep. He saw the morning star – you know – the morning star. Brighter – stranger – reminiscent – and a promise. He pointed – 'Mother', he asked me, 'what is there – beyond the stars?' A baby, a sick baby – the morning star. Next night – the finger that pointed was – (*suddenly bites her own finger*) But, yes, I am glad. He would always have tried to move and too much would hold him. Wonder would die – and he'd laugh at soaring. (*looking down, sidewise*) Though I liked his voice. So I wish you'd stay near me – for I like your voice, too.

TOM: Claire! That's (*choked*) almost too much.

CLAIRE: (*one of her swift glances – canny, almost practical*) Well, I'm glad if it is. How can I make it more? (*but what she sees brings its own change*) I know what it is you're afraid of. It's because I have so much – yes, why shouldn't I say it? – passion. You feel that in me, don't you? You think it would swamp everything. But that isn't all there is to me.

TOM: Oh, I know it! My dearest – why, it's because I know it! You think I *am* – a fool?

CLAIRE: It's a thing that's – sometimes more than I am. And yet I – I am more than it is.

TOM: I know. I know about you.

CLAIRE: I don't know that you do. Perhaps if you really knew about me – you wouldn't go away.

TOM: You're making me suffer, Claire.

CLAIRE: I know I am. I want to. Why shouldn't you suffer? (*now seeing it more clearly than she has ever seen it*) You know what I think about you? You're afraid of suffering, and so you stop this side – in what you persuade yourself is suffering. (*waits, then sends it straight*) You know – how it is – with me and Dick? (*as she sees him suffer*) Oh, no, I don't want to hurt you! Let it be you! I'll teach you – you needn't scorn it. It's rather wonderful.

TOM: Stop that, Claire! That isn't you.

CLAIRE: Why are you so afraid – of letting me be low – if that is low? You see – (*cannily*) I believe in beauty. I have the faith that can be bad as well as good. And you know why I have the faith? Because sometimes – from my lowest moments – beauty has opened as the sea. From a cave I saw immensity.

My love, you're going away –
Let me tell you how it is with me;
I want to touch you – somehow touch you once before I die –
Let me tell you how it is with me.
    I do not want to work,
I want to be;
Do not want to make a rose or make a poem –
Want to lie upon the earth and know. (*closes her eyes*)
Stop doing that! – words going into patterns;
They do it sometimes when I let come what's there.
Thoughts take pattern – then the pattern is the thing.
But let me tell you how it is with me. (*it flows again*)
All that I do or say – it is to what it comes from, –
A drop lifted from the sea.
I want to lie upon the earth and know.
But – scratch a little dirt and make a flower;
Scratch a bit of brain – something like a poem. (*covering her face*)
Stop *doing* that. Help me stop doing that!

TOM: (*and from the place where she had carried him*)
Don't talk at all. Lie still and know –
And know that I am knowing.

CLAIRE:
Yes; but we are so weak we have to talk;
To talk – to touch.
Why can't I rest in knowing I would give my life to reach you?
That has – all there is.
But I must – put my timid hands upon you,
Do something about infinity.
Oh, let what will flow into us,
And fill us full – and leave us still.
Wring me dry,
And let me fill again with life more pure.
To know – to feel,
And do nothing with what I feel and know –
That's being good. That's nearer God.
(*drenched in the feeling that has flowed through her – but surprised – helpless*)
Why, I said your thing, didn't I? Opened my life to bring you to me, and what came – is what sends you away.

TOM: No! What came is what holds us together. What came is what saves us from ever going apart. (*brokenly*) My beautiful one. You – you brave flower of all our knowing.

CLAIRE: I am not a flower. I am too torn. If you have anything – help me. Breathe. Breathe the healing oneness, and let me know in calm. (*with a sob his head rests upon her*)

CLAIRE: (*her hands on his head, but looking far*) Beauty – you pure one thing. Breathe – Let me know in calm. Then – trouble me, trouble me, for other moments – in farther calm. (*slow, motionless, barely articulate*)

TOM: (*as she does not move he lifts his head. And even as he looks at her, she does not move, nor look at him*) Claire – (*his hand out to her, a little afraid*) You went away from me then. You are away from me now.

CLAIRE: Yes, and I could go on. But I will come back. (*it is hard to do. She brings much with her*) That, too, I will give you – my by-myself-ness. That's the uttermost I can give. I never thought – to try to give it. But let us do it – the great sacrilege! Yes! (*excited, she rises; she has his hands, and bring him up beside her*) Let us take the mad chance! Perhaps it's the only way to save – what's there. How do we know? How can we know? Risk. Risk everything. From all that flows into us, let it rise! All that we never thought to use to make a moment – let it flow into what could be! Bring all into life between us – or send all down to death! Oh, do you know what I am doing? Risk, risk everything, why are you so afraid to lose? What holds you from me? Test all. Let it live or let it die. It is our chance – our chance to bear – what's there. My dear one – I will love you so. With all of me. I am not afraid now – of – all of me. Be generous. Be unafraid. Life is for *life* – though it cuts us from the farthest life. How can I make you know that's true? All that we're open to – (*hesitates, shudders*) But yes – I will, I will risk the life that waits. Perhaps only he who gives his loneliness – shall find. You never keep by holding. (*gesture of giving*) To the uttermost. And it is gone – or it is there. You do not know and – that makes the moment – (*music has begun – a phonograph downstairs; they do not heed it*) Just as I would cut my wrists – (*holding them out*) Yes, perhaps this lesser thing will tell it – would cut my wrists and let the blood flow out till all is gone if my last drop would make – would make – (*looking at them fascinated*) I want to see it doing that! Let me give my last chance for life to –

    (*He snatches her – they are on the brink of their moment; now that there are no words the phonograph from downstairs is louder. It is playing languorously the Barcarole; they become conscious of this – they do not want to be touched by the love song.*)

CLAIRE: Don't listen. That's nothing. This isn't that. (*fearing*) I tell you – it isn't that. Yes, I know – that's amorous – enclosing. I know – a little place. This isn't that. (*her arms going around him – all the lure of 'that' while she pleads against it as it comes up to them*) We will come out – to radiance – in far places (*admitting, using*) Oh, then let it be that! Go with it. Give up – the otherness. I will! And in the giving up – perhaps a door – we'd never find by searching. And if it's no more – than all have known, I only say it's worth the allness! (*her arms wrapped round him*) My love – my love – let go your pride in loneliness and let me give you joy!

TOM: (*drenched in her passion, but fighting*) It's *you*. (*in anguish*) You rare thing untouched – not – not into this – not back into this – by me – lover of your apartness.

    (*She steps back. She sees he cannot. She stands there, before what she wanted more than life, and almost had, and lost. A long moment. Then she runs down the stairs.*)

CLAIRE: (*her voice coming up*) Harry! Choke that phonograph! If you want to be lewd – do it yourselves! You tawdry things – you cheap little lewd cowards. (*a

door heard opening below) Harry! If you don't stop that music, I'll kill myself.
(*far down, steps on stairs*)

HARRY: Claire, what *is* this?

CLAIRE: Stop that phonograph or I'll –

HARRY:Why, of course I'll stop it. What – what is there to get so excited about?
Now – now just a minute, dear. It'll take a minute.

> (CLAIRE *comes back upstairs, dragging steps, face ghastly. The
> amorous song still comes up, and louder now that doors are open. She
> and* TOM *do not look at one another. Then, on a languorous swell the
> music comes to a grating stop. They do not speak or move. Quick
> footsteps* – HARRY *comes up.*)

HARRY: What in the world were you saying, Claire? Certainly you could have
asked me more quietly to turn off the Victrola. Though what harm was it doing
you – way up here? (*a sharp little sound from* CLAIRE; *she checks it, her hand
over her mouth.* HARRY *looks from her to* TOM) Well, I think you two
would better have had your dinner. Won't you come down now and have
some?

CLAIRE: (*only now taking her hand from her mouth*) Harry, tell him to come up
here – that insanity man. I – want to ask him something.

HARRY: 'Insanity man!' How absurd. He's a nerve specialist. There's a vast
difference.

CLAIRE: Is there? Anyway, ask him to come up here. Want to – ask him
something.

TOM: (*speaking with difficulty*) Wouldn't it be better for us to go down there?

CLAIRE: No. So nice up here! Everybody – up here!

HARRY: (*worried*) You'll – be yourself, will you, Claire? (*She checks a laugh,
nods.*) I think he can help you.

CLAIRE: Want to ask him to – help me.

HARRY: (*as he is starting down*) He's here as a guest to-night, you know, Claire.

CLAIRE: I suppose a guest can – help one.

TOM: (*when the silence rejects it*) Claire, you must know, it's because it is so much,
so –

CLAIRE: Be still. There isn't anything to say.

TOM: (*torn – tortured*) If it only weren't *you*!

CLAIRE: Yes, – so you said. If it weren't. I suppose I wouldn't be so – interested!
(*hears them starting up below – keeps looking at the place where they will
appear*)

> (HARRY *is heard to call*, 'Coming, Dick?' *and* DICK's *voice replies*,
> 'In a moment or two.' ADELAIDE *comes first.*)

ADELAIDE: (*as her head appears*) Well, these stairs should keep down weight.
You missed an awfully good dinner, Claire. And kept Mr Edgeworth from a
good dinner.

CLAIRE: Yes. We missed our dinner. (*her eyes do not leave the place where* DR
EMMONS *will come up*)

HARRY: (*as he and* EMMONS *appear*) Claire, this is –

CLAIRE: Yes, I know who he is. I want to ask you –

ADELAIDE: Let the poor man get his breath before you ask him anything. (*he nods, smiles, looks at* CLAIRE *with interest. Careful not to look too long at her, surveys the tower*)

EMMONS: Curious place.

ADELAIDE: Yes; it lacks form, doesn't it?

CLAIRE: What do you mean? How *dare* you?

> (*It is impossible to ignore her agitation; she is backed against the curved wall, as far as possible from them.* HARRY *looks at her in alarm, then in resentment at* TOM, *who takes a step nearer* CLAIRE.)

HARRY: (*trying to be light*) Don't take it so hard, Claire.

CLAIRE: (*to* EMMONS) It must be very interesting – helping people go insane.

ADELAIDE: Claire! How preposterous.

EMMONS: (*easily*) I hope that's not precisely what we do.

ADELAIDE: (*with the smile of one who is going to 'cover it'*.) Trust Claire to put it in the unique and – amusing way.

CLAIRE: Amusing? You are amused? But it doesn't matter. (*to the doctor*) I think it is very kind of you – helping people go insane. I suppose they have all sorts of reasons for having to do it – reasons why they can't stay sane any longer. But tell me, how do they do it? It's not so easy to – get out. How do so many manage it?

EMMONS: I'd like immensely to have a talk with you about all this some day.

ADELAIDE: Certainly this is not the time, Claire.

CLAIRE: The time? When you – can't go any farther – isn't that that –

ADELAIDE: (*capably taking the whole thing into matter-of-factness*) What I think is, Claire has worked too long with plants. There's something – not quite sound about making one thing into another thing. What we need is unity. (*from* CLAIRE *something like a moan*) Yes, dear, we do need it. (*to the doctor*) I can't say that I believe in making life *over* like this. I don't think the new species are worth it. At least I don't believe in it for Claire. If one is an intense, sensitive person –

CLAIRE: Isn't there any way to *stop* her? Always – always smothering it with the word for it?

EMMONS: (*soothingly*) But she can't smother it. Anything that's really there – she can't hurt with words.

CLAIRE: (*looking at him with eyes too bright*) Then you don't see it either. (*angry*) Yes, she can hurt it! Piling it up – always piling it up – between us and – What there. Clogging the way – always. (*to* EMMONS) I want to cease to know! That's all I ask. Darken it. Darken it. If you came to help me, strike me blind!

EMMONS: You're really all tired out, aren't you? Oh, we've got to get you rested.

CLAIRE: They – deny it saying they have it; and he (*half looks at* TOM – *quickly looks away*) – others, deny it – afraid of losing it. We're in the *way*. Can't you see the dead stuff piled in the path? (*Pointing.*)

DICK: (*voice coming up*) Me too?

CLAIRE: (*staring at the path, hearing his voice a moment after it has come*) Yes, Dick – you too. Why not – you too. (*after he has come up*) What is there any more than you are?

DICK: (*embarrassed by the intensity, but laughing*) A question not at all displeasing to me. Who can answer it?

CLAIRE: (*more and more excited*) Yes! Who can answer it? (*going to him, in terror*) Let me go with you – and be with you – and know nothing else!
ADELAIDE: (*gasping*) Why – !
HARRY: Claire! This is going a little too –
CLAIRE: Far? But you have to go far to – (*clinging to* DICK) Only a place to hide your head – what else is there to hope for? I can't stay with them – piling it up! Always – piling it up! I can't get through to – he won't let me through to – what I don't know is there! (DICK *would help her regain herself*) Don't push me away! Don't – don't stand me up, I will go back – to the worst we ever were! Go back – and remember – what we've tried to forget!
ADELAIDE: It's time to stop this by force – if there's no other way. (*the doctor shakes his head*)
CLAIRE: All I ask is to die in the gutter with everyone spitting on me. (*changes to a curious weary smiling quiet*) Still, why should they bother to do that?
HARRY: (*brokenly*) You're sick, Claire. There's no denying it. (*looks at* EMMONS, *who nods*)
ADELAIDE: Something to quiet her – to stop it.
CLAIRE: (*throwing her arms around* DICK) You, Dick. Not them. Not – any of them.
DICK: Claire, you are overwrought. You must –
HARRY: (*to* DICK, *as if only now realizing that phase of it*) I'll tell you one thing, you'll answer to me for this! (*he starts for* DICK – *is restrained by* EMMONS, *chiefly by his grave shake of the head. With* HARRY's *move to them*, DICK *has shielded* CLAIRE)
CLAIRE: Yes – hold me. Keep me. You have mercy! You will have mercy. Anything – everything – that will let me be nothing!
CURTAIN

ACT III

In the greenhouse, the same as Act I. ANTHONY *is bedding small plants where the Edge Vine grew. In the inner room the plant like caught motion glows as from a light within.* HATTIE, *the Maid, rushes in from outside.*

ANTHONY: (*turning angrily*) You are not what this place –
HATTIE: Anthony, come in the house. I'm afraid. Mr Archer, I never saw him like this. He's talking to Mr Demming – something about Mrs Archer.
ANTHONY: (*who in spite of himself is disturbed by her agitation*) And if it is, it's no business of yours.
HATTIE: You don't know how he *is*. I went in the room and –
ANTHONY: Well, he won't hurt you, will he?
HATTIE: How do I know who he'll hurt – a person's whose – (*seeing how to get him*) Maybe he'll hurt Mrs Archer.
ANTHONY: (*startled, then smiles*) No; he won't hurt Miss Claire.
HATTIE: What do you know about it? – out here in the plant house?
ANTHONY: And I don't want to know about it. This is a very important day for me. It's Breath of Life I'm thinking of today – not you and Mr Archer.

HATTIE: Well, suppose he does something to Mr Demming?

ANTHONY: Mr Demming will have to look out for himself, I am at work. (*resuming work*)

HATTIE: Don't you think I ought to tell Mrs Archer that –

ANTHONY: You let her alone! This is no day for her to be bothered by you. At eleven o'clock (*looks at watch*) she comes out here – to Breath of Life.

HATTIE: (*with greed for gossip*) Did you see any of them when they came downstairs last night?

ANTHONY: I was attending to my own affairs.

HATTIE: They was all excited. Mr Edgeworth – he went away. He was gone all night, I guess. I saw him coming back just as the milkman woke me up. Now he's packing his things. *He* wanted to get to Mrs Archer too – just a little while ago. But she won't open her door for none of them. I can't even get in to do her room.

ANTHONY: Then do some other room – and leave me alone in this room.

HATTIE: (*a little afraid of what she is asking*) Is she *sick*, Anthony – or what? (*vindicating herself, as he gives her a look*) The doctor, he stayed here late. But she'd locked herself in. I heard Mr Archer –

ANTHONY: You heard too much! (*he starts for the door, to make her leave, but* DICK *rushes in. Looks around wildly, goes to the trap-door, finds it locked*)

ANTHONY: What are you doing here?

DICK: Trying not to be shot – if you must know. This is the only place I can think of – till he comes to his senses and I can get away. Open that, will you? Rather – ignominious – but better be absurd than be dead.

HATTIE: Has he got the revolver?

DICK: Gone for it. Thought I wouldn't sit there till he got back. (*to* ANTHONY) Look here – don't you get the idea? Get me some place where he can't come.

ANTHONY: It is not what this place is for.

DICK: Any place is for saving a man's life.

HATTIE: Sure, Anthony. Mrs Archer wouldn't want Mr Demming shot.

DICK: That's right, Anthony. Miss Claire will be angry at you if you get me shot. (*he makes for the door of the inner room*)

ANTHONY: You can't go in there. It's locked.

(HARRY *rushes in from outside.*)

HARRY: I thought so! (*he has the revolver.* HATTIE *screams*)

ANTHONY: Now, Mr Archer, if you'll just stop and think, you'll know Miss Claire wouldn't want Mr Demming shot.

HARRY: You think that can stop me? You think you can stop me? (*raising the revolver*) A dog that –

ANTHONY: (*keeping squarely between* HARRY *and* DICK) Well, you can't shoot him in here. It is not good for the plants. (HARRY *is arrested by this reason*) And especially not today. Why, Mr Archer, Breath of Life may flower today. It's years Miss Claire's been working for this day.

HARRY: I never thought to see this day!

ANTHONY: No, did you? Oh, it will be a wonderful day. And how she has worked for it. She has an eye that sees what isn't right in what looks right. Many's the time I've thought – Here the form is set – and then she'd say, 'We'll try this one', and it had – what I hadn't known was there. She's like that.

HARRY: I've always been pleased, Anthony, at the way you've worked with Miss Claire. This is hardly the time to stand there eulogizing her. And she's (*can hardly say it*) things you don't know she is.

ANTHONY: (*proudly*) Oh, I know that! You think I could work with her and not know she's more than I know she is?

HARRY: Well, if you love her you've got to let me shoot the dirty dog that drags her down!

ANTHONY: Not in here. Not today. More than like you'd break the glass. And Breath of Life's in there.

HARRY: Anthony, this is pretty clever of you – but –

ANTHONY: I'm not clever. But I know how easy it is to turn life back. No, I'm not clever at all (CLAIRE *has appeared and is looking in from outside*), but I do know – there are things you mustn't hurt. (*he sees her*) Yes, here's Miss Claire. (*She comes in. She is looking immaculate.*)

CLAIRE: From the gutter I rise again, refreshed. One does, you know. Nothing is fixed – not even the gutter. (*smilingly to* HARRY *and refusing to notice revolver or agitation*) How did you like the way I entertained the nerve specialist?

HARRY: Claire! You can *joke* about it?

CLAIRE: (*taking the revolver from the hand she has shocked to limpness*) Whom are you trying to make hear?

HARRY: I'm trying to make the world hear that (*pointing*) there stands a dirty dog who –

CLAIRE: Listen, Harry. (*turning to* HATTIE, *who is over by the tall plants at right, not wanting to be shot but not wanting to miss the conversation*) You can do my room now, Hattie. (HATTIE *goes*) If you're thinking of shooting Dick, you can't shoot him while he's backed up against that door.

ANTHONY: Just what I told them, Miss Claire. Just what I told them.

CLAIRE: And for that matter, it's quite dull of you to have any idea of shooting him.

HARRY: I may be dull – I know you think I am – but I'll show you that I've enough of the man in me to –

CLAIRE: To make yourself ridiculous? If I ran out and hid my head in the mud, would you think you had to shoot the mud?

DICK: (*stung out of fear*) That's pretty cruel!

CLAIRE: Well, would you rather be shot?

HARRY: So you just said it to protect him!

CLAIRE: I change it to grass. (*nodding to* DICK) Grass. If I hid my face in the grass, would you have to burn the grass?

HARRY: Oh, Claire, how *can* you? When you know how I love you – and how I'm suffering?

CLAIRE: (*with interest*) Are you suffering?

HARRY: Haven't you *eyes*?

CLAIRE: I should think it would – do something to you.

HARRY: God! Have you no heart? (*the door opens.* TOM *comes in*)

CLAIRE: (*scarcely saying it*) Yes, I have a heart.

TOM: (*after a pause*) I came to say good-bye.

CLAIRE: God! Have you no heart? Can't you at least wait till Dick is shot?

TOM: Claire! (*now sees the revolver in her hand that is turned from him. Going to her*) Claire!

CLAIRE: And even you think this is so important? (*carelessly raises the revolver, and with her left hand out flat, tells* TOM *not to touch her*) Harry thinks it important he shoot Dick, and Dick thinks it important not to be shot, and you think I mustn't shoot anybody – even myself – and can't any of you see that none of that is as important as – where revolvers can't reach? (*putting revolver where there is no Edge Vine*) I shall never shoot myself. I'm too interested in destruction to cut it short by shooting. (*after looking from one to the other, laughs. Pointing*) One – two – three. You-love-me. But why do you bring it out here?

ANTHONY: (*who has resumed work*) It is not what this place is for.

CLAIRE: No this place is for the destruction that can get through.

ANTHONY: Miss Claire, it is eleven. At eleven we are to go in and see –

CLAIRE: Whether it has gone through. But how can we go – with Dick against the door?

ANTHONY: He'll have to move.

CLAIRE: And be shot?

HARRY: (*irritably*) Oh, he'll not be shot. Claire can spoil anything.

  (DICK *steps away from the door;* CLAIRE *takes a step nearer it.*)

CLAIRE: (*halting*) Have I spoiled everything? I don't want to go in there.

ANTHONY: We're going in together, Miss Claire. Don't you remember? Oh (*looking resentfully at the others*) don't let any little thing spoil it for you – the work of all those days – the hope of so many days.

CLAIRE: Yes – that's it.

ANTHONY: You're afraid you haven't done it?

CLAIRE: Yes, but – afraid I have.

HARRY: (*cross, but kindly*) That's just nervousness, Claire. I've had the same feeling myself about making a record in flying.

CLAIRE: (*curiously grateful*) You have, Harry?

HARRY: (*glad enough to be back in a more usual world*) Sure. I've been afraid to know, and almost as afraid of having done it as of not having done it.

  (CLAIRE *nods, steps nearer, then again pulls back.*)

CLAIRE: I can't go in there. (*she almost looks at* TOM) Not today.

ANTHONY: But, Miss Claire, there'll be things to see today we can't see tomorrow.

CLAIRE: You bring it in here!

ANTHONY: In – out from its own place? (*she nods*) And – where they are? (*again she nods. Reluctantly he goes to the door*) I will not look into the heart. No one must know before you know.

  (*In the inner room, his head a little turned away, he is seen very carefully to lift the plant which glows from within. As he brings it in, no one looks at it.* HARRY *takes a box of seedlings from a stand and puts them on the floor, that the newcomer may have a place.*)

ANTHONY: Breath of Life is here, Miss Claire.

(CLAIRE *half turns, then stops.*)

CLAIRE: Look – and see – what you see.

ANTHONY: No one should see what you've not seen.

CLAIRE: I can't see – until I know.

(ANTHONY *looks into the flower.*)

ANTHONY: (*agitated*) Miss Claire!

CLAIRE: It has come through?

ANTHONY: It has gone on.

CLAIRE: Stronger?

ANTHONY: Stronger, surer.

CLAIRE: And more fragile?

ANTHONY: And more fragile.

CLAIRE: Look deep. No – turning back?

ANTHONY: (*after a searching look*) The form is set. (*he steps back from it*)

CLAIRE: Then it is – out. (*from where she stands she turns slowly to the plant*) You weren't. You are.

ANTHONY: But come and see, Miss Claire.

CLAIRE: It's so much more than – I'd see.

HARRY: Well, I'm going to see. (*looking into it*) I never saw anything like that before! There seems something alive – inside this outer shell.

DICK: (*he too looking in and he has an artist's manner of a hand up to make the light right*) It's quite new in form. It – says something about form.

HARRY: (*cordially to* CLAIRE, *who stands apart*) So you've really put it over. Well, well, – congratulations. It's a good deal of novelty, I should say, and I've no doubt you'll have a considerable success with it – people always like something new. I'm mighty glad – after all your work, and I hope it will – set you up.

CLAIRE: (*low – and like a machine*) Will you all – go away?

(ANTHONY *goes – into the other room.*)

HARRY: Why – why, yes. But – oh, Claire! Can't you take some pleasure in your work? (*as she stands there very still*) Emmons says you need a good long rest – and I think he's right.

TOM: Can't this help you, Claire? Let this be release. This – breath of the uncaptured.

CLAIRE: (*and though speaking, she remains just as still*)
Breath of the uncaptured?
You are a novelty.
Out?
You have been brought in.
A thousand years from now, when you are but a form too long repeated,
Perhaps the madness that gave you birth will burst again,
And from the prison that is you will leap pent queernesses
To make a form that hasn't been –
To make a person new.
And this we call creation. (*very low, her head not coming up*)
Go away!

(TOM *goes;* HARRY *hesitates, looking in anxiety at* CLAIRE. *He starts to go, stops, looks at* DICK, *from him to* CLAIRE. *But goes. A moment later* DICK *moves near* CLAIRE; *stands uncertainly, then puts a hand upon her. She starts, only then knowing he is there.*)

CLAIRE: (*a slight shrinking away, but not really reached*) Um, um.

(*He goes.* CLAIRE *steps nearer her creation. She looks into what hasn't been. With her breath, and by a gentle moving of her hands, she fans it to fuller openness. As she does this* TOM *returns and from outside is looking in at her. Softly he opens the door and comes in. She does not know that he is there. In the way she looks at the flower he looks at her.*)

TOM: Claire. (*she lifts her head*) As you stood there, looking into the womb you breathed to life, you were beautiful to me beyond any other beauty. You were life and its reach and its anguish. I can't go away from you. I will never go away from you. It shall all be – as you wish. I can go with you where I could not go alone. If this is delusion, I want that delusion. It's more than any reality I could attain. (*as she does not move*) Speak to me, Claire. You – are glad?

CLAIRE: (*from far*) Speak to you? (*pause*) Do I know who you are?

TOM: I think you do.

CLAIRE: Oh, yes. I love you. That's who you are. (*waits again*) But why are you something – very far away?

TOM: Come nearer.

CLAIRE: Nearer? (*feeling it with her voice*) Nearer. But I think I am going – the other way.

TOM: No, Claire – come to me. Did you understand, dear? I am not going away.

CLAIRE: You're not going away?

TOM: Not without you, Claire. And you and I will be together. Is that – what you wanted?

CLAIRE: Wanted? (*as if wanting is something that harks far back. But the word calls to her passion*) Wanted! (*a sob, hands out, she goes to him. But before his arms can take her, she steps back*) Are you trying to pull me down into what I wanted? Are you here to make me stop?

TOM: How can you ask that? I love you because it is not in you to stop.

CLAIRE: And loving me for that – would stop me? Oh, help me see it! It is so important that I see it.

TOM: It is important. It is our lives.

CLAIRE: And more than that. I cannot see it because it is so much more than that.

TOM: Don't try to see all that it is. From peace you'll see a little more.

CLAIRE: Peace? (*troubled as we are when looking at what we cannot see clearly*) What is peace? Peace is what the struggle knows in moments very far apart. Peace – that is not a place to rest. Are you resting? What are you? You who'd take me from what I am to something else?

TOM: I thought you knew, Claire.

CLAIRE: I know – what you pass for. But are you beauty? Beauty is that only living pattern – the trying to take pattern. Are you trying?

TOM: Within myself, Claire. I never thought you doubted that.

CLAIRE: Beauty is it. (*she turns to Breath of Life, as if to learn it there, but turns away with a sob*) If I cannot go to you now – I will always be alone.

(TOM *takes her in his arms. She is shaken, then comes to rest.*)

TOM: Yes – rest. And then – come into joy. You have so much life for joy.

CLAIRE: (*raising her head, called by promised gladness*) We'll run around together. (*lovingly he nods*) Up hills. All night on hills.

TOM: (*tenderly*) All night on hills.

CLAIRE: We'll go on the sea in a little boat.

TOM: On the sea in a little boat.

CLAIRE: But – there are other boats on other seas. (*drawing back from him, troubled*) There are other boats on other seas.

TOM: (*drawing her back to him*) My dearest – not now, not now.

CLAIRE: (*her arms going round him*) Oh, I would love those hours with you. I want them. I want you! (*they kiss – but deep in her is sobbing*) Reminiscence. (*her hand feeling his arm as we touch what we would remember*) Reminiscence. (*with one of her swift changes steps back from him*) How dare you pass for what you're not? We are tired, and so we think it's you. Stop with you. Don't get through – to what you're in the way of. Beauty is not something you say about beauty.

TOM: I say little about beauty, Claire.

CLAIRE: Your life says it. By standing far off you pass for it. Smother it with a life that passes for it. But beauty – (*getting it from the flower*) Beauty is the humility breathed from the shame of succeeding.

TOM: But it may all be within one's self, dear.

CLAIRE: (*drawn by this, but held, and desperate because she is held*) When I have wanted you with all my wanting – why must I distrust you now? When I love you – with all of me, why do I know that only you are worth my hate?

TOM: It's the fear of easy satisfactions. I love you for it.

CLAIRE: (*over the flower*) Breath of Life – you here? Are you lonely – Breath of Life?

TOM: Claire – hear me! Don't go where we can't go. As there you made a shell for life within, make for yourself a life in which to live. It must be so.

CLAIRE: As you made for yourself a shell called beauty?

TOM: What is there for you, if you'll have no touch with what we have?

CLAIRE: What is there? There are the dreams we haven't dreamed. There is the long and flowing pattern. (*she follows that, but suddenly and as if blindly goes to him*) I am tired. I am lonely. I'm afraid. (*he holds her, soothing. But she steps back from him*) And because we are tired – lonely – and afraid, we stop with you. Don't get through – to what you're in the way of.

TOM: Then you don't love me?

CLAIRE: I'm fighting for my chance. I don't know – which chance.

(*Is drawn to the other chance, to Breath of Life. Looks into it as if to look through to the uncaptured. And through this life just caught comes the truth she chants.*)

I've wallowed at a coarse man's feet,
I'm sprayed with dreams we've not yet come to.
I've gone so low that words can't get there,
I've never pulled the mantle of my fears around me

And called it loneliness – And called it God.
Only with life that waits have I kept faith.
(*with effort raising her eyes to the man*)
And only you have ever threatened me.
TOM: (*coming to her, and with strength now*) And I will threaten you. I'm here to hold you from where I know you cannot go. You're trying what we can't do.
CLAIRE: What else is there worth trying?
TOM: I love you, and I will keep you – from fartherness – from harm. You are mine, and you will stay with me! (*roughly*) You hear me? You will stay with me!
CLAIRE: (*her head on his breast, in ecstasy of rest. Drowsily*) You can keep me?
TOM: Darling! I can keep you. I will keep you – safe.
CLAIRE: (*troubled by the word, but barely able to raise her head*) Safe?
TOM: (*bringing her to rest again*) Trust me, Claire.
CLAIRE: (*not lifting her head, but turning it so she sees Breath of Life*) Now can I trust – what is? (*suddenly pushing him roughly away*) No! I will beat my life to pieces in the struggle to –
TOM: To *what*, Claire?
CLAIRE: Not to stop it by seeming to have it. (*with fury*) I will keep my life low – low – that I may never stop myself – or anyone – with the thought it's what *I* have. I'd rather be the steam rising from the manure than be a thing called beautiful! (*with sight too clear*) Now I know who you are. It is you puts out the breath of life. Image of beauty – *You fill the place – should be a gate.* (*in agony*) Oh, that it is *you* – fill the place – should be a gate! My darling! That it should be you who – (*her hands moving on him*) Let me tell you something. Never was loving strong as my loving of you! Do you know that? Oh, know that! Know it now! (*her arms go around his neck*) Hours with you – I'd give my life to have! That it should be you – (*he would loosen her hands, for he cannot breathe. But when she knows she is choking him, that knowledge is fire burning its way into the last passion*) It *is* you. It is you.
TOM: (*words coming from a throat not free*) Claire! What are you doing? (*then she knows what she is doing*)
CLAIRE: (*to his resistance*) No! You are *too much*! You are *not enough*. (*still wanting not to hurt her, he is slow in getting free. He keeps stepping backward trying, in growing earnest, to loosen her hands. But he does not loosen them before she has found the place in his throat that cuts off breath. As he gasps*) Breath of Life – my gift – to you!
      (*She has pushed him against one of the plants at right as he sways, strength she never had before pushes him over backward, just as they have struggled from sight. Violent crash of glass is heard.*)
TOM: (*faint smothered voice*) No. I'm – hurt.
CLAIRE: (*in the frenzy and agony of killing*) Oh, gift! Oh, gift! (*there is no sound.*)
      CLAIRE *rises – steps back – is seen now; is looking down*) Gift.
      (*Like one who does not know where she is, she moves into the room – looks around. Takes a step toward Breath of Life; turns and goes quickly to the door. Stops, as if stopped. Sees the revolver where the Edge Vine was. Slowly goes to it. Holds it as if she cannot think what it*

is for. Then raises it high and fires above through the place in the glass left open for ventilation. ANTHONY *comes from the inner room. His eyes go from her to the body beyond.* HARRY *rushes in from outside.*)

HARRY: Who fired that?

CLAIRE: I did. Lonely.

(*Seeing* ANTHONY's *look,* HARRY's *eyes follow it.*)

HARRY: Oh! What? What? (DICK *comes running in*) Who? Claire!

(DICK *sees – goes to* TOM)

CLAIRE: Yes. I did it. MY – Gift.

HARRY: Is he – ? He isn't – ? He isn't – ?

(*Tries to go in there. Cannot – there is the sound of broken glass, of a position being changed – then* DICK *reappears.*)

DICK: (*his voice in jerks*) It's – it's no use, but I'll go for a doctor.

HARRY: No – no. Oh, I suppose – (*falling down beside* CLAIRE – *his face against her*) My darling! How can I save you now?

CLAIRE: (*speaking each word very carefully*) Saved – myself.

ANTHONY: I did it. Don't you see? I didn't want so many around. Not – what this place is for.

HARRY: (*snatching at this but lets it go*) She wouldn't let – (*looking up at* CLAIRE – *then quickly hiding his face*) And – don't you see?

CLAIRE: Out. (*a little like a child's pleased surprise*) Out.

(DICK *stands there, as if unable to get to the door – his face distorted, biting his hand.*)

ANTHONY: Miss Claire! You can do anything – won't you try?

CLAIRE: Reminiscence? (*speaking the word as if she has left even that, but smiles a little*)

(ANTHONY *takes Reminiscence, the flower she was breeding for fragrance for Breath of Life – holds it out to her. But she has taken a step forward, past them all.*)

CLAIRE: Out. (*as if feeling her way*)

Nearer,

(*Her voice now feeling the way to it.*)

Nearer –

(*Voice almost upon it.*)

– my *God*,

(*Falling upon it with surprise.*)

to Thee,

(*Breathing it.*)

Nearer – to Thee,

E'en though it be –

(*A slight turn of the head toward the dead man she loves – a mechanical turn just as far the other way.*)

a cross

That

(*Her head going down.*

raises me;

    (*Her head slowly coming up – singing it.*)
Still all my song shall be,
Nearer, my –
    (*Slowly the curtain begins to shut her out. The last word heard is the final* Nearer *– a faint breath from far.*)

CURTAIN

INHERITORS

Inheritors was first performed at the Provincetown Playhouse on April 27, 1921. It was produced for the first time in England by the Liverpool Repertory Theatre Company at the Playhouse, Liverpool, on Friday, September 25, 1925; the producer was William Armstrong, and the cast as follows:

SMITH (a young business man)	Julian Herdage
GRANDMOTHER (SILAS MORTON's mother)	Aida Jenoure
SILAS MORTON (a pioneer farmer)	Herbert Lomas
FELIX FEJEVARY, the First (an exiled Hungarian nobleman)	Hannam Clark
FELIX FEJEVARY, the Second (his son, a Harvard student)	Hugh Williams
FELIX FEJEVARY, the Second (a banker)	Hannam Clark
SENATOR LEWIS (a State Senator)	James Harcourt
HORACE FEJEVARY (son of FELIX FEJEVARY, the Second)	Hugh Williams
DORIS (a student at Morton College)	Innis Shawen
FUSSIE (another college girl)	Muriel Walker
MADELINE FEJEVARY MORTON (daughter of IRA MORTON, and granddaughter of SILAS MORTON)	Muriel Randall
ISABEL FEJEVARY (wife of FELIX FEJEVARY, the Second, and MADELINE's aunt)	Constance Pelissier
HARRY (a student clerk)	Basil Moss
HOLDEN (Professor at Morton College)	Cecil Parker
IRA MORTON (son of SILAS MORTON, and MADELINE's father	Herbert Lomas
EMIL JOHNSON (an Americanized Swede)	Gerald Pemberton

ACT I

SCENE: *Sitting-room of the Mortons' farmhouse in the Middle West – on the rolling prairie just back from the Mississippi. A room that has been long and comfortably lived in, and showing that first-hand contact with materials which was pioneer life. The hospitable table was made on the place – well and strongly made; there are braided rugs, and the wooden chairs have patchwork cushions. There is a corner closet – left rear. A picture of Abraham Lincoln. On the floor a home-made toy boat. At rise of curtain there are on the stage an old woman and a young man. GRANDMOTHER MORTON is in her rocking-chair near the open door, facing left. On both sides of door are windows, looking out on a generous land. She has a sewing basket and is patching a boy's pants. She is very old. Her hands tremble. Her spirit remembers the days of her strength.*

SMITH *has just come in and, hat in hand, is standing by the table. This was lived in the year* 1879, *afternoon of Fourth of July.*

SMITH: But the celebration was over two hours ago.

GRANDMOTHER: Oh, celebration, that's just the beginning of it. Might as well set down. When them boys that fought together all get in one square – they have to swap stories all over again. That's the worst of a war – you have to go on hearing about it so long. Here it is – 1879 – and we haven't taken Gettysburg yet. Well, it was the same way with the war of 1832.

SMITH: (*who is now seated at the table*) The war of 1832?

GRANDMOTHER: News to you that we had a war with the Indians?

SMITH: That's right – the Blackhawk war. I've heard of it.

GRANDMOTHER: Heard of it!

SMITH: Were your men in that war?

GRANDMOTHER: I was in that war. I threw an Indian in the cellar and stood on the door. I was heavier then.

SMITH: Those were stirring times.

GRANDMOTHER: More stirring than you'll ever see. This war – Lincoln's war – it's all a cut and dried business now. We used to fight with anything we could lay hands on – dish water – whatever was handy.

SMITH: I guess you believe the saying that the only good Indian is a dead Indian.

GRANDMOTHER: I dunno. We roiled them up considerable. They was mostly friendly when let be. Didn't want to give up their land – but I've noticed something of the same nature in white folks.

SMITH: Your son has – something of that nature, hasn't he?

Gettysburg: three-day battle (1–3 July 1863) fought at Gettysburg, Pennsylvania, which was one of the turning points of the American Civil War. The war was fought between the Union (North) and the Confederacy (South) during Lincoln's presidency and lasted from April 1861 until April 1865.

war of 1832 ... the Blackhawk war: mention of the Blackhawk war of 1832 sets the play in northwestern Illinois. Blackhawk was the leader of a small group of Sauk Indians who long resisted white attempts to drive them from their ancestral village and to make them settle across the Mississippi River in Iowa. He was finally defeated in a massacre on the banks of the Mississippi in August 1832.

GRANDMOTHER: He's not keen to sell. Why should he? It'll never be worth less.

SMITH: But since he has more land than any man can use, and if he gets his price –

GRANDMOTHER: That what you've come to talk to him about?

SMITH: I – yes.

GRANDMOTHER: Well, you're not the first. Many a man older than you has come to argue it.

SMITH: (*smiling*) They thought they'd try a young one.

GRANDMOTHER: Some one that knew him thought that up. Silas'd help a young one if he could. What is it you're set on buying?

SMITH: Oh, I don't know that we're set on buying anything. If we could have the hill (*looking off to the right*) at a fair price –

GRANDMOTHER: The hill above the town? Silas'd rather sell me and the cat.

SMITH: But what's he going to do with it?

GRANDMOTHER: Maybe he's going to climb it once a week.

SMITH: But if the development of the town demands its use –

GRANDMOTHER: (*smiling*) You the development of the town?

SMITH: I represent it. This town has been growing so fast –

GRANDMOTHER: This town began to grow the day I got here.

SMITH: You – you began it?

GRANDMOTHER: My husband and I began it – and our baby Silas.

SMITH: When was that?

GRANDMOTHER: 1820, that was.

SMITH: And – you mean you were here all alone?

GRANDMOTHER: No, we weren't alone. We had the Owens ten miles down the river.

SMITH: But how did you get here?

GRANDMOTHER: Got here in a wagon, how do you s'pose? (*gaily*) Think we flew?

SMITH: But wasn't it unsafe?

GRANDMOTHER: Them set on safety stayed back in Ohio.

SMITH: But one family! I should think the Indians would have wiped you out.

GRANDMOTHER: The way they wiped us out was to bring fish and corn. We'd have starved to death that first winter hadn't been for the Indians.

SMITH: But they were such good neighbours – why did you throw dish water at them?

GRANDMOTHER: That was after other white folks had roiled them up – white folks that didn't know how to treat 'em. This very land – land you want to buy – was the land they loved – Blackhawk and his Indians. They came here for their games. This was where their fathers – as they called 'em – were buried. I've seen my husband and Blackhawk climb that hill together. (*a backward point right*) He used to love that hill – Blackhawk. He talked how the red man and the white man could live together. But poor old Blackhawk – what he didn't know was how many white man there was. After the war – when he was beaten but not conquered in his heart – they took him east – Washington, Philadelphia, New York – and when he saw the white man's cities – it was a different Indian came back. He just let his heart break without ever turning a hand.

SMITH: But we paid them for their lands. (*she looks at him*) Paid them something.

GRANDMOTHER: Something. For fifteen million acres of this Mississippi Valley land – best on this globe, we paid two thousand two hundred and thirty-four dollars and fifty cents, and promised to deliver annually goods to the value of one thousand dollars. Not a fancy price – even for them days. (*children's voices are heard outside. She leans forward and looks through the door, left*) Ira! Let that cat be!

SMITH: (*looking from the window*) These, I suppose, are your grandchildren?

GRANDMOTHER: The boy's my grandson. The little girl is Madeline Fejevary – Mr Fejevary's youngest child.

SMITH: The Fejevary place adjoins on this side? (*pointing right, down*)

GRANDMOTHER: Yes. We've been neighbours ever since the Fejevarys came here from Hungary after 1848. He was a count at home – and he's a man of learning. But he was a refugee because he fought for freedom in his country. Nothing Silas could do for him was too good. Silas sets great store by learning – and freedom.

SMITH: (*thinking of his own project, looking off toward the hill – the hill is not seen from the front*) I suppose then Mr Fejevary has great influence with your son?

GRANDMOTHER: More 'an anybody. Silas thinks 'twas a great thing for our family to have a family like theirs next place to. Well – so 'twas, for we've had no time for the things their family was brought up on. Old Mrs Fejevary (*with her shrewd smile*) – she weren't stuck up – but she did have an awful ladylike way of feeding the chickens. Silas thinks – oh, my son has all kinds of notions – though a harder worker never found his bed at night.

SMITH: And Mr Fejevary – is he a veteran too?

GRANDMOTHER: (*dryly*) You don't seem to know these parts well – for one that's all stirred up about the development of the town. Yes – Felix Fejevary and Silas Morton went off together, down that road (*motioning with her hand, right*) – when them of their age was wanted. Fejevary came back with one arm less than he went with. Silas brought home everything he took – and something he didn't. Rheumatiz. So now they set more store by each other 'an ever. Seems nothing draws men together like killing other men. (*a boy's voice teasingly imitating a cat*) Madeline, make Ira let that cat be. (*a whoop from the girl – a boy's whoop*) (*looking*) There they go, off for the creek. If they set in it – (*seems about to call after them, gives this up*) Well, they're not the first. (*rather dreams over this*)

SMITH: You must feel as if you pretty near owned this country.

GRANDMOTHER: We worked. A country don't make itself. When the sun was up we were up, and when the sun went down we didn't. (*as if this renews the self of those days*) Here – let me set out something for you to eat. (*gets up with difficulty*)

SMITH: Oh, no, please – never mind. I had something in town before I came out.

GRANDMOTHER: Dunno as that's any reason you shouldn't have something here.

Hungary after 1848: the revolution of 1848, led by Lajos Kossuth, attempted to free Hungary from Austrian rule; it was finally defeated by the intervention of the Russian army, sent by Tsar Nicolas I to help Emperor Franz Joseph.

(*She goes off, right; he stands at the door, looking toward the hill until she returns with a glass of milk, a plate of cookies.*)

SMITH: Well, this looks good.

GRANDMOTHER: I've fed a lot of folks – take it by and large. I didn't care how many I had to feed in the daytime – what's ten or fifteen more when you're up and around. But to *get* up – after sixteen hours on your feet – *I* was willin', but my bones complained some.

SMITH: But did you – keep a tavern?

GRANDMOTHER: Keep a tavern? I guess we did. Every house is a tavern when houses are sparse. You think the way to settle a country is to go on ahead and build hotels? That's all you folks know. Why, I never went to bed without leaving something on the stove for the new ones that might be coming. And we never went away from home without seein' there was a-plenty for them that might stop.

SMITH: They'd come right in and take your food?

GRANDMOTHER: What else could they do? There was a woman I always wanted to know. She made a kind of bread I never had before – and left a-plenty for our supper when we got back with the ducks and berries. And she left the kitchen handier than it had ever been. I often wondered about her – where she came from, and where she went. (*as she dreams over this there is laughing and talking at the side of the house*) There come the boys.

> (MR FEJEVARY *comes in, followed by* SILAS MORTON. *They are men not far from sixty, wearing their army uniforms, carrying the muskets they used in the parade.* FEJEVARY *has a lean, distinguished face, his dark eyes are penetrating and rather wistful. The left sleeve of his old uniform is empty.* SILAS MORTON *is a strong man who has borne the burden of the land, and not for himself alone – the pioneer. Seeing the stranger, he sets his musket against the wall and holds out his hand to him, as* MR FEJEVARY *goes up to* GRANDMOTHER MORTON.)

SILAS: How do, stranger?

FEJEVARY: And how are you today, Mrs Morton?

GRANDMOTHER: I'm not abed – and don't expect to be.

SILAS: (*letting go of the balloons he has bought*) Where's Ira? and Madeline?

GRANDMOTHER: Mr Fejevary's Delia brought them home with her. They've gone down to dam the creek, I guess. This young man's been waiting to see you, Silas.

SMITH: Yes, I wanted to have a little talk with you.

SILAS: Well, why not? (*he is tying the gay balloons to his gun, then as he talks, hangs his hat in the corner closet*) We've been having a little talk ourselves. Mother, Nat Rice was there. I've not seen Nat Rice since the day we had to leave him on the road with his torn leg – him cursing like a pirate. I wanted to bring him home, but he had to go back to Chicago. His wife's dead, mother.

GRANDMOTHER: Well, I guess she's not sorry.

SILAS: Why, mother.

GRANDMOTHER: 'Why, mother.' Nat Rice is a mean, stingy, complaining man – his leg notwithstanding. Where'd you leave the folks?

SILAS: Oh – scattered around. Everybody visitin' with anybody that'll visit with them. Wish you could have gone.

GRANDMOTHER: I've heard it all. (*to* FEJEVARY) Your folks well?

FEJEVARY: All well, Mrs Morton. And my boy Felix is home. He'll stop in here to see you by and by.

SILAS: Oh, he's a fine-looking boy, mother. And think of what he knows! (*cordially including the young man*) Mr Fejevary's son has been to Harvard College.

SMITH: Well, well – quite a trip. Well, Mr Morton, I hope this is not a bad time for me to – present a little matter to you?

SILAS: (*genially*) That depends, of course, on what you're going to present. (*attracted by a sound outside*) Mind if I present a little matter to your horse? Like to uncheck him so's he can geta a bit o'grass.

SMITH: Why – yes. I suppose he would like that.

SILAS: (*going out*) You bet he'd like it. Wouldn't you, old boy?

SMITH: Your son is fond of animals.

GRANDMOTHER: Lots of people's fond of 'em – and good to 'em. Silas – I dunno, it's as if he was that animal.

FEJEVARY: He has imagination.

GRANDMOTHER: (*with surprise*) Think so?

SILAS: (*returning and sitting down at the table by the young man*) Now, what's in your mind, my boy?

SMITH: This town is growing very fast, Mr Morton.

SILAS: Yes. (*slyly – with humour*) I know that.

SMITH: I presume you, as one of the early settlers – as in fact a son of the earliest settler, feel a certain responsibility about the welfare of –

SILAS: I haven't got in mind to do the town a bit of harm. So – what's your point?

SMITH: More people – more homes. And homes must be in the healthiest places – the – the most beautiful places. Isn't it true, Mr Fejevary, that it means a great deal to people to have a beautiful outlook from their homes? A – well, an expanse.

SILAS: What is it they want to buy – these fellows that are figuring on making something out of – expanse? (*a gesture for expanse, then a reassuring gesture*) It's all right, but – just what is it?

SMITH: I am prepared to make you an offer – a gilt-edged offer for that (*pointing toward it*) hill above the town.

SILAS: (*shaking his head – with the smile of the strong man who is a dreamer*) The hill is not for sale.

SMITH: But wouldn't you consider a – particularly good offer, Mr Morton?

(SILAS, *who has turned so he can look out at the hill, slowly shakes his head.*)

SMITH: Do you feel you have the right – the moral right to hold it?

SILAS: It's not for myself I'm holding it.

SMITH: Oh, – for the children?

SILAS: Yes, the children.

SMITH: But – if you'll excuse me – there are other investments might do the children even more good.

SILAS: This seems to me – the best investment.

SMITH: But after all there are other people's children to consider.

SILAS: Yes, I know. That's it.

SMITH: I wonder if I understand you, Mr Morton?

SILAS: (*kindly*) I don't believe you do. I don't see how you could. And I can't explain myself just now. So – the hill is not for sale. I'm not making anybody homeless. There's land enough for all – all sides round. But the hill –

SMITH: (*rising*) Is yours.

SILAS: You'll see.

SMITH: I am prepared to offer you –

SILAS: You're not prepared to offer me anything I'd consider alongside what I am considering. So – I wish you good luck in your business undertakings.

SMITH: Sorry – you won't let us try to help the town.

SILAS: Don't sit up nights worrying about my chokin' the town.

SMITH: We could make you a rich man, Mr Morton. Do you think what you have in mind will make you so much richer?

SILAS: Much richer.

SMITH: Well, good-bye. Good day, sir. Good day, ma'am.

SILAS: (*following him to the door*) Nice horse you've got.

SMITH: Yes, seems all right.

(SILAS *stands in the doorway and looks off at the hill.*)

GRANDMOTHER: What are you going to do with the hill, Silas?

SILAS: After I get a little glass of wine – to celebrate Felix and me being here instead of farther south – I'd like to tell you what I want for the hill. (*to* FEJEVARY *rather bashfully*) I've been wanting to tell you.

FEJEVARY: I want to know.

SILAS: (*getting the wine from the closet*) Just a little something to show our gratitude with.

(*Goes off right for glasses.*)

GRANDMOTHER: I dunno. Maybe it'd be better to sell the hill – while they're anxious.

FEJEVARY: He seems to have another plan for it.

GRANDMOTHER: Yes. Well, I hope the other plan does bring him something. Silas has worked – all the days of his life.

FEJEVARY: I know.

GRANDMOTHER: You don't know the hull of it. But I know. (*rather to herself*) Know too well to think about it.

GRANDMOTHER: (*as SILAS returns*) I'll get more cookies.

SILAS: I'll get them, mother.

GRANDMOTHER: Get 'em myself. Pity if a woman can't get out her own cookies.

SILAS: (*seeing how hard it is for her*) I wish mother would let us do things for her.

FEJEVARY: That strength is a flame frailness can't put out. It's a great thing for us to have her, – this touch with the life behind us.

SILAS: Yes. And it's a great thing for us to have you – who can see those things and say them. What a lot I'd 'a' missed if I hadn't had what you've seen.

FEJEVARY: Oh, you only think that because you've got to be generous.

---

hull: whole?

SILAS: I'm not generous. *I'm* seeing something now. Something about you. I've been thinking of it a good deal lately – it's got something to do with – with the hill. I've been thinkin' what it's meant all these years to have a family like yours next place to. They did something pretty nice for the corn belt when they drove you out of Hungary. Funny – how things don't end the way they begin. I mean, what begins don't end. It's another thing ends. Set out to do something for your own country – and maybe you don't quite do the thing you set out to do –

FEJEVARY: No.

SILAS: But do something for a country a long way off.

FEJEVARY: I'm afraid I've not done much for any country.

SILAS: (*brusquely*) Where's your left arm – may I be so bold as to inquire? Though your left arm's nothing alongside – what can't be measured.

FEJEVARY: When I think of what I dreamed as a young man – it seems to me my life has failed.

SILAS: (*raising his glass*) Well, if your life's failed – I like failure.

(GRANDMOTHER MORTON *returns with her cookies.*)

GRANDMOTHER: There's two kinds – Mr Fejevary. These have seeds in 'em.

FEJEVARY: Thank you. I'll try a seed cookie first.

SILAS: Mother, you'll have a glass of wine?

GRANDMOTHER: I don't need wine.

SILAS: Well, I don't know as we need it.

GRANDMOTHER: No, I don't know as you do. But I didn't go to war.

FEJEVARY: Then have a little wine to celebrate that.

GRANDMOTHER: Well, just a mite to warm me up. Not that it's cold.
(FEJEVARY *brings it to her, and the cookies*) The Indians used to like cookies. I was talking to that young whippersnapper about the Indians. One time I saw an Indian watching me from a bush. (*points*) Right out there. I was never afraid of Indians when you could see the whole of 'em – but when you could see nothin' but their bright eyes – movin' through leaves – I declare they made me nervous. After he'd been there an hour I couldn't seem to put my mind on my work. So I thought, Red or White, a man's a man – I'll take him some cookies.

FEJEVARY: It succeeded?

GRANDMOTHER: So well that those leaves had eyes next day. But he brought me a fish to trade. He was a nice boy.

SILAS: Probably we killed him.

GRANDMOTHER: I dunno. Maybe he killed us. Will Owens' family was massacred just after this. Like as not my cookie Indian helped out there. Something kind of uncertain about the Indians.

SILAS: I guess they found something kind of uncertain about us.

GRANDMOTHER: Six o' one and half a dozen of another. Usually is.

SILAS: (*to* FEJEVARY) I wonder if I'm wrong. You see, I never went to school –

GRANDMOTHER: I don't know why you say that, Silas. There was two winters you went to school.

SILAS: Yes, mother, and I'm glad I did, for I learned to read there, and liked the geography globe. It made the earth so nice to think about. And one day the teacher told us all about the stars, and I had that to think of when I was driving at night. The other boys didn't believe it was so. But I knew it was so! But I mean school – the way Mr Fejevary went to school. He went to universities. In his own countries – in other countries. All the things men have found out, the wisest and finest things men have thought since first they began to think – all that was put before them.

FEJEVARY: (*with a gentle smile*) I fear I left a good deal of it untouched.

SILAS: You took a plenty. Tell in your eyes you've thought lots about what's been thought. And that's what I was setting out to say. It makes something of men – learning. A house that's full of books makes a different kind of people. Oh, of course, if the books aren't there just to show off.

GRANDMOTHER: Like in Mary Baldwin's new house.

SILAS: (*trying hard to see it*) It's not the learning itself – it's the life that grows up from learning. Learning's like soil. Like – like fertilizer. Get richer. See more. Feel more. You believe that?

FEJEVARY: Culture should do it.

SILAS: Does in your house. You somehow know how it is for the other fellow more'n we do.

GRANDMOTHER: Well, Silas Morton, when you've your wood to chop an' your water to carry, when you kill your own cattle and hogs, tend your own horses and hens, make your butter, soap, and cook for whoever the Lord sends – there's none too many hours of the day left to be polite in.

SILAS: You're right, mother. It had to be that way. But now that we buy our soap – we don't want to say what soap-making made us.

GRANDMOTHER: We're honest.

SILAS: Yes. In a way. But there's another kind o' honesty, seems to me, goes with that more seein' kind of kindness. Our honesty with the Indians was little to brag on.

GRANDMOTHER: You fret more about the Indians than anybody else does.

SILAS: To look out at that hill sometimes makes me ashamed.

GRANDMOTHER: Land sakes, you didn't do it. It was the government. And what a government does is nothing for a person to be ashamed of.

SILAS: I don't know about that. Why is *he* here? Why is Felix Fejevary not rich and grand in Hungary to-day? 'Cause he was ashamed of what his government was.

GRANDMOTHER: Well, that was a foreign government.

SILAS: A seeing how 'tis for the other person – *a bein'* that other person, kind of honesty. Joke of it, 'twould do something for *you*. 'Twould 'a' done something for us to have *been* Indians a little more. My father used to talk about Blackhawk – they was friends. I saw Blackhawk once – when I was a boy. (*to* FEJEVARY) Guess I told you. You know what he looked like? He looked like the great of the earth. Noble. Noble like the forests – and the Mississippi – and the stars. His face was long and thin and you could see the bones, and the bones were beautiful. Looked like something that's never been caught. He was something many nights in his canoe had made him. Sometimes I feel that the land itself has got a mind that the land would rather have had the Indians.

GRANDMOTHER: Well, don't let folks hear you say it. They'd think you was plum crazy.

SILAS: I s'pose they would. (*turning to* FEJEVARY) But after you've walked a long time over the earth – and you all alone, didn't you ever feel something coming up from it that's like thought?

FEJEVARY: I'm afraid I never did. But – I wish I had.

SILAS: I love land – this land. I suppose that's why I never have the feeling that I own it.

GRANDMOTHER: If you don't own it – I want to know! What do you think we come here for – your father and me? What do you think we left our folks for – left the world of white folks – schools and stores and doctors, and set out in a covered wagon for we didn't know what? We lost a horse. Lost our way – weeks longer than we thought 'twould be. You were born in that covered wagon. You know that. But what you don't know is what *that's* like – without your own roof – or fire – without –

(*She turns her face away.*)

SILAS: No. No, mother, of course not. Now – now isn't this too bad? I don't say things right. It's because I never went to school.

GRANDMOTHER: (*her face shielded*) You went to school two winters.

SILAS: Yes. Yes, mother. So I did. And I'm glad I did.

GRANDMOTHER: (*with the determination of one who will not have her own pain looked at*) Mrs Fejevary's pansy bed doing well this summer?

FEJEVARY: It's beautiful this summer. She was so pleased with the new purple kind you gave her. I do wish you could get over to see them.

GRANDMOTHER: Yes. Well, I've seen lots of pansies. Suppose it was pretty fine-sounding speeches they had in town?

FEJEVARY: Too fine-sounding to seem much like the war.

SILAS: I'd like to go to a war celebration where they never mentioned war. There'd be a way to celebrate victory. (*hearing a step, looking out*) Mother, here's Felix.

(FELIX, *a well-dressed young man, comes in.*)

GRANDMOTHER: How do, Felix?

FELIX: And how do you do, Grandmother Morton?

GRANDMOTHER: Well, I'm still here.

FELIX: Of course you are. It wouldn't be coming home if you weren't.

GRANDMOTHER: I've got some cookies for you, Felix. I set 'em out, so you wouldn't have to steal them. John and Felix was hard on the cookie jar.

FELIX: Where is John?

SILAS: (*who is pouring a glass of wine for* FELIX) You've not seen John yet? He was in town for the exercises. I bet those young devils ran off to the race-track. I heard whisperin' goin' round. But everybody'll be home some time. Mary and the girls – don't ask me where they are. They'll drive old Bess all over the country before they drive her to the barn. Your father and I come on home 'cause I wanted to have a talk with him.

FELIX: Getting into the old uniforms makes you want to talk it all over again?

SILAS: The war? Well, we did do that. But all that makes me want to talk about what's to come, about – what 'twas all for. Great things are to come, Felix. And before you are through.

FELIX: I've been thinking about them myself – walking around the town to-day. It's

grown so much this year, and in a way that means more growing – that big
glucose plant going up down the river, the new lumber mill – all that means
many more people.

FEJEVARY: And they've even bought ground for a steel works.

SILAS: Yes, a city will rise from these cornfields – a big rich place – that's bound to
be. It's written in the lay o' the land and the way the river flows. But first tell
us about Harvard College, Felix. Ain't it a fine thing for us all to have Felix
coming home from that wonderful place!

FELIX: You make it seem wonderful.

SILAS: Ah, you know it's wonderful – know it so well you don't have to say it. It's
something you've got. But to me it's wonderful the way the stars are wonderful
– this place where all that the world has learned is to be drawn from me – like
a spring.

FELIX: You almost say what Matthew Arnold says – a distinguished new English
writer who speaks of: 'The best that has been thought and said in the world'.

SILAS: 'The best that has been thought and said in the world!' (*slowly rising, and as
if the dream of years is bringing him to his feet*) That's what that hill is for!
(*pointing*) Don't you see it? End of our trail, we climb a hill and plant a
college. Plant a college, so's after we are gone that college says for us, says in
people learning has made more: 'That is why we took this land.'

GRANDMOTHER: (*incredulous*) You mean, Silas, you're going to *give the hill
away?*

SILAS: The hill at the end of our trail – how could we keep that?

GRANDMOTHER: Well, I want to know why not! Hill or level – land's land and
not a thing you give away.

SILAS: Well, don't scold *me*. I'm not giving it away. It's giving itself away, get down
to it.

GRANDMOTHER: Don't talk to me as if I was feeble-minded.

SILAS: I'm talking with all the mind I've got. If there's not mind in what I say, it's
because I've got no mind. But I have got a mind. (*to* FEJEVARY,
humorously) Haven't I? You ought to know. Seeing as you gave it to me.

FEJEVARY: Ah, no – I didn't give it to you.

SILAS: Well, you made me know 'twas there. You said things that woke things in
me and I thought about them as I ploughed. And that made me know there
had to be a college there – wake things in minds – so ploughing's more than
ploughing. What do you say, Felix?

FELIX: It – it's a big idea, Uncle Silas. I love the way you put it. It's only that I'm
wondering –

SILAS: Wondering how it can ever be a Harvard College? Well, it can't. And it
needn't be (*stubbornly*) It's a college in the cornfields – where the Indian maize
once grew. And it's for the boys of the cornfields – and the girls. There's few
can go to Harvard College – but more can climb that hill. (*turn of the head*

---

and the girls: the first co-educational college in the U.S. was Oberlin, in Ohio, which admitted
women in 1837; co-educational institutions remained limited to the Midwest until Cornell
University, in New York, admitted women in 1868. By 1879, just over half of all American
colleges and universities were co-educational.

from the hill to FELIX) Harvard on a hill? (*As* FELIX *smiles no,* SILAS *turns back to the hill*) A college should be on a hill. They can see it then from far around. See it as they go out to the barn in the morning; see it when they're shutting up at night. 'Twill make a difference – even to them that never go.

GRANDMOTHER: Now, Silas – don't be hasty.

SILAS: Hasty? It's been company to me for years. Came to me one night – must 'a' been ten years ago – middle of a starry night as I was comin' home from your place (*to* FEJEVARY) I'd gone over to lend a hand with a sick horse an' –

FEJEVARY: (*with a grateful smile*) That was nothing new.

SILAS: Well, say, I'd sit up with a sick horse that belonged to the meanest man unhung. But – there were stars that night had never been there before. Leastways I'd not seen 'em. And the hill – Felix, in all your travels east, did you ever see anything more beautiful than that hill?

FELIX: It's like sculpture.

SILAS: Hm. (*the wistfulness with which he speaks of that outside his knowledge*) I s'pose 'tis. It's the way it rises – somehow – as if it knew it rose from wide and fertile lands. I climbed the hill that night. (*to* FEJEVARY) You'd been talkin'. As we waited between medicines you told me about your life as a young man. All you'd lived through seemed to – open up to you that night – way things do at times. Guess it was 'cause you thought you was goin' to lose your horse. See, that was Colonel, the sorrel, wasn't it?

FEJEVARY: Yes. Good old Colonel.

SILAS: You'd had a long run o' off luck. Hadn't got things back in shape since the war. But say, you didn't lose him, did you?

FEJEVARY: Thanks to you.

SILAS: Thanks to the medicine I keep in the back kitchen.

FEJEVARY: You encouraged him.

GRANDMOTHER: Silas has a way with all the beasts.

SILAS: We've got the same kind of minds – the beasts and me.

GRANDMOTHER: Silas, I wish you wouldn't talk like that – and with Felix just home from Harvard College.

SILAS: Same kind of minds – except that mine goes on a little farther.

GRANDMOTHER: Well I'm glad to hear you say that.

SILAS: Well, there we sat – you an' me – middle of a starry night, out beside your barn. And I guess it came over you kind of funny you should be there with me – way off the Mississippi, tryin' to save a sick horse. Seemed to – bring your life to life again. You told me what you studied in that fine old university you loved – the Vienna, – and why you became a revolutionist. The old dreams took hold o' you and you talked – way you used to, I suppose. The years, o' course, had rubbed some of it off. Your face as you went on about the vision – you called it, vision of what life could be. I knew that night there was things I never got wind of. When I went away – knew I ought to go home to bed – hayin' at daybreak. 'Go to bed?' I said to myself. 'Strike this dead when you've never had it before, may never have it again?' I climbed the hill. Blackhawk was there.

GRANDMOTHER: Why, he was *dead*.

SILAS: He was there – on his own old hill, with me and the stars. And I said to him –

GRANDMOTHER: Silas!

SILAS: Says I to him, 'Yes – that's true; it's more yours than mine, you had it first and loved it best. But it's neither yours nor mine, – though both yours and mine. Not my hill, not your hill, but – hill of vision', said I to him. 'Here shall come visions of a better world than was ever seen by you or me, old Indian chief.' Oh, I was drunk, plum drunk.

GRANDMOTHER: I should think you was. And what about the next day's hay?

SILAS: A day in the hayfield is a day's hayin' – but a night on the hill –

FELIX: We don't have them often, do we, Uncle Silas?

SILAS: I wouldn't 'a' had that one but for your father, Felix. Thank God they drove you out o' Hungary! And it's all so dog-gone *queer*. Ain't it queer how things blow from mind to mind – like seeds. Lord A'mighty – you don't know where they'll take hold.

(Children's voices off.)

GRANDMOTHER: There come those children up from the creek – soppin' wet, I warrant. Well, I don't know how children ever get raised. But we raise more of 'em than we used to. I buried three – first ten years I was here. Needn't 'a' happened – if we'd known what we know now, and if we hadn't been alone. *(With all her strength.)* I don't know what you mean – the hill's not yours!

SILAS: It's the future's, mother – so's we can know more than we know now.

GRANDMOTHER: We know it now. 'Twas then we didn't know it. I worked for that hill! And I tell you to leave it to your own children.

SILAS: There's other land for my own children. This is for all the children.

GRANDMOTHER: What's all the children to you?

SILAS: *(derisively)* Oh, mother – what a thing for you to say! You who were never too tired to give up your own bed so the stranger could have a better bed.

GRANDMOTHER: That was different. They was folks on their way.

FEJEVARY: So are we.

(SILAS turns to him with quick appreciation.)

GRANDMOTHER: That's just talk. We're settled now. Children of other old settlers are getting rich. I should think you'd want yours to.

SILAS: I want other things more. I want to pay my debts 'fore I'm too old to know they're debts.

GRANDMOTHER: *(momentarily startled)* Debts? Huh! More talk. You don't owe any man.

SILAS: I owe him *(nodding to* FEJEVARY). And the red boys here before me.

GRANDMOTHER: Fiddlesticks.

FELIX: You haven't read Darwin, have you, Uncle Silas?

SILAS: Who?

FELIX: Darwin, the great new man – and his theory of the survival of the fittest?

SILAS: No. No, I don't know things like that, Felix.

FELIX: I think he might make you feel better about the Indians. In the struggle for existence many must go down. The fittest survive. This – had to be.

SILAS: Us and the Indians? Guess I don't know what you mean – fittest.

FELIX: He calls it that. Best fitted to the place in which one finds one's self, having

the qualities that can best cope with conditions – do things. From the
beginning of life it's been like that. He shows the growth of life from forms
that were hardly alive, the lowest animal forms – jellyfish – up to man.

SILAS: Oh, yes, that's the thing the churches are so upset about – that we come
from monkeys.

FELIX: Yes. One family of ape is the direct ancestor of man.

GRANDMOTHER: You'd better read your Bible, Felix.

SILAS: Do people believe this?

FELIX: The whole intellectual world is at war about it. The best scientists accept it.
Teachers are losing their positions for believing it. Of course, ministers can't
believe it.

GRANDMOTHER: I should think not. Anyway, what's the use believing a thing
that's so discouraging?

FEJEVARY: (*gently*) But is it that? It almost seems to me we have to accept it
because it is so encouraging. (*holding out his hand*) Why have we hands?

GRANDMOTHER: Cause God gave them to us, I s'pose.

FEJEVARY: But that's rather general, and there isn't much in it to give us
self-confidence. But when you think we have hands because ages back – before
life had taken form as man, there was an impulse to do what had never been
done – when you think that we have hands today because from the first of life
there have been adventurers – those of best brain and courage who wanted to
be more than life had been, and that from aspiration has come doing, and
doing has shaped the thing with which to do – it gives our hand a history which
should make us want to use it well.

SILAS: (*breathed from deep*) Well, by God! And you've known this all this while!
Dog-gone you – why didn't you tell me?

FEJEVARY: I've been thinking about it. I haven't known what to believe. This
hurts – beliefs of earlier years.

FELIX: The things it hurts will have to go.

FEJEVARY: I don't know about that, Felix. Perhaps in time we'll find truth in
them.

FELIX: Oh, if you feel that way, father.

FEJEVARY: Don't be kind to me, my boy, I'm not that old.

SILAS: But think what it is you've said! If it's true that we *made* ourselves – made
ourselves out of the wanting to be more – created ourselves you might say, by
our own courage – our – what is it? – aspiration. Why, I can't take it in. I
haven't got the mind to take it in. And what mind I have got says no. It's too –

FEJEVARY: It fights with what's there.

SILAS: (*nodding*) But it's like I got this (*very slowly*) other way around. From
underneath. As if I'd known it all along – but have just found out I know it!
Yes. The earth told me. The beasts told me.

GRANDMOTHER: Fine place to learn things from.

SILAS: Anyhow, haven't I seen it? (*to* FEJEVARY) In your face haven't I seen
thinking make a finer face? How long has this taken, Felix, to – well, you
might say, bring us where we are now?

FELIX: Oh, we don't know how many millions of years since earth first
stirred.

SILAS: Then we are what we are because through all that time there've been them that wanted to be more than life had been.

FELIX: That's it, Uncle Silas.

SILAS: But – why, then we aren't *finished* yet!

FEJEVARY: No. We take it on from here.

SILAS: (*slowly*) Then if we don't be – the most we can be, if we don't be more than life has been, we go back on all that life behind us; go back on – the –
(*Unable to formulate it, he looks to* FEJEVARY.)

FEJEVARY: Go back on the dreaming and the daring of a million years.
(*After a moment's pause* SILAS *gets up, opens the closet door.*)

GRANDMOTHER: Silas, what you doing?

SILAS: (*who has taken out a box*) I'm lookin' for the deed to the hill.

GRANDMOTHER: What you going to do with it?

SILAS: I'm going to get it out of my hands.

GRANDMOTHER: Get it out of your hands? (*he has it now*) Deed your father got from the government the very year the government got it from the Indians? (*rising*) Give me that! (*she turns to* FEJEVARY) Tell him he's crazy. We got the best land 'cause we was first here. We got a right to keep it.

FEJEVARY: (*going soothingly to her*) It's true, Silas, it is a serious thing to give away one's land.

SILAS: You ought to know. You did it. Are you sorry you did it?

FEJEVARY: No. But wasn't that different?

SILAS: How was it different? Yours was a fight to make life more, wasn't it? Well, let this be our way.

GRANDMOTHER: What's all that got to do with giving up the land that should provide for our own children?

SILAS: Isn't it providing for them to give them a better world to live in? Felix – you're young, I ask you, ain't it providing for them to give them a chance to be more than we are?

FELIX: I think you're entirely right, Uncle Silas. But it's the practical question that –

SILAS: If you're right, the practical question is just a thing to fix up.

FEJEVARY: I fear you don't realize the immense amount of money required to finance a college. The land would be a start. You would have to interest rich men; you'd have to have a community in sympathy with the thing you wanted to do.

GRANDMOTHER: Can't you see, Silas, that we're all against you?

SILAS: All against me? (*to* FEJEVARY) But how can you be? Look at the land we walked in and took! Was there ever such a chance to make life more? Why, the buffalo here before us was more than we if we do nothing but prosper! God damn us if we sit here rich and fat and forget man's in the makin'. (*affirming against this*) There will one day be a college in these cornfields by the Mississippi because long ago a great dream was fought for in Hungary. And I say to that old dream, Wake up, old dream! Wake up and fight! You say rich men. (*holding it out, but it is not taken*) I give you this deed to take to rich men to show them one man believes enough in this to give the best land he's got. That ought to make rich men stop and think.

GRANDMOTHER: Stop and think he's a fool.

SILAS: (*to* FEJEVARY) It's you can make them know he's not a fool. When you tell this way you can tell it, they'll feel in you what's more than them. They'll listen.

GRANDMOTHER: I tell you, Silas, folks are too busy.

SILAS: 'Too busy!' Too busy bein' nothin'? If it's true that we created ourselves out of the thoughts that came, then thought is not something *outside* the business of life. Thought – (*with his gift for wonder*) why, thought's our *chance*. I know now. Why I can't forget the Indians. We killed their joy before we killed them. We made them less. (*to* FEJEVARY, *and as if sure he is now making it clear*) I got to give it back – their hill. I give it back to joy – a better joy – joy o' aspiration.

FEJEVARY: (*moved but unconvinced*) But, my friend, there are men who have no aspiration. That's why, to me, this is as a light shining from too far.

GRANDMOTHER: (*old things waked in her*) Light shining from far. We used to do that. We never pulled the curtain. I used to want to – you like to be to yourself when night comes – but we always left a lighted window for the traveller who'd lost his way.

FELIX: I should think that would have exposed you to the Indians.

GRANDMOTHER: Yes. (*impatiently*) Well, you can't put out a light just because it may light the wrong person.

FEJEVARY: No. (*and this is as a light to him. He turns to the hill*) No.

SILAS: (*with gentleness, and profoundly*) That's it. Look again. Maybe your eyes are stronger now. Don't you see it? I see that college rising as from the soil itself, as if it was what come at the last of that thinking that breathes from the earth. I see it – but I want to know it's real before I stop knowing. Then maybe I can lie under the same sod with the red boys and not be ashamed. We're not old! Let's fight! Wake in other men what you woke in me!

FEJEVARY: And so could I pay my debt to America.

(*His hand goes out.*)

SILAS: (*giving him the deed*) And to the dreams of a million years!

(*Standing near the open door, their hands are gripped in compact.*)

CURTAIN

ACT II

SCENE: *A corridor in the library of Morton College, October of the year 1920, upon the occasion of the fortieth anniversary of its founding. This is an open place in the stacks of books, which are seen at both sides. There is a reading-table before the big rear window. This window opens out, but does not extend to the floor; only a part of its height is seen, indicating a very high window. Outside is seen the top of a tree. This outer wall of the building is on a slant, so that the entrance right is near, and the left is front. Right front is a section of a huge square column. On the rear of this, facing the window, is hung a picture of* SILAS MORTON. *Two men are standing before this portrait.*

SENATOR LEWIS *is the Midwestern state senator. He is not of the city from which Morton College rises, but of a more country community farther in-state.* FELIX

FEJEVARY, *now nearing the age of his father in the first act, is an American of the more sophisticated type – prosperous, having the poise of success in affairs and place in society.*

SENATOR: And this was the boy who founded the place, eh? It was his idea?

FEJEVARY: Yes, and his hill. I was there the afternoon he told my father there must be a college here. I wasn't any older then than my boy is now.
> (*As if himself surprised by this.*)

SENATOR: Well, he enlisted a good man when he let you in on it. I've been told the college wouldn't be what it is today but for you, Mr Fejevary.

FEJEVARY: I have a sentiment about it, and where our sentiment is, there our work goes also.

SENATOR: Yes. Well, it was those mainsprings of sentiment that won the war.
> (*He is pleased with this.*)

FEJEVARY: (*nodding*) Morton College did her part in winning the war.

SENATOR: I know. A fine showing.

FEJEVARY: And we're holding up our end right along. You'll see the boys drill this afternoon. It's a great place for them, here on the hill – shows up from so far around. They're a fine lot of fellows. You know, I presume, that they went in as strike-breakers during the trouble down here at the steel works. The plant would have had to close but for Morton College. That's one reason I venture to propose this thing of a state appropriation for enlargement. Why don't we sit down a moment? There's no conflict with the state university – they have their territory, we have ours. Ours is an important one – industrially speaking. The state will lose nothing in having a good strong college here – a one-hundred-per-cent-American college.

SENATOR: I admit I am very favourably impressed.

FEJEVARY: I hope you'll tell your committee so – and let me have a chance to talk to them.

SENATOR: Let's see, haven't you a pretty radical man here?

FEJEVARY: I wonder if you mean Holden?

SENATOR: Holden's the man. I've read things that make me question his Americanism.

FEJEVARY: Oh – (*gesture of depreciation*) I don't think he is so much a radical as a particularly human human-being.

SENATOR: But we don't want radical human beings.

FEJEVARY: He has a genuine sympathy with youth. That's invaluable in a teacher, you know. And then – he's a scholar.
> (*He betrays here his feeling of superiority to his companion, but too subtly for his companion to get it.*)

SENATOR: Oh – scholar. We can get scholars enough. What we want is Americans.

FEJEVARY: Americans who are scholars.

SENATOR: You can pick 'em off every bush – pay them a little more than they're

---

boys drill: many American colleges and universities offer R.O.T.C. (Reserve Officers' Training Corps) as an extracurricular activity.

paid in some other cheap John College. Excuse me – I don't mean this is a cheap John College.

FEJEVARY: Of course not. One couldn't think that of Morton College. But that – pay them a little more, interests me. That's another reason I want to talk to your committee on appropriations. We claim to value education and then we let highly trained, gifted men fall behind the plumber.

SENATOR: Well, that's the plumber's fault. Let the teachers talk to the plumber.

FEJEVARY: (*with a smile*) No. Better not let them talk to the plumber. He might tell them what to do about it. In fact, is telling them.

SENATOR: That's ridiculous. They can't serve both God and mammon.

FEJEVARY: Then let God give them mammon. I mean, let the state appropriate.

SENATOR: Of course this state, Mr Fejevary, appropriates no money for radicals. Excuse me, but why do you keep this man Holden?

FEJEVARY: In the scholar's world we're known because of him. And really, Holden's not a radical – in the worst sense. What he doesn't see is – expediency. Not enough the man of affairs to realize that we can't always have literally what we have theoretically. He's an idealist. Something of the – man of vision.

SENATOR: If he had the right vision he'd see that we don't every minute have literally what we have theoretically because we're fighting to keep the thing we have. Oh, I sometimes think the man of affairs has the only vision. Take you, Mr Fejevary – a banker. These teachers – books – books! (*pushing all books back*) Why, if they had to take for one day the responsibility that falls on your shoulders – big decisions to make – man among men – and all the time worries, irritations, particularly now with labour riding the high horse like a fool! I know something about these things. I went to the State House because my community persuaded me it was my duty. But I'm the man of affairs myself.

FEJEVARY: Oh yes, I know. Your company did much to develop that whole northern part of the state.

SENATOR: I think I may say we did. Well, that's why, after three sessions, I'm chairman of the appropriations committee. I know how to use money to promote the state. So – teacher? That would be a perpetual vacation to me. Now, if you want my advice, Mr Fejevary, – I think your case before the state would be stronger if you let this fellow Holden go.

FEJEVARY: I'm going to have a talk with Professor Holden.

SENATOR: Tell him it's for his own good. The idea of a college professor standing up for conscientious objectors!

FEJEVARY: That doesn't quite state the case. Fred Jordan was one of Holden's students – a student he valued. He felt Jordan was perfectly sincere in his objection.

SENATOR: Sincere in his objections! The nerve of him thinking it was his business to be sincere!

FEJEVARY: He was expelled from college – you may remember; that was how we felt about it.

SENATOR: I should hope so.

---

cheap John: inferior (literally, a travelling hawker who sells goods cheaply).

FEJEVARY: Holden fought that, but within the college. What brought him into the papers was his protest against the way the boy has been treated in prison.

SENATOR: What's the difference how he's treated? You know how I'd treat him? (*a movement as though pulling a trigger*) If I didn't know you for the American you are, I wouldn't understand your speaking so calmly.

FEJEVARY: I'm simply trying to see it all sides around.

SENATOR: Makes me see red.

FEJEVARY: (*with a smile*) But we mustn't meet red with red.

SENATOR: What's Holden fussing about – that they don't give him caviare on toast?

FEJEVARY: That they didn't give him books. Holden felt it was his business to fuss about that.

SENATOR: Well, when your own boy 'stead of whining around about his conscience, stood up and offered his life!

FEJEVARY: Yes. And my nephew gave his life.

SENATOR: That so?

FEJEVARY: Silas Morton's grandson died in France. My sister Madeline married Ira Morton, son of Silas Morton.

SENATOR: I knew there was a family connection between you and the Mortons.

FEJEVARY: (*speaking with reserve*) They played together as children and married as soon as they were grown up.

SENATOR: So this was your sister's boy? (FEJEVARY *nods*) One of the mothers to give her son!

FEJEVARY: (*speaking of her with effort*) My sister died – long ago. (*pulled to an old feeling; with an effort releasing himself*) But Ira is still out at the old place – place the Mortons took up when they reached the end of their trail – as Uncle Silas used to put it. Why, it's a hundred years ago that Grandmother Morton began – making cookies here. She was the first white woman in this country.

SENATOR: Proud woman! To have begun the life of this state! Oh, our pioneers! If they could only see us now, and know what they did! (FEJEVARY *is silent; he does not look quite happy*) I suppose Silas Morton's son is active in the college management.

FEJEVARY: No, Ira is not a social being. Fred's death about finished him. He had been – strange for years, ever since my sister died – when the children were little. It was – (*again pulled back to that old feeling*) under pretty terrible circumstances.

SENATOR: I can see that you thought a great deal of your sister, Mr Fejevary.

FEJEVARY: Oh, she was beautiful and – (*bitterly*) it shouldn't have gone like that.

SENATOR: Seems to me I've heard something about Silas Morton's son – though perhaps it wasn't this one.

FEJEVARY: Ira is the only one living here now; the others have gone farther west.

SENATOR: Isn't there something about corn?

FEJEVARY: Yes. His corn has several years taken the prize – best in the state. He's experimented with it – created a new kind. They've given it his name – Morton corn. It seems corn is rather fascinating to work with – very mutable stuff. It's a good thing Ira has it, for it's about the only thing he does care for now. Oh, Madeline, of course. He has a daughter here in the college – Madeline Morton, senior this year – one of our best students. I'd like to have you meet Madeline – she's a great girl, though – peculiar.

SENATOR: Well, that makes a girl interesting, if she isn't peculiar the wrong way. Sounds as if her home life might make her a little peculiar.

FEJEVARY: Madeline stays here in town with us a good part of the time. Mrs Fejevary is devoted to her – we all are. (*a boy starts to come through from right*) Hello, see who's here. This is my boy. Horace, this is Senator Lewis, who is interested in the college.

HORACE: (*shaking hands*) How do you do, Senator Lewis?

SENATOR: Pleased to see you, my boy.

HORACE: Am I butting in?

FEJEVARY: Not seriously; but what are you doing in the library? I thought this was a day off.

HORACE: I'm looking for a book.

FEJEVARY: (*affectionately bantering*) You are, Horace? Now how does that happen?

HORACE: I want the speeches of Abraham Lincoln.

SENATOR: You couldn't do better.

HORACE: I'll show those dirty dagoes where they get off!

FEJEVARY: You couldn't show them a little more elegantly?

HORACE: I'm going to sick the Legion on 'em.

FEJEVARY: Are you talking about the Hindus?

HORACE: Yes, the dirty dagoes.

FEJEVARY: Hindus aren't dagoes you know, Horace.

HORACE: Well, what's the difference? This foreign element gets my goat.

SENATOR: My boy, you talk like an American. But what do you mean – Hindus?

FEJEVARY: There are two young Hindus here as students. And they're good students.

HORACE: Sissies.

FEJEVARY: But they must preach the gospel of free India – non-British India.

SENATOR: Oh, that won't do.

HORACE: They're nothing but Reds, I'll say. Well, one of 'em's going back to get his. (*grins*)

FEJEVARY: There were three of them last year. One of them is wanted back home.

SENATOR: I remember now. He's to be deported.

HORACE: And when they get him – (*movement as of pulling a rope*) They hang there.

FEJEVARY: The other two protest against our not fighting the deportation of their comrade. They insist it means death to him. (*brushing off a thing that is inclined to worry him*) But we can't handle India's affairs.

---

gospel of free India: India was under direct British rule until 1947; the Congress Party (or Indian National Congress), which was chiefly Hindu, formed the main nationalist movement this century.

SENATOR: I should think not!

HORACE: Why, England's our ally! That's what I told them. But you can't argue with people like that. Just wait till I find the speeches of Abraham Lincoln!
> (*Passes through to left*)

SENATOR: Fine boy you have, Mr Fejevary.

FEJEVARY: He's a live one. You should see him in a football game. Wouldn't hurt my feelings in the least to have him a little more of a student, but –

SENATOR: Oh, well, you want him to be a regular fellow, don't you, and grow into a man among men?

FEJEVARY: He'll do that, I think. It was he who organized our boys for the steel strike – went right in himself and took a striker's job. He came home with a black eye one night, presented to him by a picket who started something by calling him a scab. But Horace wasn't thinking about his eye. According to him, it was not in the class with the striker's upper lip. 'Father,' he said, 'I gave him more red than he could swallow. The blood just –' Well, I'll spare you – but Horace's muscle is one hundred per cent American. (*going to the window*) Let me show you something. You can see the old Morton place off on that first little hill. (*pointing left*) The first rise beyond the valley.

SENATOR: The long low house?

FEJEVARY: That's it. You see, the town for the most part swung around the other side of the hill, so the Morton place is still a farm.

SENATOR: But you're growing all the while. The town'll take the cornfield yet.

FEJEVARY: Yes, our steel works is making us a city.

SENATOR: And this old boy (*turning to the portrait of* SILAS MORTON) can look out on his old home – and watch the valley grow.

FEJEVARY: Yes – that was my idea. His picture really should be in Memorial Hall, but I thought Uncle Silas would like to be up here among the books, and facing the old place. (*with a laugh*) I confess to being a little sentimental.

SENATOR: We Americans have lots of sentiment, Mr Fejevary. It's what makes us – what we are. (FEJEVARY *does not speak; there are times when the senator seems to trouble him*) Well, this is a great site for a college. You can see it from the whole country round.

FEJEVARY: Yes, that was Uncle Silas' idea. He had a reverence for education. It grew, in part, out of his feeling for my father. He was a poet – really, Uncle Silas. (*looking at the picture*) He gave this hill for a college that we might become a deeper, more sensitive people –
> (*Two girls, convulsed with the giggles, come tumbling in.*)

DORIS: (*confused*) Oh – oh, excuse us.

FUSSIE: (*foolishly*) We didn't know anybody was here.
> (MR FEJEVARY *looks at them sternly. The girls retreat.*)

SENATOR: (*laughing*) Oh, well girls will be girls. I've got three of my own.
> (HORACE *comes back, carrying an open book.*)

HORACE: Say, this must be a misprint.

FEJEVARY: (*glancing at the back of the book*) Oh, I think not.

HORACE: From his first inaugural address to Congress, March 4, 1861. (*reads*)
> 'This country with its institutions belong to the people who inhabit it.' Well, that's all right. 'Whenever they shall grow weary of the existing government

they can exercise their constitutional right of amending it' – (*after a brief consideration*) I suppose that that's all right – but listen! 'or their *revolutionary* right to dismember or overthrow it.'

FEJEVARY: He was speaking in another age. An age of different values.

SENATOR: Terms change their significance from generation to generation.

HORACE: I suppose they do – but that puts me in bad with these lice. They quoted this and I said they were liars.

SENATOR: And what's the idea? They're weary of our existing government and are about to dismember or overthrow it?

HORACE: I guess that's the dope.

FEJEVARY: Look here, Horace – speak accurately. Was it in relation to America they quoted this?

HORACE: Well, maybe they were talking about India then. But they were standing up for being revolutionists. We were giving them an earful about it, and then they spring Lincoln on us. Got their nerve – I'll say – quoting Lincoln to us.

SENATOR: The fact that they are quoting it shows it's being misapplied.

HORACE: (*approvingly*) I'll tell them that. But gee – Lincoln oughta been more careful what he said. Ignorant people don't know how to take such things.
    (*Goes back with book.*)

FEJEVARY: Want to take a look through the rest of the library? We haven't been up this way yet – (*motioning left*) We need a better scientific library. (*they are leaving now*) Oh, we simply must have more money. The whole thing is fairly bursting its shell.

DORIS: (*venturing in cautiously from the other side, looking back, beckoning*) They've gone.

FUSSIE: Sure?

DORIS: Well, are they here? And I saw them, I tell you – they went up to science.

FUSSIE: (*moving the* SENATOR*'s hat on the table*) But they'll come back.

DORIS: What if they do? We're only looking at a book. (*running her hand along the books*) Matthew Arnold.
    (*Takes a paper from* FUSSIE, *puts it in the book. They are bent with giggling as* HORACE *returns.*)

HORACE: For the love o' Pete, what's the joke? (*taking the book from the helpless girl*) Matthew Arnold. My idea of nowhere to go for a laugh. When I wrote my theme on him last week he was so dry I had to go out and get a Morton Sundee (*the girls are freshly attacked, though all of this in a subdued way, mindful of others in the library*) Say, how'd you get that way?

DORIS: Now, Horace, don't you *tell*.

HORACE: What'd I tell, except – (*seeing the paper*) Um hum – what's this?

DORIS: (*trying to get it from him*) Horace, now *don't* you (*a tussle*) You great strong mean thing! Fussie! Make him *stop*.
    (*She gets the paper by tearing it.*)

HORACE: My dad's around here – showing the college off to a politician. If you don't come across with that sheet of mystery, I'll back you both out there (*starts to do it*) and –

DORIS: Horace! You're just *horrid*.

HORACE: Sure I'm horrid. That's the way I want to be. (*takes the paper, reads*)

'To Eben
You are the idol of my dreams
I worship from afar.'
What is this?

FUSSIE: Now, listen, Horace, and don't you *tell*. You know Eben Weeks. He's the homeliest man in school. Wouldn't you say so?

HORACE: Awful jay. Like to get some of the jays out of here.

DORIS: But listen. Of course, no girl would *look* at him. So we've thought up the most *killing* joke. (*stopped by giggles from herself and* FUSSIE) Now, he hasn't handed in his Matthew Arnold dope. I heard old Mac hold him up for it – and what'd you think he said? That he'd been *ploughing*. Said he was trying to run a farm and go to college at the same time! Isn't it a *scream*?

HORACE: We oughta – make it more unpleasant for some of those jays. Gives the school a bad name.

FUSSIE: But, listen, Horace, honest – you'll just *die*. He said he was going to get the book this afternoon. Now you know what he *looks* like, but he turns to – (*both girls are convulsed*)

DORIS: It'll get him all fussed up! And for nothing at all!

HORACE: Too bad that class of people come here. I think I'll go to Harvard next year. Haven't broken it to my parents – but I've about made up my mind.

DORIS: Don't you think Morton's a good school, Horace?

HORACE: Morton's all right. Fine for the – (*kindly*) people who would naturally come here. But one gets an acquaintance at Harvard. Wher'd'y' want these passionate lines?

(FUSSIE *and* DORIS *are off again convulsed.*)

HORACE: (*eye falling on the page where he opens the book*) Say, old Bones could spill the English – what? Listen to this flyer. 'For when we say that culture is to know the best that has been thought and said in the world, we simply imply that for culture a system directly tending to that end is necessary in our reading.' (*he reads it with mock solemnity, delighting* FUSSIE *and* DORIS) 'The best that has been thought and said in the world!'

(MADELINE MORTON *comes in from right; she carries a tennis racket.*)

MADELINE: (*both critical and good-humoured*) You haven't made a large contribution to that, have you, Horace?

HORACE: Madeline, you don't want to let this sarcastic habit grow on you.

MADELINE: Thanks for the tip.

FUSSIE: Oh – *Madeline*. (*holds out her hand to take the book from* HORACE *and shows it to* MADELINE) You know –

DORIS: S–h Don't be silly. (*to cover this*) Who you playing with?

HORACE: Want me to play with you, Madeline?

MADELINE: (*genially*) I'd rather play with you than talk to you.

---

jay: greenhorn, someone inexperienced.
For when we say ... reading' quotes Arnold's 1873 Preface to *Literature and Dogma*: 'For when we say that culture is, *To know the best that has been thought and said in the world*, we imply that, for culture, a system directly tending to this end is necessary in our reading.'

HORACE: Same here.

FUSSIE: Aren't cousins affectionate?

MADELINE: (*moving through to the other part of the library*) But first I'm looking for a book.

HORACE: Well, I can tell you without your looking it up, he did say it. But that was an age of different values. Anyway, the fact that they're quoting it shows it's being misapplied.

MADELINE: (*smiling*) Father said so.

HORACE: (*on his dignity*) Oh, of course – if you don't want to be serious.

(MADELINE *laughs and passes on through.*)

DORIS: What are you two talking about?

HORACE: Madeline happened to overhear a little discussion down on the campus.

FUSSIE: Listen. You know something? Sometimes I think Madeline Morton is a highbrow in disguise.

HORACE: Say, you don't want to start anything like that. Madeline's all right. She and I treat each other rough – but that's being in the family.

FUSSIE: Well, I'll *tell* you something. I heard Professor Holden say Madeline Morton has a great deal more mind than she'd let herself know.

HORACE: Oh, well – Holden, he's erratic. Look at how popular Madeline is.

DORIS: I should *say*. What's the matter with you, Fussie?

FUSSIE: Oh, I didn't mean it really *hurt* her.

HORACE: Guess it don't hurt her much at a dance. Say, what's this new jazz they were springing last night?

DORIS: I know! Now look here, Horace – L'me show you. (*she shows him a step*)

HORACE: I get you.

(*He begins to dance with her; the book he holds slips to the floor. He kicks it under the table.*)

FUSSIE: Be *careful*. They'll be coming back here. (*glances off left*)

DORIS: Keep an eye out, Fussie.

FUSSIE: (*from her post*) They're coming! I tell you, they're *coming!*

DORIS: Horace, come *on*.

(*He teasingly keeps hold of her, continuing the dance. At sound of voices, they run off, right. FUSSIE considers rescuing the book, decides she has not time.*)

SENATOR: (*at first speaking off*) Yes, it could be done. There is that surplus, and as long as Morton College is socially valuable – right here above the steel works, and making this feature of military training – (*he has picked up his hat*) But your Americanism must be unimpeachable, Mr Fejevary. This man Holden stands in the way.

FEJEVARY: I'm going to have a talk with Professor Holden this afternoon. If he remains he will – (*it is not easy for him to say*) give no trouble. (MADELINE *returns*) Oh, here's Madeline – Silas Morton's granddaughter, Madeline Fejevary Morton. This is Senator Lewis, Madeline.

SENATOR: (*holding out his hand*) How do you do, Miss Morton. I suppose this is a great day for you.

MADELINE: Why – I don't know.

SENATOR: The fortieth anniversary of the founding of your grandfather's college? You must be very proud of your illustrious ancestor.

MADELINE: I get a bit bored with him.

SENATOR: Bored with him? My dear young lady!

MADELINE: I suppose because I've heard so many speeches about him – 'The sainted pioneer' – 'the grand old man of the prairies' – I'm sure I haven't any idea what he really was like.

FEJEVARY: I've tried to tell you, Madeline.

MADELINE: Yes.

SENATOR: I should think you would be proud to be the granddaughter of this man of vision.

MADELINE: (*her smile flashing*) Wouldn't you hate to be the granddaughter of a phrase?

FEJEVARY: (*trying to laugh it off*) Madeline! How absurd.

MADELINE: Well, I'm off for tennis.
(*Nods good-bye and passes on.*)

FEJEVARY: (*calling to her*) Oh, Madeline, if your Aunt Isabel is out there – will you tell her where we are?

MADELINE: (*calling back*) All right.

FEJEVARY: (*after a look at his companion*) Queer girl, Madeline. Rather – moody.

SENATOR: (*disapprovingly*) Well – yes.

FEJEVARY: (*again trying to laugh it off*) She's been hearing a great many speeches about her grandfather.

SENATOR: She should be proud to hear them.

FEJEVARY: Of course she should. (*looking in the direction* MADELINE *has gone*) I want you to meet my wife, Senator Lewis.

SENATOR: I should be pleased to meet Mrs Fejevary. I have heard what she means to the college – socially.

FEJEVARY: I think she has given it something it wouldn't have had without her. Certainly a place in the town that is – good for it. And you haven't met our president yet.

SENATOR: Guess, I've met the real president.

FEJEVARY: Oh – no. I'm merely president of the board of trustees.

SENATOR: 'Merely!'

FEJEVARY: I want you to know President Welling. He's very much the cultivated gentleman.

SENATOR: Cultivated gentlemen are all right. I'd hate to see a world they ran.

FEJEVARY: (*with a laugh*) I'll just take a look up here, then we can go down the shorter way.
(*He goes out right.* SENATOR LEWIS *turns and examines the books. FUSSIE slips in, looks at him, hesitates, and then stoops under the table for the Matthew Arnold (and her poem) which* HORACE *has kicked there. He turns.*)

FUSSIE: (*not out from under the table*) Oh, I was just looking for a book.

SENATOR: Quite a place to look for a book.

FUSSIE: (*crawling out*) Yes, it got there. I thought I'd put it back. Somebody – might want it.

SENATOR: I see, young lady, that you have a regard for books.

FUSSIE: Oh, yes, I do have a regard for them.

SENATOR: (*holding out his hand*) And what is your book?

FUSSIE: Oh – it's – it's nothing.

> (*As he continues to hold out his hand, she reluctantly gives the book.*)

SENATOR: (*solemnly*) Matthew Arnold? Nothing?

FUSSIE: Oh, I didn't mean *him*.

SENATOR: A master of English! I am glad, young woman, that you value this book.

FUSSIE: Oh yes, I'm – awfully fond of it.

> (*Growing more and more nervous as in turning the pages he nears the poem.*)

SENATOR: I am interested in you young people of Morton College.

FUSSIE: That's so good of you.

SENATOR: What is your favourite study?

FUSSIE: Well – (*an inspiration*) I like all of them.

SENATOR: Morton College is coming on very fast, I understand.

FUSSIE: Oh yes, it's getting more and more of the right people. It used to be a little jay, you know. Of course, the Fejevarys give it class. Mrs Fejevary – isn't she wonderful?

SENATOR: I haven't seen her yet. Waiting here now to meet her.

FUSSIE: (*worried by this*) Oh, I must – must be going. Shall I put the book back? (*holding out her hand*)

SENATOR: No, I'll just look it over a bit. (*sits down*)

FUSSIE: (*unable to think of any way of geting it*) This is where it belongs.

SENATOR: Thank you.

> (*Reluctantly she goes out. SENATOR LEWIS pursues Matthew Arnold with the conscious air of a half literate man reading a 'great book'. The FEJEVARYS come in*)

FEJEVARY: I found my wife, Senator Lewis.

AUNT ISABEL: (*she is a woman of social distinction and charm*) How do you do, Senator Lewis? (*They shake hands.*)

SENATOR: It's a great pleasure to meet you, Mrs Fejevary.

AUNT ISABEL: Why don't we carry Senator Lewis home for lunch?

SENATOR: Why, you're very kind.

AUNT ISABEL: I'm sure there's a great deal to talk about, so why not talk comfortably, and really get acquainted? And we want to tell you the whole story of Morton College – the good old American spirit behind it.

SENATOR: I am glad to find you an American, Mrs Fejevary.

AUNT ISABEL: Oh, we are that. Morton College is one hundred per cent American. Our boys –

> (*Her boy HORACE rushes in.*)

HORACE: (*wildly*) Father! Will you go after Madeline? The police have got her!

FEJEVARY: *What!*

AUNT ISABEL: (*as he is getting his breath*) What absurd thing are you saying, Horace?

HORACE: Awful row down on the campus. The Hindus. I told them to keep their mouths shut about Abraham Lincoln. I told them the fact they were quoting him –

FEJEVARY: Never mind what you told them! What happened?

HORACE: We started – to rustle them along a bit. Why, they had *handbills* (*holding one up as if presenting incriminating evidence* – *the* SENATOR *takes it from him*) telling America what to do about deportation! Not on this campus – I say. So we were – we were putting a stop to it. They resisted – particularly the fat one. The cop at the corner saw the row – came up. He took hold of Bakhshish, and when the dirty anarchist didn't move along fast enough, he took hold of him – well, a bit rough, you might say, when up rushes Madeline and calls to the cop, 'Let that boy alone!' Gee – I don't know just what did happen – awful mix-up. Next thing I knew Madeline hauled off and pasted the policeman a fierce one with her tennis racket!

SENATOR: She *struck* the officer?

HORACE: I should say she did. Twice. The second time –

AUNT ISABEL: *Horace.* (*looking at her husband*) I – I can't believe it.

HORACE: I could have squared it, even then, but for Madeline herself. I told the policeman that she didn't understand – that I was her cousin, and apologized for her. And she called over at me, 'Better apologize for yourself!' As if there was any sense to that – that she – she looked like a *tiger.* Honest, everybody was afraid of her. I kept right on trying to square it, told the cop she was the granddaughter of the man that founded the college – that you were her uncle – he would have gone off with just the Hindu, fixed this up later, but Madeline balled it up again – didn't care who was her uncle – Gee! (*he throws open the window*) There! You can see them, at the foot of the hill. A *nice* thing – member of our family led off to the police station!

FEJEVARY: (*to the* SENATOR) Will you excuse me?

AUNT ISABEL: (*trying to return to the manner of pleasant social things*) Senator Lewis will go on home with me, and you – (*he is hurrying out*) come when you can. (*to the* SENATOR) Madeline is such a high-spirited girl.

SENATOR: If she had no regard for the living, she might – on this day of all others – have considered her grandfather's memory.

(*Raises his eyes to the picture of* SILAS MORTON.)

HORACE: Gee! Wouldn't you *say* so?

CURTAIN

ACT III

SCENE: *The same as Act II three hours later.* PROFESSOR HOLDEN *is seated at the table, books before him. He is a man in the fifties. At the moment his care-worn face is lighted by that lift of the spirit which sometimes rewards the scholar who has imaginative feeling.* HARRY, *a student clerk, comes hurrying in. Looks back.*

HARRY: Here's Professor Holden, Mr Fejevary.

HOLDEN: Mr Fejevary is looking for me?

HARRY: Yes.

(He goes back, a moment later MR FEJEVARY enters. He has his hat, gloves, stick; seems tired and disturbed.)

HOLDEN: Was I mistaken? I thought our appointment was for five.

FEJEVARY: Quite right. But things have changed, so I wondered if I might have a little talk with you now.

HOLDEN: To be sure. *(rising)* Shall we go downstairs?

FEJEVARY: I don't know. Nice and quiet up here. *(to HARRY, who is now passing through)* Harry, the library is closed now, is it?

HARRY: Yes, it's locked.

FEJEVARY: And there's no one in here?

HARRY: No, I've been all through.

FEJEVARY: There's a committee downstairs. Oh, this is a terrible day. *(putting his things on the table)* We'd better stay up here. Harry, when my niece – when Miss Morton arrives – I want you to come and let me know. Ask her not to leave the building without seeing me.

HARRY: Yes, sir. *(he goes out)*

FEJEVARY: Well, *(wearily)* it's been a day. Not the day I was looking for.

HOLDEN: No.

FEJEVARY: You're very serene up here.

HOLDEN: Yes, I wanted to be – serene for a little while.

FEJEVARY: *(looking at the books)* Emerson. Whitman. *(with a smile)* Have they anything new to say on economics?

HOLDEN: Perhaps not; but I wanted to forget economics for a time. I came up here by myself to try and celebrate the fortieth anniversary of the founding of Morton College. *(answering the other man's look)* Yes, I confess I've been disappointed in the anniversary. As I left Memorial Hall after the exercises this morning, Emerson's words came into my mind –
'Give me truth,
For I am tired of surfaces
And die of inanition.'
Well, then I went home – *(stops, troubled)*

FEJEVARY: How is Mrs Holden?

HOLDEN: Better, thank you, but – not strong.

FEJEVARY: She needs the very best of care for a time, doesn't she?

HOLDEN: Yes. *(silent a moment)* Then, this is something more than the fortieth anniversary, you know. It's the first of the month.

FEJEVARY: And illness hasn't reduced the bills?

HOLDEN: *(shaking his head)* I didn't want this day to go like that; so I came up here to try and touch what used to be here.

FEJEVARY: But you speak despondently of us. And there's been such a fine note of optimism in the exercises. *(speaks with the heartiness of one who would keep himself assured)*

'*Give me truth . . . inanition*' misquotes the opening lines of Emerson's poem 'Blight': ' Give me truths;/For I am weary of the surfaces,/And die of inanition.'
exercises: ceremonies on special occasions, such as graduation.

HOLDEN: I didn't seem to want a fine note of optimism. (*with roughness*) I wanted
– a gleam from reality.

FEJEVARY: To me this is reality – the robust spirit created by all these young
people.

HOLDEN: Do you think it is robust? (*hand affectionately on the book before him*)
I've been reading Whitman.

FEJEVARY: This day has to be itself. Certain things go – others come; life is
change.

HOLDEN: Perhaps it's myself I'm discouraged with. Do you remember the tenth
anniversary of the founding of Morton College.

FEJEVARY: The tenth? Oh yes, that was when this library was opened.

HOLDEN: I shall never forget your father, Mr Fejevary, as he stood out there and
said the few words which gave these books to the students. Not many books,
but he seemed to baptize them in the very spirit from which books are born.

FEJEVARY: He died the following year.

HOLDEN: One felt death near. But that didn't seem the important thing. A student
who had fought for liberty for mind. Of course his face would be sensitive.
You must be very proud of your heritage.

FEJEVARY: Yes. (*a little testily*) Well, I have certainly worked for the college. I'm
doing my best now to keep it a part of these times.

HOLDEN: (*as if this has not reached him*) It was later that same afternoon I talked
with Silas Morton. We stood at this window and looked out over the valley to
the lower hill that was his home. He told me how from that hill he had for
years looked up to this one, and why there had to be a college here. I never
felt America as that old farmer made me feel it.

FEJEVARY: (*drawn by this, then shifting in irritation because he is drawn*) I'm sorry
to break in with practical things, but alas, I am a practical man – forced to be.
I too have made a fight – though the fight to finance never appears an idealistic
one. But I'm deep in that now, and I must have a little help; at least, I must
not have – stumbling-blocks.

HOLDEN: Am I a stumbling-block?

FEJEVARY: Candidly (*with a smile*) you are a little hard to finance. Here's the
situation. The time for being a little college has passed. We must take our
place as one of the important colleges – I make bold to say one of the
important universities – of the Middle West. But we have to enlarge before we
can grow. (*answering* HOLDEN's *smile*) Yes, it is ironic, but that's the way of
it. It was a nice thing to open the anniversary with fifty thousand from the steel
works – but fifty thousand dollars – nowadays – to an institution? (*waves the
fifty thousand aside*) They'll do more later, I think, when they see us coming
into our own. Meanwhile, as you know, there's this chance for an
appropriation from the state. I find that the legislature, the members who
count, are very friendly to Morton College. They like the spirit we have here.
Well, now I come to you, and you are one of the big reasons for my wanting to
put this over. Your salary makes me blush. It's all wrong that a man like you
should have these petty worries, particularly with Mrs Holden so in need of the
things a little money can do. Now this man Lewis is a reactionary. So,
naturally, he doesn't approve of you.

HOLDEN: So naturally I am to go.

FEJEVARY: Go? Not at all. What have I just been saying?

HOLDEN: Be silent, then.

FEJEVARY: Not that either – not – not really. But – be a little more discreet.
(*seeing him harden*) This is what I want to put up to you. Why not give things a
chance to mature in your own mind? Candidly, I don't feel you know just what
you do think; is it so awfully important to express – confusion?

HOLDEN: The only man who knows just what he thinks at the present moment is
the man who hasn't done any new thinking in the past ten years.

FEJEVARY: (*with a soothing gesture*) You and I needn't quarrel about it. I
understand you, but I find it a little hard to interpret you to a man like Lewis.

HOLDEN: Then why not let a man like Lewis go to thunder?

FEJEVARY: And let the college go to thunder? I'm not willing to do that. I've
made a good many sacrifices for this college. Given more money than I could
afford to give; given time and thought that I could have used for personal gain.

HOLDEN: That's true, I know.

FEJEVARY: I don't know just why I've done it. Sentiment, I suppose. I had a very
strong feeling about my father, Professor Holden. And this friend Silas
Morton. This college is the child of that friendship. Those are noble words in
our manifesto: 'Morton College was born because there came to this valley a
man who held his vision for mankind above his own advantage; and because
that man found in this valley a man who wanted beauty for his fellow-men as
he wanted no other thing.'

HOLDEN: (*taking it up*) 'Born of the fight for freedom and the aspiration to richer
living, we believe that Morton College – rising as from the soil itself – may
strengthen all those here and everywhere who fight for the life there is in
freedom, and may, to the measure it can, loosen for America the beauty that
breathes from knowledge.' (*moved by the words he has spoken*) Do you know,
I would rather do that – really do that – than – grow big.

FEJEVARY: Yes. But you see, or rather, what you don't see is, you have to look at
the world in which you find yourself. The only way to stay alive is to grow big.
It's been hard, but I have tried to – carry on.

HOLDEN: And so have I tried to carry on. But it is very hard – carrying on a
dream.

FEJEVARY: Well, I'm trying to make it easier.

HOLDEN: Make it easier by destroying the dream?

FEJEVARY: Not at all. What I want is scope for dreams.

HOLDEN: Are you sure we'd have the dreams after we've paid this price for the
scope?

FEJEVARY: Now let's not get rhetorical with one another.

HOLDEN: Mr Fejevary, you have got to let me be as honest with you as you say
you are being with me. You have got to let me say what I feel.

FEJEVARY: Certainly. That's why I wanted this talk with you.

HOLDEN: You say you have made sacrifices for Morton College. So have I.

FEJEVARY: How well I know that.

HOLDEN: You don't know all of it. I'm not sure you understand any of it.

FEJEVARY: (*charmingly*) Oh, I think you're hard on me.

HOLDEN: I spoke of the tenth anniversary. I was a young man then, just home from Athens. (*pulled back into an old feeling*) I don't know why I felt I had to go to Greece. I knew then that I was going to teach something within sociology, and I didn't want anything I felt about beauty to be left out of what I formulated about society. The Greeks –

FEJEVARY: (*as* HOLDEN *has paused before what he sees*) I remember you told me the Greeks were the passion of your student days.

HOLDEN: Not so much because they created beauty, but because they were able to let beauty flow into their lives – to create themselves in beauty. So as a romantic young man (*smiles*), it seemed if I could go where they had been – what I had felt might take form. Anyway, I had a wonderful time there. Oh, what wouldn't I give to have again that feeling of life's infinite possibilities!

FEJEVARY: (*nodding*) A youthful feeling.

HOLDEN: (*softly*) I like youth. Well, I was just back, visiting my sister here, at the time of the tenth anniversary. I had a chance then to go to Harvard as instructor. A good chance, for I would have been under a man who liked me. But that afternoon I heard your father speak about books. I talked with Silas Morton. I found myself telling him about Greece. No one had ever felt it as he felt it. It seemed to become of the very bone of him.

FEJEVARY: (*affectionately*) I know how he used to do.

HOLDEN: He put his hands on my shoulders. He said, 'Young man, don't go away. We need you here. Give us this great thing you've got!' And so I stayed, for I felt that here was soil in which I could grow, and that one's whole life was not too much to give to a place with roots like that. (*a little bitterly*) Forgive me if this seems rhetoric.

FEJEVARY: (*a gesture of protest. Silent a moment*) You make it – hard for me. (*with exasperation*) Don't you think I'd like to indulge myself in an exalted mood? And why don't I? I can't afford it – not now. Won't you have a little patience? And faith – faith that the thing we want will be there for us after we've worked our way through the woods. We are in the woods now. It's going to take our combined brains to get us out. I don't mean just Morton College.

HOLDEN: No – America. As to getting out, I think you are all wrong.

FEJEVARY: That's one of your sweeping statements, Holden. Nobody's all wrong. Even you aren't.

HOLDEN: And in what ways am I wrong – from the standpoint of your Senator Lewis?

FEJEVARY: He's not my Senator Lewis, he's the state's, and we have to take him as he is. Why, he objects, of course, to your radical activities. He spoke of your defence of conscientious objectors.

HOLDEN: (*slowly*) I think a man who is willing to go to prison for what he believes has stuff in him no college needs turn its back on.

FEJEVARY: Well, he doesn't agree with you – nor do I.

HOLDEN: (*still quietly*) And I think a society which permits things to go on which I can prove go on in our federal prisons had better stop and take a fresh look at itself. To stand for that and then talk of democracy and idealism – oh, it shows no mentality, for one thing.

FEJEVARY: (*easily*) I presume the prisons do need a cleaning up. As to Fred

Jordan, you can't expect me to share your admiration. Our own Fred – my nephew Fred Morton, went to France and gave his life. There's some little courage, Holden, in doing that.

HOLDEN: I'm not trying to belittle it. But he had the whole spirit of his age with him – fortunate boy. The man who stands outside the idealism of this time –

FEJEVARY: Takes a good deal upon himself, I should say.

HOLDEN: There isn't any other such loneliness. You know in your heart it's a noble courage.

FEJEVARY: It lacks – humility. (HOLDEN *laughs scoffingly*) And I think you lack it. I'm asking you to co-operate with me for the good of Morton College.

HOLDEN: Why not do it the other way? You say enlarge that we may grow. That's false. It isn't of the nature of growth. Why not do it the way of Silas Morton and Walt Whitman – each man being his purest and intensest self. I was full of this fervour when you came in. I'm more and more disappointed in our students. They're empty – flippant. No sensitive moment opens them to beauty. No exaltation makes them – what they hadn't known they were. I concluded some of the fault must be mine. The only students I reach are the Hindus. Perhaps Madeline Morton – I don't quite make her out. I too must have gone into a dead stratum. But I can get back. Here alone this afternoon – (*softly*) I was back.

FEJEVARY: I think we'll have to let the Hindus go

HOLDEN: (*astonished*) *Go?* Our best students?

FEJEVARY: This college is for Americans. I'm not going to have foreign revolutionists come here and block the things I've spent my life working for.

HOLDEN: I don't seem to know what you mean at all.

FEJEVARY: Why, that disgraceful performance this morning. I can settle Madeline all right. (*looking at his watch*) She should be here by now. But I'm convinced our case before the legislature will be stronger with the Hindus out of here.

HOLDEN: Well, I seem to have missed something – disgraceful performance – the Hindus, Madeline – (*stops, bewildered*)

FEJEVARY: You mean to say you don't know about the disturbance out here?

HOLDEN: I went right home after the address. Then came up here alone.

FEJEVARY: Upon my word, you do lead a serene life. While you've been sitting here in contemplation I've been to the police court – trying to get my niece out of jail. That's what comes of having radicals around.

HOLDEN: What happened?

FEJEVARY: One of our beloved Hindus made himself obnoxious on the campus. Giving out handbills about freedom for India – howling over deportation. Our American boys wouldn't stand for it. A policeman saw the fuss – came up and started to put the Hindu in his place.Then Madeline rushes in, and it ended in her pounding the policeman with her tennis racket.

HOLDEN: Madeline Morton did that!

FEJEVARY: (*sharply*) You seem pleased.

HOLDEN: I am – interested.

FEJEVARY: Well, I'm not interested. I'm disgusted. My niece mixing up in a free-for-all fight and getting taken to the police station! It's the first disgrace we've ever had in our family.

HOLDEN: (*as one who has been given courage*) Wasn't there another disgrace?
FEJEVARY: What do you mean?
HOLDEN: When your father fought his government and was banished from his country.
FEJEVARY: That was not a disgrace!
HOLDEN: (*as if in surprise*) Wasn't it?
FEJEVARY: See here, Holden, you can't talk to me like that.
HOLDEN: I don't admit you can talk to me as you please and that I can't talk to you. I'm a professor – not a servant.
FEJEVARY: Yes, and you're a damned difficult professor. I certainly have tried to –
HOLDEN: (*smiling*) Handle me?
FEJEVARY: I ask you this. Do you know any other institution where you could sit and talk with the executive head as you have here with me?
HOLDEN: I don't know. Perhaps not.
FEJEVARY: Then be reasonable. No one is entirely free. That's naïve. It's rather egotistical to want to be. We're held by our relations to others – by our obligations to the (*vaguely*) – the ultimate thing. Come now – you admit certain dissatisfactions with yourself, so – why not go with intensity into just the things you teach – and not touch quite so many other things?
HOLDEN: I couldn't teach anything if I didn't feel free to go wherever that thing took me. Thirty years ago I was asked to come to this college precisely because my science was not in isolation, because of my vivid feeling of us as a moment in a long sweep, because of my faith in the greater beauty our further living may unfold.
            (HARRY *enters.*)
HARRY: Excuse me. Miss Morton is here now, Mr Fejevary.
FEJEVARY: (*frowns, hesitates*) Ask her to come up here in five minutes (*After* HARRY *has gone*) I think we've thrown a scare into Madeline. I thought as long as she'd been taken to jail it would be no worse for us to have her stay there awhile. She's been held since one o'clock. That ought to teach her reason.
HOLDEN: Is there a case against her?
FEJEVARY: No, I got it fixed up. Explained that it was just college girl foolishness – wouldn't happen again. One reason I wanted this talk with you first, if I do have any trouble with Madeline I want you to help me.
HOLDEN: Oh, I can't do that.
FEJEVARY: You aren't running out and clubbing the police. Tell her she'll have to think things over and express herself with a little more dignity.
HOLDEN: I ask to be excused from being present while you talk with her.
FEJEVARY: But why not stay in the library – in case I should need you. Just take your books over to the east alcove and go on with what you were doing when I came in.
HOLDEN: (*with a faint smile*) I fear I can hardly do that. As to Madeline –
FEJEVARY: You don't want to see the girl destroy herself, do you? I confess I've always worried about Madeline. If my sister had lived – But Madeline's mother died, you know, when she was a baby. Her father – well, you and I talked that

over just the other day – there's no getting to him. Fred never worried me a bit – just the fine normal boy. But Madeline – (*with an effort throwing it off*) Oh, it'll be all right, I haven't a doubt. And it'll be all right between you and me, won't it? Caution over a hard strip of the road, then – bigger things ahead.

HOLDEN: (*slowly, knowing what it may mean*) I shall continue to do all I can toward getting Fred Jordan out of prison. It's a disgrace to America that two years after the war closes he should be kept there – much of the time in solitary confinement – because he couldn't believe in war. It's small – vengeful – it's the Russia of the Czars. I shall do what is in my power to fight the deportation of Gurkul Singh. And certainly I shall leave no stone unturned if you persist in your amazing idea of dismissing the other Hindus from college. For what – I ask you? Dismissed – for *what?* Because they love liberty enough to give their lives to it! The day you dismiss them, burn our high-sounding manifesto, Mr Fejevary, and admit that Morton College now sells her soul to the – committee on appropriations!

FEJEVARY: Well, you force me to be as specific as you are. If you do these things, I can no longer fight for you.

HOLDEN: Very well then, I go.

FEJEVARY: Go where?

HOLDEN: I don't know – at the moment.

FEJEVARY: I fear you'll find it harder than you know. Meanwhile, what of your family?

HOLDEN: We will have to manage some way.

FEJEVARY: It is not easy for a woman whose health – in fact, whose life – is a matter of the best of care to 'manage some way'. (*with real feeling*) What is an intellectual position alongside that reality? You'd like, of course, to be just what you want to be – but isn't there something selfish in that satisfaction? I'm talking as a friend now – you must know that. You and I have a good many ties, Holden. I don't believe you know how much Mrs Fejevary thinks of Mrs Holden.

HOLDEN: She has been very, very good to her.

FEJEVARY: And will be. She cares for her. And our children have been growing up together – I love to watch it. Isn't that the reality? Doing for them as best we can, making sacrifices of – of *every* kind. Don't let some tenuous, remote thing destroy this flesh and blood thing.

HOLDEN: (*as one fighting to keep his head above water*) Honesty is not a tenuous, remote thing.

FEJEVARY: There's a kind of honesty in selfishness. We can't always have it. Oh, I used to – go through things. But I've struck a pace – one does – and goes ahead.

HOLDEN: Forgive me, but I don't think you've had certain temptations to – selfishness.

FEJEVARY: How do you know what I've had? You have no way of knowing what's in me – what other thing I might have been? You know my heritage; you think that's left nothing? But I find myself here in America. I love those dependent on me. My wife – who's used to a certain manner of living; my children – who are to become part of the America of their time. I've never said this to another human being – I've never looked at myself – but it's pretty arrogant to think you're the only man who has made a sacrifice to fit himself into the age in which he lives. I hear Madeline. This hasn't left me in very good form for talking with her. Please don't go away. Just –

    (MADELINE *comes in, right. She has her tennis racket. Nods to the two men.* HOLDEN *goes out, left.*)

MADELINE: (*looking after* HOLDEN – *feeling something going on. Then turning to her uncle, who is still looking after* HOLDEN) You wanted to speak to me, Uncle Felix?

FEJEVARY: Of course I want to speak to you.

MADELINE: I feel just awfully sorry about – banging up my racket like this. The second time it came down on this club. Why do they carry those things? Perfectly fantastic, I'll say, going around with a club. But as long as you were asking me what I wanted for my birthday –

FEJEVARY: Madeline, I am not here to discuss your birthday.

MADELINE: I'm sorry – (*smiles*) to hear that.

FEJEVARY: You don't seem much chastened.

MADELINE: Chastened? Was that the idea? Well, if you think that keeping a person where she doesn't want to be chastens her! I never felt less 'chastened' than when I walked out of that slimy spot and looked across the street at your nice bank. I should think you'd hate to – (*with friendly concern*) Why, Uncle Felix, you look tired out.

FEJEVARY: I am tired out, Madeline. I've had a nerve-racking day.

MADELINE: Isn't that too bad? Those speeches were so boresome, and that old senator person – wasn't he a stuff? But can't you go home now and let auntie give you tea and –

FEJEVARY: (*sharply*) Madeline, have you no intelligence? Hasn't it occurred to you that your performance would worry me a little?

MADELINE: I suppose it was a nuisance. And on such a busy day. (*changing*) But if you're going to worry, Horace is the one you should worry about. (*answering his look*) Why, he got it all up. He made me ashamed!

FEJEVARY: And you're not at all ashamed of what you have done?

MADELINE: Ashamed? Why – no.

FEJEVARY: Then you'd better be! A girl who rushes in and assaults an officer!

MADELINE: (*earnestly explaining it*) But, Uncle Felix, I had to stop him. No one else did.

FEJEVARY: Madeline, I don't know whether you're trying to be naïve –

MADELINE: (*angrily*) Well, I'm *not*. I like that! I think I'll go home.

FEJEVARY: I think you will not! It's stupid of you not to know this is serious. You could be dismissed from school for what you did.

MADELINE: Well, I'm good and ready to be dismissed from any school that would dismiss for that!

FEJEVARY: (*in a new manner – quietly, from feeling*) Madeline, have you no love for this place?

MADELINE: (*doggedly, after thinking*) Yes, I have. (*she sits down*) And I don't know why I have.

FEJEVARY: Certainly it's not strange. If ever a girl had a background, Morton

College is Madeline Fejevary Morton's background. (*he too now seated by the table*) Do you remember your Grandfather Morton?

MADELINE: Not very well. (*a quality which seems sullenness*) I couldn't bear to look at him. He shook so.

FEJEVARY: (*turning away, real pain*) Oh – how cruel!

MADELINE: (*surprised, gently*) Cruel? Me – cruel?

FEJEVARY: Not just you. The way it passes – (*to himself*) so *fast* it passes.

MADELINE: I'm sorry. (*troubled*) You see, he was too old then –

FEJEVARY: (*his hand up to stop her*) I wish I could bring him back for a moment, so you could see what he was before he (*bitterly*) shook so. He was a powerful man, who was as real as the earth. He was strangely of the earth, as if something went from it to him. (*looking at her intently*) Queer you should be the one to have no sentiment about him, for you and he – sometimes when I'm with you it's as if – he were near. He had no personal ambition, Madeline. He was ambitious for the earth and its people. I wonder if you can realize what it meant to my father – in a strange land, where he might so easily have been misunderstood, pushed down, to find a friend like that? It wasn't so much the material things – though Uncle Silas was always making them right – and as if – oh, hardly conscious what he was doing – so little it mattered. It was the way he *got* father, and by that very valuing kept alive what was there to value. Why, he literally laid this country at my father's feet – as if that was what this country was for, as if it made up for the hard early things – for the wrong things.

MADELINE: He must really have been a pretty nice old party. No doubt I would have hit it off with him all right. I don't seem to hit it off with the – speeches about him. Somehow I want to say, 'Oh, give us a rest.'

FEJEVARY: (*offended*) And that, I presume, is what you want to say to me.

MADELINE: No, no, I didn't mean you, Uncle. Though (*hesitatingly*) I was wondering how you could think you were talking on your side.

FEJEVARY: What do you mean – my side?

MADELINE: Oh, I don't – exactly. That's nice about him being – of the earth. Sometimes when I'm out for a tramp – way off by myself – yes, I know. And I wonder if that doesn't explain his feeling about the Indians. Father told me how grandfather took it to heart about the Indians.

FEJEVARY: He felt it as you'd feel it if it were your brother. So he must give his choicest land to the thing we might become. 'Then maybe I can lie under the same sod with the red boys and not be ashamed.'

(MADELINE *nods, appreciatively.*)

MADELINE: Yes, that's really – all right.

FEJEVARY: (*irritated by what seems charily stated approval*) 'All right!' Well, I am not willing to let this man's name pass from our time. And it seems rather bitter that Silas Morton's granddaughter should be the one to stand in my way.

MADELINE: Why, Uncle Felix, I'm not standing in your way. Of course I wouldn't do that. I – (*rather bashfully*) I love the Hill. I was thinking about it in jail. I got fuddled on direction in there, so I asked the woman who hung around which way was College Hill. 'Right through there', she said. A blank wall. I sat and looked through that wall – long time. (*she looks front, again looking through that blank wall*) It was all – kind of funny. Then later she came and told me you were out there, and I thought it was corking of you to come and tell them they couldn't put that over on College Hill. And I know Bakhshish will appreciate it too. I wonder where he went?

FEJEVARY: Went? I fancy he won't go much of anywhere to-night.

MADELINE: What do you mean?

FEJEVARY: Why, he's held for this hearing, of course.

MADELINE: You mean – you came and got just me – and left him there?

FEJEVARY: Certainly.

MADELINE: (*rising*) Then I'll have to go and get him!

FEJEVARY: Madeline, don't be so absurd. You don't get people out of jail by stopping in and calling for them.

MADELINE: But you got me.

FEJEVARY: Because of years of influence. At that, it wasn't simple. Things of this nature are pretty serious nowadays. It was only your ignorance got you out.

MADELINE: I do seem ignorant. While you were fixing it up for me, why didn't you arrange for him too?

FEJEVARY: Because I am not in the business of getting foreign revolutionists out of jail.

MADELINE: But he didn't do as much as I did.

FEJEVARY: It isn't what he did. It's what he is. We don't want him here.

MADELINE: Well, I guess I'm not for that!

FEJEVARY: May I ask why you have appointed yourself guardian of these strangers?

MADELINE: Perhaps because they are strangers.

FEJEVARY: Well, they're the wrong kind of strangers.

MADELINE: Is it true that the Hindu who was here last year is to be deported? Is America going to turn him over to the government he fought?

FEJEVARY: I have an idea they will all be deported. I'm not so sorry this thing happened. It will get them into the courts – and I don't think they have money to fight.

MADELINE: (*giving it clean and straight*) Gee, I think that's rotten!

FEJEVARY: Quite likely your inelegance will not affect it one way or the other.

MADELINE: (*she has taken her seat again, is thinking it out*) I'm twenty-one next Tuesday. Isn't it on my twenty-first birthday I get that money Grandfather Morton left me?

FEJEVARY: What are you driving at?

MADELINE: (*simply*) They can have my money.

FEJEVARY: Are you crazy? What *are* these people to you?

MADELINE: They're people from the other side of the world who came here believing in us, drawn from the far side of the world by things we say about ourselves. Well, I'm going to pretend – just for fun – that the things we say about ourselves are true. So if you'll – arrange so I can get it, Uncle Felix, as soon as it's mine.

FEJEVARY: And this is what you say to me at the close of my years of trusteeship! If you could know how I've nursed that little legacy along – until now it is – (*breaking off in anger*) I shall not permit you to destroy yourself!

MADELINE: (*quietly*) I don't see how you can keep me from 'destroying myself'.

FEJEVARY: (*looking at her, seeing that this may be true. In genuine amazement, and hurt*) Why – but it's incredible. Have I – has my house – been nothing to you all these years?

MADELINE: I've had my best times at your house. Things wouldn't have been – very gay for me – without you all – though Horace gets my goat!

FEJEVARY: And does your Aunt Isabel – 'get your goat'?

MADELINE: I love auntie. (*rather resentfully*) You know that. What has that got to do with it?

FEJEVARY: So you are going to use Silas Morton's money to knife his college.

MADELINE: Oh, Uncle Felix, that's silly.

FEJEVARY: It's a long way from silly. You know a little about what I'm trying to do – this appropriation that would assure our future. If Silas Morton's granddaughter casts in her lot with revolutionists, Morton College will get no help from the state. Do you know enough about what you are doing to assume this responsibility?

MADELINE: I am not casting 'in my lot with revolutionists'. If it's true, as you say, that you have to have money in order to get justice –

FEJEVARY: I didn't say it!

MADELINE: Why, you did, Uncle Felix. You said so. And if it's true that these strangers in our country are going to be abused because they're poor, – what else could I do with my money and not feel like a skunk?

FEJEVARY: (*trying a different tack, laughing*) Oh, you're a romantic girl, Madeline – skunk and all. Rather nice, at that. But the thing is perfectly fantastic, from every standpoint. You speak as if you had millions. And if you did, it wouldn't matter, not really. You are going against the spirit of this country; with or without money, that can't be done. Take a man like Professor Holden. He's radical in his sympathies – but does he run out and club the police?

MADELINE: (*in a smouldering way*) I thought America was a democracy.

FEJEVARY: We have just fought a great war for democracy.

MADELINE: Well, is that any reason for not having it?

FEJEVARY: I should think you would have a little emotion about the war – about America – when you consider where your brother is.

MADELINE: Fred had – all kinds of reasons for going to France. He wanted a trip. (*answering his exclamation*) Why, he *said* so. Heavens, Fred didn't make speeches about himself. Wanted to see Paris – poor kid, he never did see Paris. Wanted to be with a lot of fellows – knock the Kaiser's block off – end war, get a French girl. It was all mixed up – the way things are. But Fred was a pretty decent sort. I'll say so. He had such kind, honest eyes. (*this has somehow said itself; her own eyes close and what her shut eyes see makes feeling hot*) One thing I do know! Fred never went over the top and out to back up the argument you're making now!

FEJEVARY: (*stiffly*) Very well, I will discontinue the argument I'm making now. I've been trying to save you from – pretty serious things. The regret of having stood in the way of Morton College – (*his voice falling*) the horror of having driven your father insane.

MADELINE: *What?*

FEJEVARY: One more thing would do it. Just the other day I was talking with
Professor Holden about your father. His idea of him relates back to the
pioneer life – another price paid for this country. The lives back of him were
too hard. Your great-grandmother Morton – the first white woman in this
region – she dared too much, was too lonely, feared and bore too much. They
did it, for the task gave them a courage for the task. But it – left a scar.

MADELINE: And father is that – (*can hardly say it*) – scar. (*fighting the idea*) But
Grandfather Morton was not like that.

FEJEVARY: No; he had the vision of the future; he was robust with feeling for
others. (*gently*) But Holden feels your father is the – dwarfed pioneer child.
The way he concentrates on corn – excludes all else – as if unable to free
himself from their old battle with the earth.

MADELINE: (*almost crying*) I think it's pretty terrible to – wish all that on poor
father.

FEJEVARY: Well, my dear child, it's life has 'wished it on him'. It's just one other
way of paying the price for his country. We needn't get it for nothing. I feel
that all our chivalry should go to your father in his – heritage of loneliness.

MADELINE: Father couldn't always have been – dwarfed. Mother wouldn't have
cared for him if he had always been – like that.

FEJEVARY: No, if he could have had love to live in. But no endurance for losing it.
Too much had been endured just before life got to him.

MADELINE: Do you know, Uncle Felix – I'm afraid that's true? (*he nods*)
Sometimes when I'm with father I feel those things near – the – the too much –
the too hard, – feel them as you'd feel the cold. And now that it's different –
easier – he can't come into the world that's been earned. Oh, I wish I could
help him!

> (*As they sit there together, now for the first time really together, there
> is a shrill shout of derision from outside.*)

MADELINE: What's that? (*a whistled call*) Horace! That's Horace's call. That's for
his gang. Are they going to start something now that will get Atma in jail?

FEJEVARY: More likely he's trying to start something. (*they are both listening
intently*) I don't think our boys will stand much more.

> (*A scoffing whoop.* MADELINE *springs to the window; he reaches it
> ahead and holds it.*

FEJEVARY: This window stays closed.

> (*She starts to go away, he takes hold of her.*)

MADELINE: You think you can keep me in here?

FEJEVARY: Listen, Madeline – plain, straight truth. If you go out there and get in
trouble a second time, I can't make it right for you.

MADELINE: You needn't!

FEJEVARY: You don't know what it means. These things are not child's play – not
today. You could get twenty years in prison for things you'll say if you rush out
there now. (*she laughs*) You laugh because you're ignorant. Do you know that
in America today there are women in our prisons for saying no more than
you've said here to me!

MADELINE: Then you ought to be ashamed of yourself!

FEJEVARY: I? Ashamed of myself?

MADELINE: Yes! Aren't you an American? (*a whistle*) Isn't that a policeman's whistle? Are *they* coming back? Are they hanging around here to – (*pulling away from her uncle as he turns to look, she jumps up in the deep sill and throws open the window. Calling down*) Here – Officer – *You* – Let that boy alone!

FEJEVARY: (*going left, calling sharply*) Holden. Professor Holden – here – quick!

VOICE: (*coming up from below, outside*) Who says so?

MADELINE: I say so!

VOICE: And who are you talking for?

MADELINE: I am talking for Morton College!

FEJEVARY: (*returning – followed, reluctantly, by* HOLDEN) Indeed you are not. Close that window or you'll be expelled from Morton College.
    (*Sounds of a growing crowd outside.*)

VOICE: Didn't I see you at the station?

MADELINE: Sure you saw me at the station. And you'll see me there again, if you come bullying around here. You're not what this place is for! (*her uncle comes up behind, right, and tries to close the window – she holds it out*) My grandfather gave this hill to Morton College – a place where anybody – from any land – can come and say what he believes to be true! Why, you poor simp – this is America! Beat it from here! Atna! Don't let him take hold of you like that! He has no right to – Oh, let me *down* there!
    (*Springs down, would go off right, her uncle spreads out his arms to block that passage. She turns to go the other way.*)

FEJEVARY: Holden! Bring her to her senses. Stand there. (HOLDEN *has not moved from the place he entered, left, and so blocks the doorway*) Don't let her pass.
    (*Shouts of derision outside.*)

MADELINE: You think you can keep me in here – with that going on out there?
    (*Moves nearer* HOLDEN, *stands there before him, taut, looking him straight in the eye. After a moment, slowly, as one compelled, he steps aside for her to pass. Sound of her running footsteps. The two men's eyes meet. A door slams.*)
                    CURTAIN

ACT IV

SCENE: *At the* MORTON *place, the same room in which* SILAS MORTON *told his friend* FELIX FEJEVARY *of his plan for the hill. The room has not altogether changed since that day in 1879. The table around which they dreamed for the race is in its old place. One of the old chairs is there, the other two are modern chairs. In a corner is the rocker in which* GRANDMOTHER MORTON *sat. This is early afternoon, a week after the events of Act II.*

MADELINE *is sitting at the table, in her hand a torn, wrinkled piece of brown paper – peering at writing almost too fine to read. After a moment her hand goes out to a beautiful dish on the table – an old dish of coloured Hungarian glass. She is about to take something from this, but instead lets her hand rest an instant on the dish itself.*

Then turns and through the open door looks out at the hill, sitting where her
GRANDFATHER MORTON *sat when he looked out at the hill.*
Her father, IRA MORTON, *appears outside, walking past the window, left. He
enters, carrying a grain sack, partly filled. He seems hardly aware of* MADELINE,
*but taking a chair near the door, turned from her, opens the sack and takes out a
couple of ears of corn. As he is bent over them, examining in a shrewd, greedy way,*
MADELINE *looks at that lean, tormented, rather desperate profile, the look of one
confirming a thing she fears. Then takes up her piece of paper.*

MADELINE: Do you remember Fred Jordan, father? Friend of our Fred – and of
    mine?
IRA: (*not wanting to take his mind from the corn*) No. I don't remember him. (*his
    voice has that timbre of one not related to others*)
MADELINE: He's in prison now.
IRA: Well I can't help that. (*after taking out another ear*) This is the best corn I ever
    had. (*he says it gloatingly to himself*)
MADELINE: He got this letter out to me – written on this scrap of paper. They
    don't give him paper. (*peering*) Written so fine I can hardly read it. He's in
    what they call 'the hold', father – a punishment cell. (*with difficulty reading it*)
    It's two and a half feet at one end, three feet at the other, and six feet long.
    He'd been there ten days when he wrote this. He gets two slices of bread a
    day; he gets water; that's all he gets. This because he balled the deputy warden
    out for chaining another prisoner up by the wrists.
IRA: Well, he'd better a-minded his own business. And you better mind yours. I've
    got no money to spend in the courts. (*with excitement*) I'll not mortgage this
    farm! It's been clear since the day my father's father got it from the
    government – and it stays clear – till I'm gone. It grows the best corn in the
    state – best corn in the Mississippi Valley. Not for *anything* – you hear me? –
    would I mortgage this farm my father handed down to me.
MADELINE: (*hurt*) Well, father, I'm not asking you to.
IRA: Then go and see your Uncle Felix. Make it up with him. He'll help you – if you
    say you're sorry.
MADELINE: I'll not go to Uncle Felix.
IRA: Who will you go to then? (*pause*) Who will help you then? (*again he waits*)
    You come before this United States Commissioner with no one behind you,
    he'll hold you for the grand jury. Judge Watkins told Felix there's not a doubt
    of it. You know what that means? It means you're on your way to a cell. Nice
    thing for a Morton, people who've had their own land since we got it from the
    Indians. What's the matter with your uncle? Ain't he always been good to
    you? I'd like to know what things would 'a' been for you without Felix and
    Isabel and all their friends. You want to think a little. You like good times too
    well to throw all that away.
MADELINE: I do like good times. So does Fred Jordan like good times. (*smooths
    the wrinkled paper*) I don't know anybody – unless it is myself – loves to be
    out, as he does. (*she tries to look out, but cannot; sits very still, seeing what it is
    pain to see. Rises, goes to that corner closet, the same one from which* SILAS
    MORTON *took the deed to the hill. She gets a yard stick, looks in a box and*

finds a piece of chalk. On the floor she marks off FRED JORDAN's *cell. Slowly, at the end left unchalked, as for a door, she goes in. Her hand goes up as against a wall; looks at her other hand, sees it is out too far, brings it in, giving herself the width of the cell. Walks its length, halts, looks up.*) And one window – too high up to see out.

> (*In the moment she stands there, she is in that cell; she is all the people who are in those cells.* EMIL JOHNSON *appears from outside; he is the young man brought up on a farm, a crudely Americanized Swede.*)

MADELINE: (*stepping out of the cell door, and around it*) Hello, Emil.

EMIL: How are you, Madeline? How do, Mr Morton. (IRA *barely nods and does not turn. In an excited manner he begins gathering up the corn he has taken from the sack.* EMIL *turns back to* MADELINE) Well, I'm just from the courthouse. Looks like you and I might take a ride together, Madeline. You come before the Commissioner at four.

IRA: What have you got to do with it?

MADELINE: Oh, Emil has a courthouse job now, father. He's part of the law.

IRA: Well, he's not going to take you to the law! Anybody else – not Emil Johnson!

MADELINE: (*astonished – and gently, to make up for his rudeness*) Why – father, why not Emil? Since I'm going, I think it's nice to go in with someone I know – with a neighbour like Emil.

IRA: If *this* is what he lived for! If this is why –
> (*He twists the ear of corn until some of the kernels drip off.*
> MADELINE *and* EMIL *look at one another in bewilderment.*)

EMIL: It's too bad anybody has to take Madeline in. I should think your uncle could fix it up. (*low*) And with your father taking it like this – (*to help* IRA) That's fine corn, Mr Morton. My corn's getting better all the time, but I'd like to get some of this for seed.

IRA: (*rising and turning on him*) *You* get my corn? I raise this corn for you? (*not to them – his mind now going where it is shut off from any other mind*) If I could make the *wind* stand still! I want to *turn the wind around*.

MADELINE: (*going to him*) Why – father. I don't understand at all.

IRA: Don't understand. Nobody understands. (*a curse with a sob in it*) God damn the wind!
> (*Sits down, his back to them.*)

EMIL: (*after a silence*) Well, I'll go. (*but he continues to look at* IRA, *who is holding the sack of corn shut, as if someone may take it*) Too bad – (*stopped by a sign from* MADELINE, *not to speak of it*) Well, I was saying, I have go on to Beard's Crossing. I'll stop for you on my way back. (*confidentially*) Couldn't you telephone your uncle? He could do something. You don't know what you're going up against. You heard what the Hindus got, I suppose.

MADELINE: No. I haven't seen anyone to-day.

EMIL: They're held for the grand jury. They're locked up now. No bail for *them*. I've got the inside dope about them. They're going to get what this country can hand 'em; then after we've given them a nice little taste of prison life in America, they're going to be sent back home – to see what India can treat them to.

MADELINE: Why are you so pleased about this, Emil?

EMIL: Pleased? It's nothin' to me – I'm just telling you. Guess you don't know much about the Espionage Act or you'd go and make a little friendly call on your uncle. When your case comes to trial – and Judge Lenon may be on the bench – (*whistles*) He's one fiend for Americanism. But if your uncle was to tell the right parties that you're just a girl, and didn't realize what you were saying –

MADELINE: I did realize what I was saying, and every word you've just said makes me know I meant what I said. I said if this was what our country has come to, then I'm not for our country. I said that – and a-plenty more – and I'll say it again!

EMIL: Well – gee, you don't know what it means.

MADELINE: I do know what it means, but it means not being a coward.

EMIL: Oh, well – Lord, you can't say everything you think. If everybody did that, things'd be worse off than they are now.

MADELINE: Once in a while you have to say what you think – or hate yourself.

EMIL: (*with a grin*) Then hate yourself.

MADELINE: (*smiling too*) No thank you; it spoils my fun.

EMIL: Well, look-a-here, Madeline, aren't you spoiling your fun now? You're a girl who liked to be out. Ain't I seen you from our place, with this one and that one, sometimes all by yourself, strikin' out over the country as if you was crazy about it? How'd you like to be where you couldn't even see out?

MADELINE: (*a step nearer the cell*) There oughtn't to be such places.

EMIL: Oh, well – Jesus, if you're going to talk about that –! You can't change the way things are.

MADELINE: (*quietly*) Why can't I?

EMIL: Well, say, who do you think you are?

MADELINE: I think I'm an American. And for that reason I think I have something to say about America.

EMIL: Huh! America'll lock you up for your pains.

MADELINE: All right. If it's come to that, maybe I'd rather be a locked-up American than a free American.

EMIL: I don't think you'd like the place, Madeline. There's not much tennis played there. Jesus – what's Hindus?

MADELINE: You aren't really asking Jesus, are you, Emil? (*smiles*) You mightn't like his answer.

EMIL: (*from the door*) Take a tip. Telephone your uncle.
                    (*He goes.*)

IRA: (*not looking at her*) There might be a fine, and they'd come down on me and take my land.

MADELINE: Oh, no, father, I think not. Anyway, I have a little money of my own. Grandfather Morton left me something. Have you forgotten that?

IRA: No. No, I know he left you something. (*the words seem to bother him*) I know he left you something.

MADELINE: I get it to-day. (*wistfully*) This is my birthday, father. I'm twenty-one.

IRA: Your birthday? Twenty-one? (*in pain*) Was that twenty-one years ago? (*it is not to his daughter this has turned him*)

MADELINE: It's the first birthday I can remember that I haven't had a party.

IRA: It was your Aunt Isabel gave you your parties.

MADELINE: Yes.

IRA: Well, you see now.

MADELINE: (*stoutly*) Oh, well, I don't need a party. I'm grown up now.
    (*She reaches out for the old Hungarian dish on the table; holding it,
    she looks to her father, whose back is still turned. Her face tender, she
    is about to speak when he speaks.*)

IRA: Grown up now – and going off and leaving me alone. You too – the last one.
    And – *what for?* (*turning, looking around the room as for those long gone*)
    There used to be so many in this house. My grandmother. She sat there.
    (*pointing to the place near the open door*) Fine days like this – in that chair
    (*points to the rocker*) she'd sit there – tell me stories of the Indians. Father. It
    wasn't ever lonely where father was. Then Madeline Fejevary – my Madeline
    came to this house. Lived with me in this house. Then one day she – walked
    out of this house. Through that door – through the field – out of this house.
    (*bitter silence*) Then Fred – out of this house. Now you. With Emil Johnson!
    (*insanely, and almost with relief at leaving things more sane*) Don't let him
    touch my corn. If he touches one kernel of this corn! (*with the suspicion of the
    tormented mind*) I wonder where he went? How do I know he went where he
    said he was going? (*getting up*) I dunno as that south bin's locked.

MADELINE: Oh – father!

IRA: I'll find out. How do I know what he's doing?
    (*He goes out, turning left. MADELINE goes to the window and looks
    after him. A moment later, hearing someone at the door, she turns and
    finds her AUNT ISABEL, who has appeared from right. Goes swiftly
    to her, hands out.*)

MADELINE: Oh, *auntie* – I'm glad you came! It's my birthday, and I'm – lonely.

AUNT ISABEL: You dear little girl! (*again giving her a hug, which MADELINE
    returns, lovingly*) Don't I know it's your birthday? Don't think that day will
    ever get by while your Aunt Isabel's around. Just see what's here for your
    birthday. (*hands her the package she is carrying*)

MADELINE: (*with a gasp – suspecting from its shape*) Oh! (*her face aglow*) Why – is
    it?

AUNT ISABEL: (*laughing affectionately*) Foolish child, open it and see.
    (*MADELINE loosens the paper and pulls out a tennis racket.*)

MADELINE: (*excited, and moved*) Oh, aunt Isabel! that was dear of you. I
    shouldn't have thought you'd – quite do that.

AUNT ISABEL: I couldn't imagine Madeline without a racket. (*gathering up the
    paper, lightly reproachful*) But be a little careful of it, Madeline. It's meant for
    tennis balls. (*they laugh together*)

MADELINE: (*making a return with it*) It's a *peach.* (*changing*) Wonder where I'll
    play now.

AUNT ISABEL: Why, you'll play on the courts at Morton College. Who has a
    better right?

MADELINE: Oh, I don't know. It's pretty much balled up, isn't it?

AUNT ISABEL: Yes; we'll have to get it straightened out. (*gently*) It was really dreadful of you, Madeline, to rush out a second time. It isn't as if they were people who were anything to you.

MADELINE: But, auntie, they are something to me.

AUNT ISABEL: Oh, dear, that's what Horace said.

MADELINE: What's what Horace said?

AUNT ISABEL: That you must have a case on one of them.

MADELINE: That's what Horace would say. That makes me sore!

AUNT ISABEL: I'm sorry I spoke of it. Horace is absurd in some ways.

MADELINE: He's a –

AUNT ISABEL: (*stopping it with her hand*) No, he isn't. He's a headstrong boy, but a very loving one. He's dear with me, Madeline.

MADELINE: Yes. You are good to each other. (*her eyes are drawn to the cell*)

AUNT ISABEL: Of course we are. We'd be a pretty poor sort if we weren't. And these are days when we have to stand together – all of us who are the same kind of people must stand together because the thing that makes us the same kind of people is threatened.

MADELINE: Don't you think we're rather threatening it ourselves, auntie?

AUNT ISABEL: Why, no, we're fighting for it.

MADELINE: Fighting for what?

AUNT ISABEL: For Americanism; for – democracy.

MADELINE: Horace is fighting for it?

AUNT ISABEL: Well, Horace does go at it as if it were a football game, but his heart's in the right place.

MADELINE: Somehow, I don't seem to see my heart in that place.

AUNT ISABEL: In what place?

MADELINE: Where Horace's heart is.

AUNT ISABEL: It's too bad you and Horace quarrel. But you and I don't quarrel, Madeline.

MADELINE: (*again drawn to the cell*) No. You and I don't quarrel. (*she is troubled*)

AUNT ISABEL: Funny child! Do you want us to?

> (MADELINE *turns, laughing a little, takes the dish from the table, holds it out to her aunt.*)

MADELINE: Have some fudge, auntie.

AUNT ISABEL: (*taking the dish*) Do you *use* them? – the old Hungarian dishes? (*laughingly*) I'm not allowed to – your uncle is so choice of the few pieces we have. And here are you with fudge in one of them.

MADELINE: I made the fudge because – oh, I don't know, I had to do something to celebrate my birthday.

AUNT ISABEL: (*under her breath*) Dearie!

MADELINE: And then that didn't seem to – make a birthday, so I happened to see this, way up on a top shelf, and I remembered that it was my mother's. It was nice to get it down and use it – almost as if mother was giving me a birthday present.

---

to have a case on: to be infatuated with or enamoured of (OED Supp.)

AUNT ISABEL: And how she would love to give you a birthday present.

MADELINE: It was her mother's, I suppose, and they brought it from Hungary.

AUNT ISABEL: Yes. They brought only a very few things with them, and left –_oh, so many beautiful ones behind.

MADELINE: (*quietly*) Rather nice of them, wasn't it? (*her aunt waits inquiringly*) To leave their own beautiful things – their own beautiful life behind – simply because they believed life should be more beautiful for more people.

AUNT ISABEL: (*with constraint*) Yes. (*gayly turning it*) Well, now, as to the birthday. What do you suppose Sarah is doing this instant? Putting red frosting on white frosting. (*writing it with her finger*) Madeline. And what do you suppose Horace is doing? (*this a little reproachfully*) Running around buying twenty-one red candles. Twenty-two – one to grow on. Big birthday cake. Party to-night.

MADELINE: But, auntie, I don't see how I can be there.

AUNT ISABEL: Listen, dear. Now, we've got to use our wits and all pull together. Of course we'd do anything in the world rather than see you – left to outsiders. I've never seen your uncle as worried, and – truly, Madeline, as sad. Oh, my dear, it's these human things that count! What would life be without the love we have for each other?

MADELINE: The love we have for each other?

AUNT ISABEL: Why, yes, dearest. Don't turn away from me Madeline. Don't – don't be strange. I wonder if you realize how your uncle has worked to have life a happy thing for all of us? Be a little generous to him. He's had this great burden of bringing something from another day on into this day. It is not as simple as it may seem. He's done it as best he could. It will hurt him as nothing has ever hurt him if you now undo that work of his life. Truly, dear, do you feel you know enough about it to do that? Another thing: people are a little absurd out of their own places. We need to be held in our relationships – against our background – or we are – I don't know – grotesque. Come now, Madeline, where's your sense of humour? Isn't it a little absurd for you to leave home over India's form of government?

MADELINE: It's not India. It's America. A sense of humour is nothing to hide behind!

AUNT ISABEL: (*with a laugh*) I knew I wouldn't be a success at world affairs – better leave that to Professor Holden. (*a quick keen look from* MADELINE) They've driven on to the river – they'll be back for me, and then he wants to stop in for a visit with you while I take Mrs Holden for a further ride. I'm worried about her. She doesn't gain strength at all since her operation. I'm going to try keeping her out in the air all I can.

MADELINE: It's dreadful about families!

AUNT ISABEL: Dreadful? Professor Holden's devotion to his wife is one of the most beautiful things I've ever seen.

MADELINE: And is that all you see it in?

AUNT ISABEL: You mean the – responsibility it brings? Oh, well – that's what life is. Doing for one another. Sacrificing for one another.

MADELINE: I hope I never have a family.

AUNT ISABEL: Well, I hope you do. You'll miss the best of life if you don't.
Anyway, you have a family. Where is your father?

MADELINE: I don't know.

AUNT ISABEL: I'd like to see him.

MADELINE: There's no use seeing him today.

AUNT ISABEL: He's –?

MADELINE: Strange – shut in – afraid something's going to be taken from him.

AUNT ISABEL: Poor Ira. So much has been taken from him. And now you. Don't
hurt him again, Madeline. He can't bear it. You see what it does to him.

MADELINE: He has – the wrong idea about things.

AUNT ISABEL: 'The wrong idea!' Oh, my child – that's awfully young and hard.
It's so much deeper than that. Life has made him into something – something
he can't escape.

MADELINE: (*with what seems sullenness*) Well, I don't want to be made into that
thing.

AUNT ISABEL: Of course not. But you want to help him, don't you? Now, dear –
about your birthday party –

MADELINE: The United States Commissioner is giving me my birthday party.

AUNT ISABEL: Well, he'll have to put his party off. Your uncle has been thinking
it all out. We're to go to his office and you'll have a talk with him and with
Judge Watkins. He's off the state supreme bench now – practising again, and
as a favour to your uncle he will be your lawyer. You don't know how relieved
we are at this, for Judge Watkins can do – anything he wants to do, practically.
Then you and I will go on home and call up some of the crowd to come in and
dance to-night. We have some beautiful new records. There's a Hungarian
waltz –

MADELINE: And what's the price of all this, auntie?

AUNT ISABEL: The – Oh, you mean – Why, simply say you felt sorry for the
Hindu students because they seemed rather alone; that you hadn't realized –
what they were, hadn't thought out what you were saying –

MADELINE: And that I'm sorry and will never do it again.

AUNT ISABEL: I don't know that you need say that. It would be gracious, I think,
to indicate it.

MADELINE: I'm sorry you – had the cake made. I suppose you can eat it, anyway.
I (*turning away*) – can't eat it.

AUNT ISABEL: Why – Madeline.

(*Seeing how she has hurt her,* MADELINE *goes out to her aunt.*)

MADELINE: Auntie, dear! I'm sorry – if I hurt your feelings.

AUNT ISABEL: (*quick to hold out a loving hand, laughing a little*) They've been
good birthday cakes, haven't they, Madeline?

MADELINE: (*she now trying not to cry*) I don't know – what I'd have done without
them. Don't know – what I will do without them. I don't – see it.

AUNT ISABEL: Don't try to. Please don't see it! Just let me go on helping you.
That's all I ask. (*she draws* MADELINE *to her*) Ah, dearie, I held you when
you were a little baby without your mother. All those years count for
something, Madeline. There's just nothing to life if years of love don't count
for something. (*listening*) I think I hear them. And here are we, weeping like

two idiots. (MADELINE *brushes away tears,* AUNT ISABEL *arranges her veil, regaining her usual poise*) Professor Holden was hoping you'd take a tramp with him. Wouldn't that do you good? Anyway, a talk with him will be nice. I know he admires you immensely, and really – perhaps I shouldn't let you know this – sympathizes with your feeling. So I think his maturer way of looking at things will show you just the adjustment you need to become a really big and useful person. There's so much to be done in the world, Madeline. Of course we ought to make it a better world. (*in a manner of agreement with* MADELINE) I feel very strongly about all that. Perhaps we can do some things together. I'd love that. Don't think I'm hopeless! Way down deep we have the same feeling. Yes, here's Professor Holden.

    (HOLDEN *comes in. He seems older.*)

HOLDEN: And how are you, Madeline? (*holding out his hand*)

MADELINE: I'm – all right.

HOLDEN: Many happy returns of the day. (*embarrassed by her half laugh*) The birthday.

AUNT ISABEL: And did you have a nice look up the river?

HOLDEN: I never saw this country as lovely as it is to-day. Mary is just drinking it in.

AUNT ISABEL: You don't think the further ride will be too much?

HOLDEN: Oh, no – not in that car.

AUNT ISABEL: Then we'll go on – perhaps as far as Laughing Creek. If you two decide on a tramp – take that road and we'll pick you up. (*smiling warmly, she goes out*)

HOLDEN: How good she is.

MADELINE: Yes. That's just the trouble.

HOLDEN: (*with difficulty getting past this*) How about a little tramp? There'll never be another such day.

MADELINE: I used to tramp with Fred Jordan. This is where he is now. (*stepping inside the cell*) He doesn't even see out.

HOLDEN: It's all wrong that he should be where he is. But for you to stay indoors won't help him, Madeline.

MADELINE: It won't help him, but – today – I can't go out.

HOLDEN: I'm sorry, my child. When this sense of wrongs done first comes down upon one, it does crush.

MADELINE: And later you get used to it and don't care.

HOLDEN: You care. You try not to destroy yourself needlessly. (*he turns from her look*)

MADELINE: Play safe.

HOLDEN: If it's playing safe it's that one you love more than yourself be safe. It would be a luxury to – destroy one's self.

MADELINE: That sounds like Uncle Felix. (*seeing she has hurt him, she goes over and sits across from him at the table*) I'm sorry. I say the wrong things today.

HOLDEN: I don't know that you do.

MADELINE: But isn't uncle funny? His left mind doesn't know what his right mind is doing. He has to think of himself as a person of sentiment – idealism, and – quite a job, at times. Clever – how he gets away with it. The war must have been a godsend to people who were in danger of getting on to themselves. But I should think you could fool all of yourself all the time.

HOLDEN: You don't. (*he is rubbing his hand on the table*)

MADELINE: Grandfather Morton made this table. I suppose he and Grandfather Fejevary used to sit here and talk – they were great old pals. (*slowly* HOLDEN *turns and looks out at the hill*) Yes. How beautiful the hill must have been – before there was a college there. (*he looks away from the hill*) Did you know Grandfather Morton?

HOLDEN: Yes, I knew him. (*speaking of it against his will*) I had a wonderful talk with him once; about Greece – and the cornfields, and life.

MADELINE: I'd like to have been a pioneer! Some ways they had it fierce, but think of the fun they had! A whole big land to open up! A big new life to begin! (*her hands closing in from wideness to a smaller thing*) Why did so much get shut out? Just a little way back – anything might have been. What happened?

HOLDEN: (*speaking with difficulty*) It got – set too soon.

MADELINE: (*all of her mind open, trying to know*) And why did it? Prosperous, I suppose. That seems to set things – set them in fear. Silas Morton wasn't afraid of Felix Fejevary, the Hungarian revolutionist. He laid this country at that refugee's feet! That's what Uncle Felix says himself – with the left half of his mind. Now – the Hindu revolutionists –! (*pause*) I took a walk late yesterday afternoon. Night came, and for some reason I thought of how many nights have come – nights the earth has known long before we knew the earth. The moon came up and I thought of how moonlight made this country beautiful before any man knew that moonlight was beautiful. It gave me a feeling of coming from something a long way back. Moving toward – what will be here when I'm not here. Moving. We seem here, now, in America, to have forgotten we're moving. Think it's just *us* – just now. Of course, that would make us afraid, and – ridiculous.

        (*Her father comes in.*)

IRA: Your Aunt Isabel – did she go away – and leave you?

MADELINE: She's coming back.

IRA: For you?

MADELINE: She – wants me to go with her. This is Professor Holden, father.

HOLDEN: How do you do, Mr Morton?

IRA: (*nods, not noticing* HOLDEN's *offered hand*) How'do. When is she coming back?

MADELINE: Soon.

IRA: And then you're going with her?

MADELINE: I – don't know.

IRA: I say you go with her. You want them all to come down on us? (*to* HOLDEN) What are you here for?

MADELINE: Aunt Isabel brought Professor Holden, father.

'*You could fool ... all the time*' perhaps alludes to a famous quotation attributed to Lincoln: 'You can fool all the people some of the time, and some of the people all of the time, but you cannot fool all the people all the time.'

IRA: Oh. Then you – you tell her what to do. You make her do it. (*he goes into the room at left*)

MADELINE: (*sadly, after a silence*) Father's like something touched by an early frost.

HOLDEN: Yes. (*seeing his opening and forcing himself to take it*) But do you know, Madeline, there are other ways of that happening – 'touched by an early frost'. I've seen it happen to people I know – people of fine and daring mind. They do a thing that puts them apart – it may be the big, brave thing – but the apartness does something to them. I've seen it many times – so many times – so many times, I fear for you. You do this thing and you'll find yourself with people who in many ways you don't care for at all; find yourself apart from people who in most ways are your own people. You're many-sided, Madeline. (*moves her tennis racket*) I don't know about it's all going to one side. I hate to see you, so young, close a door on so much life. I'm being just as honest with you as I know how. I myself am making compromises to stay within. I don't like it, but there are – reasons for doing it. I can't see you leave that main body without telling you all it is you are leaving. It's not a clean-cut case – the side of the world or the side of the angels. I hate to see you lose the – fullness of life.

MADELINE: (*a slight start, as she realizes the pause. As one recalled from far*) I'm sorry. I was listening to what you were saying – but all the time – something else was happening. Grandfather Morton, big and – oh, terrible. He was here. And we went to that walled-up hole in the ground – (*rising and pointing down at the chalked cell*) – where they keep Fred Jordan on bread and water because he couldn't be a part of nations of men killing each other – and Silas Morton – only he was all that is back of us, tore open that cell – it was his voice tore it open – his voice as he cried, 'God damn you, this is America!' (*sitting down, as if rallying from a tremendous experience*) I'm sorry – it should have happened, while you were speaking. Won't you – go on?

HOLDEN: That's a pretty hard thing to go on against. (*after a moment*) I can't go on.

MADELINE: You were thinking of leaving the college, and then – decided to stay? (*he nods*) And you feel there's more – fullness of life for you inside the college than outside?

HOLDEN: No – not exactly. (*again a pause*) It's very hard for me to talk to you.

MADELINE: (*gently*) Perhaps we needn't do it.

HOLDEN: (*something in him forcing him to say it*) I'm staying for financial reasons.

MADELINE: (*kind, but not going to let the truth get away*) You don't think that – having to stay within – or deciding to, rather, makes you think these things of the – blight of being without?

HOLDEN: I think there is danger to you in – so young, becoming alien to society.

MADELINE: As great as the danger of staying within – and becoming like the thing I'm within?

HOLDEN: You wouldn't become like it.

MADELINE: Why wouldn't I? That's what it does to the rest of you. I don't see it – this fullness of life business. I don't see that Uncle Felix has got it – or even Aunt Isabel, and you – I think that in buying it you're losing it.

HOLDEN: I don't think you know what a cruel thing you are saying.

MADELINE: There must be something pretty rotten about Morton College if you have to sell your soul to stay in it!

HOLDEN: You don't 'sell your soul'. You persuade yourself to wait.

MADELINE: (*unable to look at him, as if feeling shame*) You have had a talk with Uncle Felix since that day in the library you stepped aside for me to pass.

HOLDEN: Yes; and with my wife's physician. If you sell your soul – it's to love you sell it.

MADELINE: (*low*) That's strange. It's love that – brings life along, and then it's love – holds life back.

HOLDEN: (*and all the time with this effort against hopelessness*) Leaving me out of it, I'd like to see you give yourself a little more chance for detachment. You need a better intellectual equipment if you're going to fight the world you find yourself in. I think you will count for more if you wait, and when you strike, strike more maturely.

MADELINE: Detachment. (*pause*) This is one thing they do at this place. (*she moves to the open door*) Chain them up to the bars – just like this. (*in the doorway where her two grandfathers once pledged faith with the dreams of a million years, she raises clasped hands as high as they will go*) Eight hours a day – day after day. Just hold your arms up like this one hour then sit down and think about – (*as if tortured by all who have been so tortured, her body begins to give with sobs, arms drop, the last word is a sob*) detachment.

    HOLDEN *is standing helplessly by when her father comes in.*

IRA: (*wildly*) Don't cry. No! Not in this house! I can't – Your aunt and uncle will fix it up. The law won't take you this time – and you won't do it again.

MADELINE: Oh, what does *that* matter – what they do to *me?*

IRA: What are you crying about then?

MADELINE: It's – the *world.* It's –

IRA: The *world?* If that's all you've got to cry about! (*to* HOLDEN) Tell her that's nothing to cry about. What's the matter with you. Mad'line? That's crazy – cryin' about the world! What good has ever come to this house through carin' about the world? What good's that college? Better we had that hill. Why is there no one in this house to-day but me and you? Where's your mother? Where's your brother? The *world.*

HOLDEN: I think your father would like to talk to you. I'll go outside – walk a little, and come back for you with your aunt. You must let us see you through this, Madeline. You couldn't bear the things it would bring you to. I see that now. (*as he passes her in the doorway his hand rests an instant on her bent head*) You're worth too much to break.

IRA: (*turning away*) I don't want to talk to you. What good comes of talking? (*In moving, he has stepped near the sack of corn. Takes hold of it.*) But not with Emil Johnson! That's not – what your mother died for.

MADELINE: Father, you must talk to me. What did my mother die for? No one has ever told me about her – except that she was beautiful – not like other people here. I got a feeling of – something from far away. Something from long ago. Rare. Why can't Uncle Felix talk about her? Why can't you? Wouldn't she want me to know her? Tell me about her. It's my birthday and I need my mother.

IRA: (*as if afraid he is going to do it*) How can you touch – what you've not touched in nineteen years? Just once – in nineteen years – and that did no good.

MADELINE: Try. Even though it hurts. Didn't you use to talk to her? Well, I'm her daughter. Talk to me. What has she to do with Emil Johnson?

IRA: (*the pent-up thing loosed*) What has she to do with him? She died so he could live. He lives because she's dead. (*in anguish*) And what is *he* alongside her? Yes. Something from far away. Something from long ago. Rare. How'd you know that? Finding in me – what I didn't know was there. Then *she* came – that ignorant Swede – Emil Johnson's mother – running through the cornfield like a crazy woman – 'Miss Morton! Miss Morton! Come help me! My children are choking!' Diphtheria they had – the whole of 'em – but out of this house she ran – my Madeline, leaving you – her own baby – running as fast as she could through the cornfield after that immigrant woman. She stumbled in the rough field – fell to her knees. That was the last I saw of her. She choked to death in that Swede's house. They lived.

MADELINE: (*going to him*) Oh – father. (*voice rich*) But how lovely of her.

IRA: Lovely? Lovely to leave you without a mother – leave me without her after I'd had her? Wasn't she worth more than them.

MADELINE: (*proudly*) Yes. She was worth so much that she never stopped to think how much she was worth.

IRA: Ah, if you'd known her you couldn't take it like that. And now you cry about the world! That's what the world is – all coming to nothing. My father used to sit there at the table and talk about the world – my father and her father. They thought 'twas all for something – that what you were went on into something more than you. That's the talk I always heard in this house. But it's just talk. The rare thing that came here was killed by the common thing that came here. Just happens – and happens cruel. Look at your brother! Gone – (*snaps his fingers*) like that. I told him not to go to war. He didn't have to go – they'd been glad enough to have him stay here on the farm. But no, – he must – make the world safe for democracy! Well, you see how safe he made it, don't you? Now I'm alone on the farm and he – buried on some Frenchman's farm. That is, I hope they buried him – I hope they didn't just – (*tormented*)

MADELINE: Oh, father – of course not. I know they did.

IRA: How do you know? What do you care – once they got him? *He* talked about the world – better world – end war. Now he's in his grave – I hope he is – and look at the front page of the paper! No such thing – war to end war!

MADELINE: But he thought there was, father. Fred believed that – so what else could he do?

IRA: He could 'a' minded his own business.

MADELINE: No – oh, no. It was fine of him to give his life to what he believed should be.

IRA: The light in his eyes as he talked of it, now – eyes gone – and the world he died for all hate and war. Waste. Waste. Nothin' but waste – the life of this house. Why, folks to-day'd laugh to hear my father talk. He gave his best land for ideas to live. Thought was going to make us a better people. What was his word? (*waits*) Aspiration. (*says it as if it is a far-off thing*) Well, look at your friend, young Jordan. Kicked from the college to prison for ideas of a better world. (*laughs*) His 'aspiration' puts him in a hole on bread and water! So – mind your own business, that's all that's so in this country. (*constantly tormented anew*) Oh, I told your brother all that – the night I tried to keep him. Told him about his mother – to show what come of running to other folks. And he said – standing right there – (*pointing*) eyes all bright, he said, 'Golly, I think that's great!' And then *he* – walked out of this house. (*fear takes him*) Madeline! (*she stoops over him, her arm around him*) Don't you leave me – all alone in this house – where so many was once. What's Hindus – alongside your own father – and him needing you? It won't be long. After a little I'll be dead – or crazy – or something. But not here alone where so many was once.

MADELINE: Oh – father. I don't know what to do.

IRA: Nothing stays at home. Not even the corn stays at home. If only the wind wouldn't blow! Why can't I have my field to myself? Why can't I keep what's mine? All these years I've worked to make it better. I wanted it to be – the most that it could be. My father used to talk about the Indians – how our land was their land, and how we must be more than them. He had his own ideas of bein' more – well, what's that come to? The Indians lived happier than we – wars, strikes, prisons. But I've made the corn more! This land that was once Indian maize now grows corn – I'd like to have the Indians see my corn! I'd like to see them side by side! – their Indian maize, my corn. And how'd I get it? Ah, by thinkin' – always tryin', changin', carin'. Plant this corn by that corn, and the pollen blows from corn to corn – the golden dust it blows, in the sunshine and of nights – blows from corn to corn like a – (*the word hurts*) gift. No, you don't understand it, but (*proudly*) corn don't stay what it is! You can make it anything – according to what you do, 'cording to the corn it's alongside. (*changing*) But that's it. I want it to stay in my field. It goes away. The prevailin' wind takes it on to the Johnsons – them Swedes that took my Madeline! I hear it! Oh, nights when I can't help myself – and in the sunshine I can *see* it – pollen – soft golden dust to make new life – goin' on to *them*, – and them too ignorant to know what's makin' their corn better! I want my field to myself. What'd I work all my life for? Work that's had to take the place o' what I lost – is that to go to Emil Johnson? No! The wind shall stand still! I'll make it. I'll find a way. Let me alone and I – I'll think it out. Let me alone, I say.

> (*A mind burned to one idea, with greedy haste he shuts himself in the room at left. MADELINE has been standing there as if mist is parting and letting her see. And as the vision grows power grows in her. She is thus flooded with richer life when her AUNT and Professor HOLDEN come back. Feeling something new, for a moment they do not speak.*)

AUNT ISABEL: Ready, dear? It's time for us to go now.

MADELINE: (*with the quiet of plentitude*) I'm going in with Emil Johnson.

AUNT ISABEL: Why – Madeline. (*falteringly*) We thought you'd go with us.

MADELINE: No. I have to be – the most I can be. I want the wind to have something to carry.

AUNT ISABEL: (*after a look at Professor* HOLDEN, *who is looking intensely at* MADELINE) I don't understand.

MADELINE: The world is all a – moving field. (*her hands move, voice too is of a moving field*) Nothing is to itself. If America thinks so – America is like father. I don't feel alone any more. The wind has come through – wind rich from lives now gone. Grandfather Fejevary, gift from a field far off. Silas Morton. No, not alone any more. And afraid? I'm not even afraid of being absurd!

AUNT ISABEL: But Madeline – you're leaving your father?

MADELINE: (*after thinking it out*) I'm not leaving – what's greater in him than he knows.

AUNT ISABEL: You're leaving Morton College?

MADELINE: That runt on a high hill? Yes, I'm leaving grandfather's college – then maybe I can one day lie under the same sod with him, and not be ashamed. Though I must tell you (*a little laugh*) under the sod is my idea of no place to be. I want to be a long time – where the wind blows.

AUNT ISABEL: (*who is trying not to cry*) I'm afraid it won't blow in prison, dear.

MADELINE: I don't know. Might be the only place it would blow. (EMIL *passes the window, hesitates at the door*) I'll be ready in just a moment, Emil.
(*He waits outside.*)

AUNT ISABEL: Madeline, I didn't tell you – I hoped it wouldn't be necessary, but your uncle said – if you refused to do it his way, he could do absolutely nothing for you, not even – bail.

MADELINE: Of course not. I wouldn't expect him to.

AUNT ISABEL: He feels so deeply about these things – America – loyalty, he said if you didn't come with us it would be final, Madeline. Even – (*breaks*) between you and me.

MADELINE: I'm sorry, auntie. You know how I love you. (*and her voice tells it*) But father has been telling me about the corn. It gives itself away all the time – the best corn a gift to other corn. What you are – that doesn't stay with you. Then – (*not with assurance, but feeling her way*) be the most you can be, so life will be more because you were. (*freed by the truth she has found*) Oh – do that! Why do we three go apart? Professor Holden, his beautiful trained mind; Aunt Isabel – her beautiful love, love that could save the world if only you'd – throw it to the winds. (*moving nearer* HOLDEN, *hands out to him*) Why do – (*seeing it is not to be, she turns away. Low, with sorrow for that great beauty lost*) Oh, have we brought mind, have we brought heart, up to this place – only to turn them against mind and heart?

HOLDEN: (*unable to bear more*) I think we – must go. (*going to* MADELINE, *holding out his hand and speaking from his sterile life to her fullness of life*) Good-bye, Madeline. Good luck.

MADELINE: Good-bye, Professor Holden. (*hesitates*) Luck to you.
(*Shaking his head, stooped, he hurries out.*)

MADELINE: (*after a moment when neither can speak*) Good-bye – auntie dearest. Thank you – for the birthday present – the cake – everything. Everything – all the years.
(*There is something* AUNT ISABEL *would say, but she can only hold*

tight to MADELINE's *hands. At last, with a smile that speaks for love, a little nod, she goes.* EMIL *comes in.*)

EMIL: You better go with them, Madeline. It'd make it better for you.

MADELINE: Oh no, it wouldn't. I'll be with you in an instant, Emil. I want to – say good-bye to my father.

(*But she waits before that door, a door hard to go through. Alone,* EMIL *looks around the room. Sees the bag of corn, takes a couple of ears and is looking at them as* MADELINE *returns. She remains by the door, shaken with sobs, turns, as if pulled back to the pain she has left.*)

EMIL: Gee. This is great corn.

MADELINE: (*turning now to him*) It is, isn't it, Emil?

EMIL: None like it.

MADELINE: And you say – your corn is getting better?

EMIL: Oh, yes – I raise better corn every year now.

MADELINE: (*low*) That's nice. I'll be right out, Emil.

(*He puts the corn back, goes out. From the closet* MADELINE *takes her hat and wrap. Putting them on, she sees the tennis racket on the table. She goes to it, takes it up, holds it a moment, then takes it to the closet, puts it carefully away, closes the door behind it. A moment she stands there in the room, as if listening to something. Then she leaves that house.*)

CURTAIN

THE PLAYS OF SUSAN GLASPELL

August, 1915	*Suppressed Desires* (with George Cram Cook)	Wharf Theatre
August 8, 1916	*Trifles*	Wharf Theatre
March 9, 1917	*The People*	Playwrights' Theatre
November 2, 1917	*Close the Book*	Playwrights' Theatre
December 28, 1917	*The Outside*	Playwrights' Theatre
April 26, 1918	*Woman's Honor*	Playwrights' Theatre
December 20, 1918	*Tickless Time* (with George Cram Cook)	Provincetown Playhouse
March 21, 1919	*Bernice*	Provincetown Playhouse
April 27, 1921	*Inheritors*	Provincetown Playhouse
November 14, 1921	*The Verge*	Provincetown Playhouse
April 27, 1922	*Chains of Dew*	Provincetown Playhouse
June 24, 1928	*The Comic Artist* (with Norman Matson)	Strand Theatre
December 1, 1930	*Alison's House*	Civic Repertory Theatre

SELECT BIBLIOGRAPHY

NON-DRAMATIC WRITING
STORIES

'Tom and Towser', *Davenport Weekly Outlook* (December 26, 1896), 8.
'The Tragedy of a Mind', *The Delphic*, 14 (February, 1898), 98–102.
'On the Second Down', *Author's Magazine*, 3 (November, 1902), 3–11.
'The Girl from Downtown', *Youth's Companion*, 77 (April 2, 1903), 160–1.
'In the Face of His Constituents', *Harper's*, 107 (October, 1903), 757–62.
'The Intrusion of the Personal', *Frank Leslie's Monthly* (April, 1904), 629–32.
'The Man of Flesh and Blood', *Harper's*, 108 (May, 1904), 957.
'Contrary to Precedent', *Booklovers* (January–June, 1904), 235–56.
'Freckles M'Grath', *Munsey's*, 31 (July, 1904), 481.
'The Return of Rhoda', *Youth's Companion*, 79 (January 26, 1905), 40.
'For Tomorrow', *Booklovers*, 5 (March, 1905), 559–70.
'For Love of the Hills', *Black Cat*, 11 (October, 1905), 1–11.
'At the Turn of the Road', *Speaker*, 2 (1906), 359–61.
'A Boycott on Caroline', *Youth's Companion*, 80 (March 22, 1906), 137–8.
'How the Prince Saw America', *American*, 62 (July, 1906), 274.
'From A–Z', *American*, 65 (October, 1909), 543.
'According to his Lights', *American*, 72 (June, 1911), 153–62.
Lifted Masks, New York, 1912.
'At the Source', *Woman's Home Companion*, 39 (May, 1912), 5–6.
'The Anarchist: His Dog', *American*, 74 (June, 1912), 145–54.
'A Boarder of Art', *Ladies' Home Journal*, 29 (October, 1912), 11, 92–3.
'The Resurrection and the Life', *Smart Set* (September, 1913), 65–8.
'Whom Mince Pie Hath Joined Together', *Ladies' Home Journal*, 30 (November, 1913), 10, 71–3.
'The Rules of the Institution', *Harper's*, 128 (January, 1914), 198–208.
'Looking After Clara', *Ladies' Home Journal*, 31 (August, 1914), 9, 35–7.
'The Manager of Crystal Sulphur Springs', *Harper's*, 131 (July, 1915), 176–84.
'Agnes at Cape's End', *American*, 80 (September, 1915), 5–7, 67–72.
'Unveiling Brenda', *Harper's*, 133 (June, 1916), 14–16.
'"Finality" in Freeport', *Pictorial Review*, 17 (July, 1916), 14–15, 32.
'Her Heritage of Ideals', *Canadian*, 48 (November, 1916), 63–8.
'Miss Jessie's Trip Abroad', *Woman's Home Companion*, 48 (November, 1916), 9–10, 79.

'The Hearing Ear', *Harper's*, 134 (January, 1917), 234–41.
'A Jury of Her Peers', *Everyweek* (March 5, 1917).
'Everything You Want to Plant', *Everyweek* (August 13, 1917), 20–1.
'A Matter of Gesture', *McClure's* (August, 1917), 36.
'Poor Ed', *Liberator*, 1 (March, 1918), 675–9.
'Beloved Husband', *Harper's*, 136 (April, 1918).
'Good Luck', *Good Housekeeping*, 67 (September, 1918), 44–6, 122–6.
'The Busy Duck', *Harper's*, 137 (November, 1918), 828–36.
'Pollen', *Harper's*, 138 (March, 1919), 446–51.
'The Escape', *Harper's*, 140 (December, 1919), 29–38.
'The Nervous Pig', *Harper's*, 140 (February, 1920), 209–20.
'His Smile', *Pictorial Review*, 22 (January, 1921), 15.
'The Faithless Shepherd', *Cornhill*, 60 (January, 1926), 51–9.
'Rose in the Sand', *Pall Mall*, 1927.

NOVELS

The Glory of the Conquered, New York, 1909.
The Visioning, New York, 1911.
Fidelity, Boston, 1915.
Brook Evans, New York, 1928.
Fugitive's Return, New York, 1929.
Ambrose Holt and Family, New York, 1931.
The Morning is Near Us, New York, 1939.
Cherished and Shared of Old, New York, 1940.
Norma Ashe, New York, 1942.
Judd Rankin's Daughter, New York, 1945.

PLAYS

Suppressed Desires (with Cook) in *Plays*, Boston, 1920.
Trifles in *Plays*, Boston, 1920.
The People in *Plays*, Boston, 1920.
Close the Book in *Plays*, Boston, 1920.
The Outside in *Plays*, Boston, 1920.
Woman's Honor in *Plays*, Boston, 1920.
Tickless Time (with Cook) in *Plays*, Boston, 1920.
Bernice in *Plays*, Boston, 1920.
Inheritors, Boston, 1921. London, 1924.
The Verge, Boston, 1922. London, 1924.
The Comic Artist, with Norman Matson, New York, 1927. London, 1927.
Alison's House, New York, 1930.
Chains of Dew (unpublished).

BOOKS AND ARTICLES ABOUT SUSAN GLASPELL

Gerhard Bach, *Susan Glaspell und die Provincetown Players: eine Studie zur Fruhphase des modernen amerikanischen Dramas und Theaters*, Marburg, 1971.

C. W. E. Bigsby, *A Critical Introduction to Twentieth Century American Drama: Volume I 1900–1940*, Cambridge, 1982.

Floyd Dell, *Homecoming*, New York, 1933.

Helen Deutsch and Stella Hanau, *The Provincetown: A Story of the Theatre*, New York, 1931.

Thomas H. Dickinson, *Playwrights of the New American Theatre*, New York, 1925.

Isaac Goldberg, *The Drama of Transition*, Cincinnati, 1922.

Jean Gould, *Modern American Playwrights*, New York, 1966.

Ludwig Lewisohn, *Expression in America*, New York, 1932.

Marcia Noe, 'A Critical Biography of Susan Glaspell', unpublished Ph.D thesis, University of Iowa, 1976.

Oliver M. Sayler, *Our American Theater 1908–1923*, New York, 1923.

Mary Heaton Vorse, *Time and the Town*, New York, 1942.

Arthur E. Waterman, *Susan Glaspell*, New York, 1966.